Domestic Architecture, Literature and the
Sexual Imaginary in Europe, 1850–1930

Nineteenth-Century and Neo-Victorian Cultures
Series editors: Ruth Heholt and Joanne Ella Parsons

Editorial Board
Rosario Arias, University of Malaga, Spain
Katherine Bowers, University of British Columbia, Canada
Jessica Cox, Brunel University, UK
Laura Eastlake, Edge Hill University, UK
Kate Hext, University of Exeter, UK
Elizabeth Ho, University of Hong Kong, Hong Kong
Tara MacDonald, University of Idaho, USA
Charlotte Mathieson, University of Surrey, UK
Royce Mahawatte, Central Saint Martins, University of the Arts London, UK
John Miller, University of Sheffield, UK
Grace Moore, University of Otago, New Zealand
Antonija Primorac, University of Rijeka, Croatia

Recent books in the series:
Domestic Architecture, Literature and the Sexual Imaginary in Europe, 1850–1930
Aina Martí-Balcells

Forthcoming
Lost and Revenant Children 1850–1940
Tatiana Kontou
Olive Schreiner and the Politics of Print Culture, 1883–1920
Clare Gill
Michael Field's Revisionary Poetics
Jill Ehnenn
Literary Illusions: Performance Magic and Victorian Literature
Christopher Pittard
Pastoral in Early-Victorian Fiction: Environment and Modernity
Mark Frost
Spectral Embodiments of Child Death in the Long Nineteenth Century
Jen Baker
The Idler's Club: Humor and Mass Readership from Jerome K. Jerome to P. G. Wodehouse
Laura Fiss
Women's Activism in the Transatlantic Consumers' Leagues, 1885–1920
Flore Janssen
Assessing Intelligence: The Bildungsroman and the Politics of Human Potential in Britain, 1860–1919
Sara Lyons
Life Writing and the Nineteenth-Century Market
Sean Grass

Domestic Architecture, Literature and the Sexual Imaginary in Europe, 1850–1930

Aina Martí-Balcells

EDINBURGH
University Press

Edinburgh University Press is one of the leading university presses in the UK. We publish academic books and journals in our selected subject areas across the humanities and social sciences, combining cutting-edge scholarship with high editorial and production values to produce academic works of lasting importance. For more information visit our website: edinburghuniversitypress.com

© Aina Martí-Balcells 2022, 2024

Cover image: *Woman Standing in Doorway*, 1894. Sir William Rothenstein. Oil paint on canvas © Tate Images
Cover design: www.hayesdesign.co.uk

Edinburgh University Press Ltd
The Tun – Holyrood Road
12(2f) Jackson's Entry
Edinburgh EH8 8PJ

First published in hardback by Edinburgh University Press 2022

Typeset in 11/13pt Sabon
by Cheshire Typesetting Ltd, Cuddington, Cheshire

A CIP record for this book is available from the British Library

ISBN 978 1 4744 6307 2 (hardback)
ISBN 978 1 4744 6308 9 (paperback)
ISBN 978 1 4744 6309 6 (webready PDF)
ISBN 978 1 4744 6310 2 (epub)

The right of Aina Martí-Balcells to be identified as the author of this work has been asserted in accordance with the Copyright, Designs and Patents Act 1988, and the Copyright and Related Rights Regulations 2003 (SI No. 2498).

Contents

Series Preface	vi
Introduction	1
1. Adultery and the Subversion of Architectural Prescriptiveness in *Madame Bovary* and *The Return of the Native*	16
2. Sexual Accessibility and Exhibitionism: Glass in *La Curée*	49
3. Glass Dwellings and the Dissolution of Adultery in Fontane's *L'Adultera*	81
4. Domestic and Sexual Circulation in Huysmans' *En ménage*	111
5. Vienna: Towards a New Domestic Imaginary	146
Bibliography	179
Index	192

Series Preface

This interdisciplinary series provides space for full and detailed scholarly discussions on nineteenth-century and Neo-Victorian cultures. Drawing on radical and cutting-edge research, the volumes explore and challenge existing discourses, providing an engaging reassessment of the time period. The series encourages debates about decolonising nineteenth-century cultures, histories, and scholarship, as well as raising questions about diversities. Encompassing art, literature, history, performance, theatre studies, film and TV studies, medical and the wider humanities, *Nineteenth-Century and Neo-Victorian Cultures* is dedicated to publishing pioneering research that focuses on the Victorian era in its broadest and most diverse sense.

To my father, who made this possible.

Introduction

In the last decades of the nineteenth century, two phenomena were taking place in the main European capitals: an unprecedented number of large-scale building projects that shifted the urban landscape, and another seemingly unprecedented proliferation of sexual discourses by the emergent field of sexology. These two events, apparently so unrelated to each other, appear to have strong connections when observed through the lenses of literature. In *Pot-Bouille* (1882), Zola fills a new apartment building with hysterical women that by osmosis resemble the domestic spaces in which they live. The notion of sick building syndrome appears in its embryonic form in Zola's text. But *Pot-Bouille* also makes a display of new sexual neuroses that were being taxonomised at the same time that new private residences appeared as a symbol of the new Paris of the Second Empire. By placing a range of sexual pathologies within a new apartment building aimed for the middle classes, Zola is hinting at a relationship between new architectural designs and sexuality. In *Pot-Bouille*, new architectures and sexual pathologies meet at the space of domesticity. Home is the place par excellence where we observe the interplay between sexuality and architecture; not in terms of gendered spaces but in the ways in which sexual pathologies and architectural forms shape each other.[1]

A wide range of literary production unearths the not so obvious relationship between domestic architecture and sexuality, both architectural and sexual discourses embedded within the medical parameters of the normal/normative and the abnormal or pathological. While literature conforms the imagined spaces in which the relationships between sexuality and domestic architecture become visible, it is through the application of the concept of normality to the usages of the space and the body that both sexuality and home partake in the same prescriptive pattern. Thus, at a conceptual level, architecture relates to the medical field through notions of the normal and normativity. Considering the appropriation architects made of medical terminology on a large scale, this is not surprising. Architects approached their practice as a medical discipline, which resulted in a strong prescriptive field that aimed at regulating how people lived and used their domestic spaces. Sharing his rhetoric with physicians, French architect Léonce Reynaud employed the term 'distribution vicieuse' (vicious distribution) to refer to an inappropriate architectural design (Reynaud 1867: 1), echoing a faulty biological organisation of the human body. As Peter Cryle and Elizabeth Stephens highlight, doctors used the word 'vicieuse' to refer to sexual pathology before the word 'perversity' came into more regular use, talking of 'organisation vicieuse' (vicious organisation) (Cryle and Stephens 2017: 134). We find the term perversity in the work of English architect Robert Kerr (1823–1904), who argues that rooms be designed 'according to [their] purpose, [and] shall be for that purpose satisfactorily contrived, so as to be free from perversities of their own' (Kerr 1865: 70). The use of 'perversity' is an important conceptual choice because it indicates that Kerr saw architectural transgression as part of a wider set of practices that included sexual perversities, envisaging home not only as a gendered space but also as the facilitator of pathological sexual practices. Architecture is in Kerr a reality with agency that presents a constant threat to the enactment of the domestic ideal. The body, both inhabitant of a room and the locus of sexuality, is subjected to the prescriptiveness of both architecture and medicine that together create a set of regulations in the realm of private life. The misuse of the body in its movements, crossing and using rooms, and in the sexual act itself is what is at stake here. In Kerr, the former finds a correlation with the latter. They are intertwined realities that cannot be separated.

Following Foucault, I define normative sexuality as the normalised sexual practices within the legal framework of marriage, what he refers to as sexuality with 'feu' (fire/fireplace) and 'loi' (law): 'ce qui n'est pas ordonné à la génération ou transfiguré par elle n'a plus ni feu ni loi' (that which does not lead to procreation has no fire or law) (Foucault 1976: 10). Harry Oosterhuis mentions, for example, how 'by naming and classifying virtually all non-procreative sexuality, [Krafft-Ebing] synthesised the new psychiatric knowledge about perversion' (Oosterhuis 2012). Procreative sexuality was the ideal sexual practice configuring domesticity and, as Foucault suggests, there was a relationship between architecture and non-normative sexuality in the nineteenth century: the latter was not meant to be placed within the boundaries of domestic space. Similarly, Rita Felski argues how sexological and psychiatric discourses identified 'the sexual deviant [. . .] with a transgressive extremity of experience beyond the boundaries of everyday social and sexual norms' (Felski 1995: 174). Normative sexuality was formulated through its opposition to perverse sexual practices that were theoretically opposed to domesticity. In order to identify perversities, I will use as reference the medical texts that started configuring the discipline of sexology in the 1880s, with particular attention to Sigmund Freud (1856–1939) and the Austrian psychiatrist Richard von Krafft-Ebing (1840–1902). I am well aware that some of the literary texts I will be analysing here were published before 1880 but I approach medical texts as a reflection and representation of generalised perceptions on ideas of normal sexuality as opposed to notions of 'perversion', 'perversity' or 'the perverse'. We will need to wait until Freud to see how this binary opposition between the normal and the perverse erodes and the concepts start merging into each other. This movement from a binary to a seamless connection of the pathological to the normal will be very important for my analysis of the conflation between bourgeois sexuality and other kinds of sexualities such as those associated to prostitution. In this regard, we will see how Huysmans' *En ménage* (1881) and Schnitzler's *Traumnovelle* (1927) imagine the conflation of the idea of the wife and that of the prostitute by dissolving architectural boundaries.

Architecture as a prescriptive practice is explored and represented in several literary works of the second half of the nineteenth century.[2] Thomas Hardy's narrative poem 'How I Built Myself a House' (1865) illustrates the frustrating experience of the narrator when he is confronted with architectural norms:

> We were told the only possible size we could have the rooms, the only way we should be allowed to go upstairs, and the exact quantity of wine we might order at once, so as to fit the wine-cellar [the architect] had in his head. (Hardy [1865] 2004: 5)

'How I Built Myself a House' highlights architecture as a strong regulator, whereby the architect becomes what Sylviane Agacinski calls 'le tyran-architecte' (tyrant-architect) (1992: 38). In architecture scholarship, Annmarie Adams uses the term prescriptiveness in her article 'The Eichler Home: Intention and Experience in Postwar Suburbia' (1995) to illustrate how the dwellers of a house do not follow the indications of the architect and his original plans which consisted in creating and using spaces for the surveillance of children, and for isolating the house from the rest of the neighbouring houses. But Adams does not reflect on the consequences of transgressing that norm and the cultural significance this has for home life.

Architectural prescriptiveness emerged from discourses that addressed questions of usage (such as who should be present in each room of the house, what activities should be undertaken in each room, or at which moment of the day the room should be used) and questions of design (the size, position and number of windows in a room, the number of rooms according to the size of the house, or the position of doors). The concept of prescriptiveness acquires a significant relevance in light of Bernard Tschumi's architectural theory. In his work *Architecture Concepts: Red is Not a Color* (2012), architecture, Tschumi argues, 'generate[s] ideas and concepts about the world we live in [. . .]. Nevertheless, architecture's inescapable materiality is what makes it different from philosophy, mathematics, or literature. By its very nature, architecture involves the materialization of concepts or ideas' (Tschumi 2012: 6). The generation of ideas, however, does not solely involve the architect; the subject who inhabits the space is extremely important in the making of concepts. This fact will be of paramount importance for my literary analysis in the chapters that follow for three main reasons. First of all, it shows how, by transgressing the usages of domestic space, new meanings are created. This implicitly involves a tension between the inhabitant and the rules of architecture that is only possible due to the prescriptive nature of the latter. Secondly, it highlights the role of literature in the making of architectural theory. Literature does not only illustrate the many ways in which architecture is used but it also displays the range of consequences that has been imagined from such misuse of space. By doing so, literary texts unfold the ways in which the usages of domestic architecture shaped sexual perversities or normality. My use of the term transgression is based on what Tschumi theorises in terms of violence:

> Entering a building may be a delicate act, but it violates the balance of a precisely ordered geometry [...]. Bodies carve all sorts of new and unexpected spaces through fluid or erratic motions. Architecture, then, is only an organism engaged in constant intercourse with users, whose bodies rush against the carefully established rules of architectural thought. No wonder the human body has always set limits to the most extreme architectural ambitions. The body disturbs the purity of architectural order. (Tschumi 2012: 75)

The architectural norm is subjected to the ways in which the subject uses – respects or transgresses – the space. In Flaubert's *Madame Bovary* (1856), for example, Emma Bovary transgresses the architecture she inhabits when she uses rooms, doors and windows in the wrong way. We will see how, from an architectural perspective, adultery becomes an act of rebellion against the 'purity of architectural order' that runs parallel with the transgression of the purity of the female body. But we will also see how the act of adultery is imagined breaking architectural conventions. What Emma Bovary does with her body is to expand the limits of architecture and, with it, of her sexual body.

Finally, the importance of approaching architecture as a generator of concepts lies in the fact that it was the literary representation of architecture, and not architecture itself, that first showed the potentialities of architectural design in modifying sexual and domestic cultures. In Zola's *La Curée* (1871), we will see how the use of glass impacts on, and shapes a set of sexual practices such as voyeurism, exhibitionism and promiscuity, and also wider sexual notions that form part of sexual culture and are not specific practices. Thus, the dissolution of boundaries between the interior and the outside world that started modifying notions of female sexuality as belonging to the private sphere are configured through the images of glass. All these ideas were being shaped in architectural discussions and literature due to an increased use of glass. While architects hinted at, and speculated about the potential danger that glass can pose to privacy, literature enacted a whole set of consequences in the realm of sexuality. Architecture shaped the sexual imagination through practices, usages, discourses and representations. Literature shows how the consequence of architectural transgression is in fact a sexual transgression. Thus, architectural prescriptiveness was embedded with notions of sexuality and had consequences far more important than a mere misuse of space. The added value of literature lies, precisely, in materialising the consequences of breaking architectural prescriptiveness. The analysis of the novels in the following chapters will show to what extent domestic architecture participated in the formation of the sexual imaginary in a moment of important shifts both in domestic culture and architectural designs. By unveiling the theoretical connections between the theory of architecture and the ideas shaping sexual culture in a particular historical moment, my aim is to bring to light the ways in which the theory, practice and representations of domestic architecture were an essential part in the making of normative sexuality.

But what was behind the prescriptive nature of domestic architecture? Throughout the nineteenth century but particularly in the second half, architects had been concerned about how to best preserve the normativity of domestic life (Marcus 1999: 138). In Marcus's words, architects 'strove to materialise domestic ideology' (1999: 101). The norm against which domesticity was measured had to do with the fact that gender was a production of space and all architectural regulations aimed at producing gendered spaces (Baydar 2005; Chase and Levenson 2000), and, in that way, strengthening the notions of gender difference. But in the same way that space can produce strict and inflexible notions of gender, it can also dissolve them, and it can design a layout that invites the practice of non-normative sexual acts. Thus, we will see how in early twentieth-century Vienna, architect Adolf Loos (1870–1933) changed the normative use of windows, which consisted, not in letting light and air in, as was the case in most treatises, but in looking through at a semi-naked female body. Voyeurism became the result of architectural prescriptiveness, which, at the same time, showed a tendency towards the normalisation of such a practice. It is the actual materiality of architecture that generates and normalises concepts and practices. In this context, the last part of the book will show how spatial regulations also reflected and facilitated the production of theories and ideas of sexuality by modifying the meaning of architectural prescriptiveness strongly related to that of normative sexuality.

In this book, I will use the term 'ideal' to refer to what many scholars, such as Marcus herself, call 'ideology'. My choice of word aims to highlight the state of perfection 'ideal' implies and that by its very definition is unreachable. By using this term, I also want to avoid the political connotations of 'ideology' as domestic culture is a complex phenomenon that cannot be reduced to a political project, as Elisabeth Badinter argues (1980: 139), but is intertwined with the feelings, expectations and imagination that come to represent a way of living. The protagonists of domesticity were supposed to be those who configured a household, which, ideally, would be formed by 'the occupier of the house, the householder, master, husband, or father; while the other members of the family are the wife, children, servants, relatives, visitors, and persons constantly or accidentally in the house' (Chase and Levenson 2000: xxxiv). The successful accomplishment of the domestic ideal has been strongly questioned. Studies of representations of home in nineteenth-century literature have mainly moved towards a revisionist analysis of the domestic ideal, and the ways in which such an ideal was not representative of reality. While it did permeate the middle classes' daily life, it did not configure a homogeneous way of living (Bryden and Floyd 1999). This contradiction between the ideal and the practice, and the desired homogenisation of ways of living has been extensively explored by Chase and Levenson (2000), who note how the official definition of family at the time escaped many households. Architect Charles Rice has defined such opposition with the term 'doubleness' (Rice 2007: 2): the simultaneous presence of an image of domesticity and its contradictory reality. Rice notes that both representations of the interior and spatial practices did not adjust to each other, rather, they doubled, concluding that the emergence of the interior in the nineteenth century did happen in this doubleness: the image or idea versus the practice. This opposition has even informed literary theory; Marcus, for example, places the contradiction between theory and practice at the heart of haunted house stories, which, she argues, 'exposed the ways that the ideal failed to materialise in homes filled with ghosts' (Marcus 1999: 127). The tensions between the theory and practice of domesticity will be at the heart of my analysis throughout this book. But instead of exposing the contradictions of the domestic ideal in terms of the subjective experience (how the individual feels and lives), I will place the conflict on the very materiality of architecture, that is, how the individual uses domestic space and what the consequences are. This grounds my literary analysis in the history and theory of domestic architecture and shows how it is the breaking of architectural norms that puts at risk the domestic ideal and its associated notions of normative sexuality.

In all the literary texts analysed in this book, women are the main transgressors of the 'purity of the architectural order' (Tschumi 2012: 75). The fact that the weight of transgression is placed on women shows the specific role and space given to them: changes in domesticity were articulated through women, and so were shifts in sexual culture. Authors such as French historian Jules Michelet (1798–1874) defined the woman in strict relation to home: '[la femme] est dans toute l'histoire l'élément de fixité. Le bon sens dit assez pourquoi: non-seulement parce qu'elle est mère, qu'elle est le foyer, la maison' (in all history she is the element of stability. Common sense sufficiently explains the reason for this. It is not only because she is the mother, the embodiment of the family and the household) (1870: 80). Michelet was a representative of a domestic culture – the seventh edition of *L'amour* came out in 1870 – that placed women at the centre of the private sphere. But this was not a French phenomenon solely. Michelet's words echoed those of other authors from different fields in other European countries: in *The Angel in the House* (1862), Coventry Patmore (1823–1896) praised the female ideal as a wife devoted to her husband and domestic duties. In 1886, Krafft-Ebing defined womanhood only in relation to domestic life: 'Das Ziel und Ideal des Weibes, auch des in Schmutz und Laster verkommenen, ist und bleibt die Ehe' (The ultimate aim, the ideal, of woman, even when she is dragged in the mire of vice, ever is and will be marriage) (Krafft-Ebing 1894: 16). While in England, Kerr associated the specialisation and division of rooms with privacy and the isolation of women:

> One of the most important points involved in the improvement of plan has been that of domestic privacy. There are two forms in which [. . .] this is especially cared for; namely, the separation of the family from the servants, and the still further retirement of the female sex; and it may appear wonderful that ideas now so axiomatic in their nature as these should have required any considerable time. (Kerr 1865: 26–7)

The images of home as woman and woman as home were not only present across countries but they also crossed disciplinary boundaries; they configured a pattern. It was this association that strengthened the identification between the domestic interior and female sexuality. In *Sex and Real Estate: Why We Love Houses* (2000), Marjorie Garber looks at the history of representations of the home in Britain and North America from the eighteenth to the twenty-first century, arguing how the association between house and woman could be partly due to a reading of female sexuality as enclosed and interior, making the Victorians not only locate the woman at home, but also see the woman as home. It is this image of female sexuality as enclosed and interior that will be of interest for us as it establishes a correlation between modifications on female sexuality and domestic architecture: at a conceptual level, a change to one impacts on the other. Although Garber does not reach this point, she approaches it when she states that architecture did 'reflect and produc[e] sexual law and morality' (Garber 2000: 76) – something that Foucault already suggests in *La volonté de savoir* (1976), discussing eighteenth-century boarding schools and architecture's capacity to construct and/or express sexual norms:

Soient les collèges d'enseignement au XVIIIe siècle. Globalement, on peut avoir l'impression que du sexe on n'y parle pratiquement pas. Mais il suffit de jeter un coup d'œil sur les dispositifs architecturaux, sur les règlements de discipline et toute l'organisation intérieure: il ne cesse pas d'y être question du sexe. (Foucault 1976: 39)

(Let us take as examples eighteenth-century schools. Overall, there is the impression that sex is hardly talked about. But looking at the architectural devices, the disciplinary regulations and the internal organization: it is all about sex.)

According to Foucault, architecture displays its mechanisms of control in order to organise and structure the sexual life of its inhabitants. This is already present in Rousseau's domestic representations in *Julie, ou la nouvelle Heloïse* (1761). Once married, Julie's household is an example of domestic virtue based on the separation of the sexes: 'la maxime de Mad de Wolmar se soutient très bien par l'exemple de sa maison. Chacun étant pour ainsi dire tout à son sexe, les femmes y vivent très séparées des hommes') (The norm of Madam de Wolmar is very well expressed through her house. Everyone lives, so to say, according to his or her sex, women live separated from men (Rousseau [1761] 1993: 65).

This sexual division was in fact seen as a natural condition: 'ce qui nous sépare des hommes, c'est la nature elle-même qui nous prescrit des occupations différentes' (That which separates us from men is nature itself, which gives us different occupations) ([1761] 1993: 121). Mark Wigley delves even earlier in history, placing the representation of a new sexuality in the Renaissance, when ideas of privacy appeared: 'the new sexuality is produced in the very moment of its privatization. All of the ensemble of strategic mechanisms that define and constitute the house are involved in the production of this sexuality as such' (Wigley 1992: 346). But it is in *Julie*, where the relationship between domestic architecture and sexuality appears to be essential to the construction of an image of domesticity that will prevail throughout and beyond the nineteenth century.

In the following chapters, we will see the importance of female agency in motivating changes in domestic and sexual culture. And, in fact, Rousseau's Julie is a female protagonist on which the creation of the bourgeois household relies. Thus, women were at the centre of a new domestic culture in the eighteenth century and they remained key for any consequent modification of domesticity. The sense of movement inherent to the idea of transgression also illustrates how women were theorised as static bodies, as we have seen in Michelet. Thus, transgressing meant crossing a spatial boundary which was imagined both as the house and the body. This transgression, precisely, *seemed* to break the association between the house and the female body but in the end did not: it perpetuated the domestic imaginary, as both the idea of home and that of womanhood were modified at the same time. This is one of the paradoxes this book argues: changes in sexual culture were actually based in the fact that the image of the female body as house never did really dissolve. In fact, Garber notes the contemporaneity of the woman-home association, and, therefore, of the domestic ideal:

> One of the ways we have of making things modern – or postmodern – is to scramble up the 'laws' of the house-as-body, turning the conventions of the house inside out, rearranging functional spaces in new – and often playful – ways. But if pleasure comes [. . .] from flirting with transgression or excess, the very possibility of transgression comes [. . .] from our acceptance of and dependence upon the old metaphor. (Garber 2000: 79–80)

Like Garber, feminist philosophy and geography claim the persistence and continuation of the home-house identification in the twentieth century. Luce Irigaray states that woman has been defined in terms of space and container, as mother and wife (Irigaray 1983: 11). Rose Gillian claims that 'Place is represented as Woman' by being seen as 'conflict-free, caring, nurturing' (Gillian 2007: 56) in a male-dominated field of geography – representations of place and home with which, Gillian argues, many women fail to identify. Doreen Massey states how 'particular ways of thinking about space and place are tied up with, both directly and indirectly, particular social constructions of gender relations' (Massey 2007: 2). Massey argues for dynamic spaces and unstable boundaries (if any) in order to end with static definitions of gender and home. The continuation between the interior and exterior is one of Massey's arguments, and such continuation means exactly the opposite to the separation of spheres that aimed at organising ways of living in the nineteenth century. In this context, I will illustrate how theories of space – or of the organisation of space – find a correlation with approaches to sexuality. Thus, we will see how anxieties around the use of glass, for example, related to a theoretical dissolution of the boundary between inside and outside that was ultimately perceived as the dissolution of a sexual boundary, and of the image of the body as house.

But with regard to the importance placed on representations of women, their sexuality and domestic experiences, another question arises: where did men stand in a context of domestic and sexual change? As this introduction suggests, scholarship has traditionally focused on women while showing a tendency to understate the male experience. But men were also engaged in the making of domesticity. With the purpose of presenting a more balanced analysis, the last two chapters of the book shift the focus from female to male approaches, to domestic changes and the alienating experience such changes produce in men. The shift in gender perspective in representations of the domestic crisis shows the unsettlement of a traditional male position within the domestic realm due a shift in gender roles. In *En ménage* and *Traumnovelle*, we will see how the main male characters André and Fridolin long for the domestic ideal, strongly grounded in their imagination. The main reason for the impossibility of accomplishing the domestic ideal appears to be the wives of André and Fridolin. In both cases, an unsettling female sexuality causes movement and a sense of homelessness in both men, whose movement towards the outside turns their domestic position into a dependent one: both texts show how men cannot be domestic, or feel at home, without a woman whose sexuality and desires are strongly regulated.

Having said that, we should be very careful in assuming, in a general way, that the nineteenth-century European bourgeoisies were subjected to a repressive sexual life. Even if sexual discourses were being produced with a strong prescriptive style, we should not jump to conclusions about what happened in the bedroom. Peter Gay, in his history of private life in the nineteenth century, presents a rather different version of the ways in which the middle classes actually lived their sexuality. In *Schnitzler's Century: The Making of Middle-Class Culture, 1815–1914* (2002), Gay notes the openness surrounding Victorian sexual practices by noting how some sexologists such as J. F. Albrecht already considered female sexuality in a positive way, advising husbands on how to satisfy women. Other doctors such as Krafft-Ebing, Paolo Mantegazza and William Acton, however, had a different discourse, which indeed was exploited later on by Victorian detractors, and became our inherited view on the Victorians (Gay 2002: 81–3). Gay provides a series of letters written between spouses and examples of surveys of middle-class sexuality (Gay 2002: 86) that testify to the importance given to sex by doctors who certainly approach it as an important and healthy topic:

> It is in that most secluded of domains, the sexual life of the married Victorian bourgeoisie, that the gap between legend and truth yawns most widely. Given the Victorian's passion for privacy, the door to their bedroom remained firmly closed [. . .]. What we do know [. . .] should leave little doubt that respectable middle-class couples often shared their erotic pleasures in passionate gratification. (Gay 2002: 286)

Gay does accept the importance of privacy in the nineteenth century, however, his claims about the open sexual life of the middle classes contradict many of the premises of feminist studies, particularly regarding the alienating aspect of female sexuality. In fact, Gay suggests that our view on the Victorians responds to some kind of ideological motivation that chose some medical tradition over another. My choice of focusing on Krafft-Ebing is due to the systematic aspect of his work – his catalogue of perversions – which I read as a symptomatic discourse of a wider cultural moment. In the nineteenth century, knowledge was produced in a systematic way, through classifications, catalogues and labels. Thus, we will see the formal similarities between architectural and medical discourses, both sustaining a worldview based on strict definitions and oppositions that while aiming to regulate transgression, also made it possible. However, Krafft-Ebing also stands out for representing the foundation of modern sexuality and has informed our views on the topic. Oosterhuis argues how we owe the recognition of sexual diversity to the work of Krafft-Ebing, which also understood sexual deviance as a medical condition rather than an immoral act, advocating for the decriminalising of the so-called perverts (Oosterhuis 2012).

Similarly to Gay, Felski notes the empowering effects of sexological discourses on female sexuality: 'the discourse of sexology was ultimately enabling for women in acknowledging their status as desiring subjects [...]. The sexualisation of culture brought with it a gradual process of democratization' (Felski 1995: 181). This, however, should be taken carefully as Krafft-Ebing, for example, still tends to deny an open sexual desire in women. Freud would be the first to ascertain more clearly and with enough popularity the existence of a strong female desire. But I agree with Felski that an emerging sexual democratisation was taking place, especially from the 1880s, that enabled women to acknowledge their sexuality in a stronger way. This topic will occupy us in the last three chapters where female sexual desires are represented as potential threats to the domestic ideal. Female eroticism is an important motif in modifying the domestic experience. At the same time, the erotic becomes part of marriage and domesticity, configuring a cultural change. If, as Alain Corbin notes, 'au XIXe siècle, l'érotisme conjugal [...] se lie étroitement à l'adultère' (in the nineteenth century, the erotic life in marriage [...] is strongly related to adultery) (Corbin 2008: 440), by the end of the century, the erotic is placed within marriage. On one hand, this affected the concept of normal sexuality, as the erotic was not associated with reproduction. On the other hand, we will see how the introduction of the erotic in late nineteenth-century marriage finds a correlation with the dissolution of adultery as a literary topic.

*

The first chapter will present a comparative analysis of *Madame Bovary* and *The Return of the Native* in order to illustrate how literature imagined a correlation between the misuse of domestic space and that of the sexual body, throwing light on the sexual norm hidden in architectural practices in France and England. This chapter will also trace analogies of content and form between *The Gentleman's House* and *Psychopathia Sexualis* in order to illustrate the prescriptive nature of architecture and the use of medico-sexual terms by architects. In this context, the analysis of *Madame Bovary* and *The Return of the Native* illustrates how the breaking of the architectural norm leads to the act of adultery.

The second chapter will read the domestic spaces in *La Curée* against its architectural background, when important urban renovations were taking place in Paris. I argue that Zola's text engages with the architects' anxieties about the use of glass in new domestic designs. In *La Curée*, glass deregulates the hegemonic sexual norm, antedating new sexual and domestic cultures. These are characterised by the introduction of notions of sexual accessibility and the exhibition of the female body.

Chapter Three will focus on Fontane's *L'Adultera*. This chapter contrasts discourses of glass for private residences found in architectural texts and in *L'Adultera*. Like *La Curée*, Fontane's work is contextualised in a moment of intense building in Berlin in which the wider inclusion of glass was a characteristic of the new private residences. I argue that, by showing awareness of glass, *L'Adultera* articulates new possibilities of dwelling, organising family life and representing female sexuality. This chapter also defines the concept of a glass house as representative of domestic and sexual cultures in which honesty becomes fundamental to establish a household, signposting contemporary relationships.

Chapter Four shows how *En ménage* represents the correlation between the deregulation of sexual normativity and a constant home moving. Sexuality and domesticity present a sense of mobility that breaks with the static definition of home articulated by the domestic ideal, which is deconstructed by presenting the interior as a representation. The chapter shows the introduction of a new cultural paradigm based on mobility and ephemerality that the text represents by associating change of sexual partners with change of homes. Issues of ownership arise as movement and circulation handicap male possessions such as houses and women. This chapter continues discussions on glass by showing how glass relates to a crisis of hegemonic representations of masculinity.

Finally, the last chapter will analyse Schnitzler's *Traumnovelle* and private spaces designed by Otto Wagner, Joseph Frank and Adolf Loos. I will analyse the production of a new sexual discourse being built at the intersection of literature, architecture and psychoanalysis. This chapter will argue that the new architecture gave form to a new sexual norm by facilitating the enactment of sexual perversions, while the concept of sexual perversion itself was undergoing modifications through psychoanalytical discourse. This chapter develops further the question of the eroticisation of marriage and the representation of the bourgeois woman as an erotic subject.

Notes

1 The relation between domestic architecture and sexuality in eighteenth-, nineteenth- and twentieth-century Europe has been widely covered in terms of gendered spaces, paying special attention to the creation and distribution of rooms according to the sexes. See Baydar 2005; Brown 2008; Chase and Levenson 2000; Colomina 1992; Downey 2013; Foster 2002; Heynen 2005; Reed 1996; Rosner 2005; Wigley 1992.
2 See Rudolph 2015.

I

Adultery and the Subversion of Architectural Prescriptiveness in *Madame Bovary* and *The Return of the Native*

Amongst Hardy's novels, *The Return of the Native* (1878) is not considered a rich example of architectural descriptions.[1] The text tells the story of Eustacia Vye, a young woman who feels trapped in the provinciality of Egdon Heath and marries Clym Yeobright with the hope of moving to Paris with him. However, her dreams are broken when Clym shows no intention to move back to the French capital. Eustacia starts then an affair with Damon Wildeve that will lead to her own destruction. There are striking resemblances between Hardy's main female character and Emma Bovary. In many instances, Eustacia seems to have been inspired by the character of Emma: dreams about Paris, fashion, ambition and their approaches to marriage as a way to accomplish their goals are present in both heroines. Emma and Eustacia, although different in nature, see their aspirations buried in the provincial towns of Yonville and Egdon Heath respectively. In fact, after marrying Clym, we know that '[Eustacia] had represented Paris [. . .] as in all likelihood their future home. Her hopes were bound up in this dream' (Hardy [1878] 2008: 234). It is precisely the image of Paris and its fantasies that first drives Eustacia to marry Clym: 'a young and clever man was coming into that lonely heath from, of all contrasting places in the world, Paris. It was like a man coming from heaven' (Hardy [1878] 2008: 108). Clym opens up the possibility of Eustacia leaving Egdon Heath for a fashionable and amusing city, in the same way as Charles Bovary is seen with the potentiality of realising all of Emma's romantic dreams. For Eustacia, 'to be loved to madness [. . .] was her great desire' (Hardy [1878] 2008: 69), while Emma, once married, 'ne pouvait s'imaginer [. . .] que ce calme où elle vivait fut le bonheur qu'elle avait rêvé' (could not believe [...] that the quietness in which she lived was the happiness she had dreamt of) (Flaubert [1856] 2001: 90). The strong longings for passion and love of Eustacia and Emma are placed in marriage, which is eventually turned into a delusion and a self-destructive experience.

Both the French and English texts also present remarkably similar episodes in which Emma and Eustacia engage with the architecture of domestic space in transgressive ways in order to either consummate their desires or to subvert their status quo. Descriptions of domestic spaces in the texts of Flaubert and Hardy also conform to paramount examples of the principles that should inform domestic architecture, as reflected in Robert Kerr's *The Gentleman's House* (1864). This, as we will see, illustrates the many influences between French and English architects and the ways in which a normative way of living was being defined in both countries since much earlier than the 1860s. The fact that the English and French domestic spaces represented in the chosen texts respond to Kerr's paradigmatic work allows for the identification of architectural transgression and its imagined consequences. Thus, the reading of the novels in light of *The Gentleman's House* shows that the subversion of architectural normativity was imagined to serve non-regulated female sexuality, leading to the consummation of adultery. In architectural terms, female adultery evokes the contamination of the domestic space, a contained space that echoes the enclosure of the female body. The fact that contamination can only come from a foreign element immediately brings into play notions of the inside and the outside, in this case, through the sexual use of the female body. The adulteress embodies the boundaries of domestic space: she lets the intruder in and out the house both literally and metaphorically. She threatens the organisation of domestic architecture, or, in Tschumi's words, the purity of the architectural order, by recreating the boundaries of domestic space. These architectural boundaries will literally and progressively open throughout the last decades of the century and during the early twentieth century. The transgressions of Emma and Eustacia are, thus, interpreted as opening the possibility to new ways of living by illustrating the alienating nature of a prescriptive architecture in the second half of the nineteenth century.

Hardy himself was trained as an architect; he mostly worked on restoration and designed what would become his home, Max

Gate, in 1885. However, 'he carefully emphasises that he had little interest in the practical side of architecture' (Rimmer 2004: 137). In fact, Hardy was not acclaimed for his architectural works but for his writing. Paul Turner mentions how Hardy 'went on to apply his structural instincts to verse-forms, fictional plots, and a massive historical drama' (2001: 5). Architecture did imbue Hardy's writing, as Turner notes, mentioning how Hardy's first surviving poem, 'Domicilium', 'a blank-verse description of his home written in his late teens, already showed an interest in structure and proportion' (2001: 5). If 'Domicilium' testified to Hardy's architectural sensibility, his first prose fiction did so to no lesser extent. In 'How I Built Myself a House' (1865) the narrator describes his frustration as he envisages a house for himself and his family but becomes subject to the architect's prescriptiveness. A very similar situation takes place in another of Hardy's poems 'Heiress and Architect' (1867) which U. C. Knoepflmacher analyses in terms of a clash between architectural prescriptiveness and the female desire for a different way of dwelling: '[the heiress's] naïveté about life, [the architect] insists on showing, invalidates the various shapes into which she tries to enclose her desire for a place of her own' (1990: 1058). The heiress's alienating experience of domestic space epitomises the clash between female sexuality and architecture; a clash that resonates with the disappointment of Emma and Eustacia with their much dreamed of notions of married life. Hardy's texts oppose the narrator's imagined architecture with the tyrannical reality of architecture and its limitations. In light of such architectural experience, adultery is both the outcome and an act of rebellion against architectural prescriptiveness.

How to live: the prescriptive practices of Kerr, Krafft-Ebing and M. Homais

Kerr's *The Gentleman's House* was published at a moment of architectural uncertainty in England. Many scholars have referred to the state of architecture in the second half of the nineteenth century as 'the battle of styles' (Mays 2014), when Victorian architects tried to identify a proper style for the time. The battle of styles was mostly divided into two tendencies: on the one hand, the strict followers of Gothic forms, and on the other hand, those who advocated for a new, modern style (Mays 2014: 4), although without totally abandoning the Gothic. The situation was similar in France; however, it was not until the early 1860s, with the work of Eugène Viollet-Le-Duc (1814–1879), that historicism, the revival of antique Greek and Roman styles, was openly questioned. Under the Second Empire, France mostly followed classical models, while in England, Greek and Roman models were perceived as foreign and were rejected. Thus, English historicism was characterised by the Gothic Revival. There were two tendencies in England that represented different elaborations of Gothic architecture, rather than constituting two clearly separate styles. In this context, in 1859 the *Art Journal* introduced the difference between 'Victorian Gothic' and 'Medieval Gothic' in order to differentiate between the modern, in the first case, and the old, in the second case (Mays 2014: 6). The difference between Victorian and Medieval Gothic was claimed to be the latter's failure 'to accommodate or reflect modern "conditions" and "requirements"; "Victorian notions of health and comfort" or "the varying circumstances, feelings, associations, [and] requirements of advancing times"' (Mays 2014: 6). Some leading architects of both tendencies were George Gilbert Scott (1811–1878), defender of the Victorian Gothic, and Augustus W. N. Pugin (1812–1852), who aimed at strict reproductions of the Medieval Gothic.

Jill Franklin notes Pugin's importance in the Gothic Revival in domestic architecture until the late 1860s (1981: 8). John Ruskin (1819–1900) was another very important figure whose *Seven Lamps of Architecture* (1st edn 1849, 2nd edn 1853) was highly influential (Crook 1987: 69). Ruskin mostly imitated the Italian Gothic, and put the emphasis on aesthetics, which he associated with morality, rather than on architectural structure (Crook 1987: 69). In this polemical context, Kerr's work is remarkable for the introduction of a strong architectural organisation rather than for introducing innovations in the field. Mark Girouard defines Kerr as an architect whose designs recollected and reflected the habits of the time rather than introducing any novelties in architectural structure. Kerr stands as representative of the new Victorian tendency to organise, classify and subdivide domestic space to a high degree (Girouard 1979: 29), reflecting what Girouard calls the properly Victorian: 'The Victorians had a genius for analysis and definition; everything was to be divided up into departments' (16). This tendency to divide and classify the whole is well represented in Kerr's work:

> The FAMILY DEPARTMENT may be subdivided thus: –
> The Day-rooms.
> The Sleeping-rooms.
> The Children's rooms.
> The Supplementaries.
> The Thoroughfares.
> The SERVANTS' DEPARTMENT may be subdivided in this manner: –
> The Kitchen Offices.
> The Upper Servants' Offices.
> The Lower Servants' Offices.
> The Laundry Offices.
> The Bakery and Brewery Offices.
> The Cellars, Storage, and Outhouses.
> The Servants' private rooms.
> The Supplementaries.
> The Thoroughfares.
>
> (1865: 64)

The wide range of specialised rooms that Kerr notes in his book respond to a strict sense of architectural use. It was clear to Kerr that houses were not places left to free and spontaneous use: 'all the uses and purposes of the establishment [should] be carried on in perfect harmony, – with a place for everything and everything in its place [. . .], with one obvious way of accomplishing an object, and that the right way' (1865: 71). The dweller's imagination had little, if any, role to play when it came to inhabiting the house's rooms and even deciding on the usages of his or her domestic objects and furniture. 'With one obvious way of accomplishing an object, and that the right way' (1865: 71), purpose becomes a prominent concept in architecture that relates to notions of convenience, and it must be both defined by, and accomplished through, architectural form: rooms designed 'according to [their] purpose, shall be for that purpose satisfactorily contrived, so as to be free from perversities of [their] own [. . .]. This might be called *convenience*, as regards the Room' (1865: 70). The term convenience plays a prominent role in setting the strong prescriptive tone of Kerr's work, and in fleshing out the relationship between sexuality and architecture as it is suggested by the employment of the term 'perversities'. It is interesting to note the formal similarities of *The Gentleman's House* and Krafft-Ebing's *Psychopathia*

Adultery and the Subversion of Architectural Prescriptiveness 21

Sexualis (1894), where classification and definition play a prominent role in understanding and regulating sexual practices. The first consistent catalogue of perversities looks strikingly similar to Kerr's tables:

> Schema der sexualen Neurosen.
> I. Periphere Neurosen.
> 1) Sensible.
> a) Anästhesie. b) Hyperästhesie. c) Neuralgie.
> 2. Secretorische.
> a) Aspermie. b) Polyspermie.
> 3. Motorische.
> a) Pollutionen (Krampf). b) Spermathorrhöe (Lähmung).
> (1894: 35)

As introduction to a number of definitions and pathological cases, Krafft-Ebing's previous scheme classifies the nature of sexual perversions, which the author approaches as pathological: 'Perversion des Geschlechtstriebs ist [...] nicht zu verwechseln mit Perversität geschlechtlichen Handelns [...]. Um zwischen Krankheit (Perversion) und Laster (Perversität) unterscheiden zu können, muss auf die Gesammtpersönlichkeit des Handelnden und auf die Triebfeder seines perversen Handelns zurückgegangen werden' (Perversion of the sexual instinct is [...] not to be confused with the perversity of sexual behaviour. In order to be able to differentiate between illness (perversion) and vice (perversity), one has to go back to the overall personality of the subject and to the origin of his perverse action) (Krafft-Ebing 1894: 56). For Krafft-Ebing, the concepts of perversion and perversity differ according to the subject's health: while perversion is an illness, perversity is the vicious attitude of a healthy subject. Vice, i.e., perversity, however, although not pathological, was also a medical concern. Degeneration theory in the late nineteenth century illustrated the risk of vice becoming a permanent and inheritable trait. Charles Féré notes how 'sous l'influence de l'habitude, les défauts d'éducation entrainent des perversions qui deviennent tout aussi constitutionnelles que les perversions congénitales' (Under the influence of habit, defects in education lead to perversions that become as constitutional as congenital perversions) (1899: 18). Perversity, then, also needed to be observed and treated to restore the subject's health. Kerr's short reference to the practice of restoration includes an illustrative analogy between architecture and medicine: 'no doubt it is very much a question of the nature of the disease and the skill of the doctor how far an old house may be remodelled with success' (1865: 280). A healthy house should enact privacy: 'being, indeed, the basis of our primary classification [that of privacy]. It is a first principle with the better classes of English people that the Family Rooms shall be essentially private [...]. It becomes the foremost of all maxims' (Kerr 1865: 67). Kerr is identifying the architect's responsibility in diagnosing the health of a house in order to make it a successful habitat, probably avoiding terminological misunderstandings, and consequently, potential misuses. A discussion found in an 1856 article in *The Builder* exemplifies the importance of architectural terminology as it relates to the representation of purpose. On one occasion an architect feels the need to defend himself against the belief that he was inaccurate in associating form and function in the Abbey Kitchen at Fontevrault:

> As to the use or destination of the building, I did not pretend to offer any opinion whatever [...]. I observe that although [Turner] speaks of the building decidedly as a kitchen [...], he adds that it is 'commonly called the octagon chapel or tower of Evrault' [...]. And to show that I did not intend to assert positively that it was a chapel, I added, 'if it be one, for I do not know that its purpose has been asserted'. (1856: 73b)

Excusing himself, the architect tries to argue that he was careful when using the term 'chapel' as he was unsure of the purpose of that specific part of the building: it might have been a kitchen. The reference invites us to think that in the twelfth century, the part in question was designed like a tower but served as a kitchen.[2] In the mid-nineteenth century, many architects might have found this form-function relationship unsettling, and indeed, the passage above shows how the fact of naming in such a way as to express both purpose and form becomes the core issue: in this case, form did not seem to meet purpose as well as it should. This implicitly raises questions about nineteenth-century restoration practices and the impact architectural form might have had on renovated old buildings that escape the purpose of this book.

At the core of the discussion about the Abbey Kitchen at Fontevrault lies the law of convenience, that is, that rooms designed 'according to [their] purpose, shall be for that purpose satisfactorily contrived' (Kerr 1965: 70). Convenience does not only define the proper use of a room, i.e., its normative and normal use, but it also illustrates the classificatory purposes of architecture and its medical approaches. In France, the importance of 'convenances' in the use of rooms is noted by Léonce Reynaud who, in the 1867 edition of his seminal work *Traité d'architecture* (1850), defines architecture as 'l'art des convenances' (the art of convenience) (1867: 1), defining a bad distribution as 'distribution vicieuse' (vicious distribution) (1) when form does not meet purpose. Reynaud insists in his writing: 'De même que dans les êtres sortis de la main de Dieu il existe [en architecture] un rapport intime entre la forme et la fonction; que l'extérieur est le résultat de la composition de l'intérieur' (Just as in the creatures made by God, there exists [in architecture] an intimate relationship between form and function; the exterior is the result of the interior's composition) (10). Both Kerr and Reynaud approach dwelling in medical terms: perversity is in architecture, as in medicine, a *contra-natura* act shaped by the inadequate use of a form. For Reynaud, it constitutes a vice (a word also used by Krafft-Ebing above) when purpose is not defined by form. Reynaud's definition of vicious space echoes nineteenth-century approaches to inversion in which the body's form did not adjust to the interior being. Rosario defines how inversion was perceived in the nineteenth century as 'a radical contradiction between the interior being and the superficial appearance' (1997: 71). As Krafft-Ebing states, acting against nature is something which can be defined, identified and readdressed. Kerr, in order to avoid perversity and enact convenience, proceeds with each room in the same way: 'having first made a complete classified list of the rooms, with [their] approximate dimensions', Kerr instructs architects to 'cut out to scale small pieces of paper which shall represent these rooms individually; and mark and classify the whole' (1865: 76). Through his extensive labour, Kerr cancels any act of spatial interpretation and the freedom to pursue new ways of dwelling, hence turning the act of inhabiting into a normative practice.

Convenience would continue to appear in architectural and design books later in the century. French art historian Henry Havard (1838–1921) made 'convenance' one of the conditions for a home to be habitable in his design book *L'Art dans la maison: grammaire de l'ameublement* (1884). Havard's work, addressed to housewives, covers a wide range of topics including the adequate use of architectural materials, the layout of rooms, and the way in which each space should be inhabited. Finding a proximity to Kerr, Havard mentions: 'on donne, en matière d'ameublement, le nom de convenance, au rapport exact qui doit exister entre l'objet et sa destination, entre la forme de cet objet et l'usage auquel il s'adapte' (regarding furniture, we name convenience the exact relationship that must exist between an object and its purpose, between the object's shape and its use) (1884: 246). While Kerr refers more explicitly to the architectural design and structure of the rooms, Havard introduces the same idea of convenience in furniture and objects, that is, in the mobile configuration of the room. In the 1880s, this extension of the concept of convenience in Paris seems rather a reaction against an emergent domestic culture based on circulation. As we will see in detail in Chapter Four, the experience of home became more intertwined with notions of mobility and ephemerality, but theoreticians still strived to maintain the basic principles of convenience and even stability. Juxtaposing the architectural and medical terms of convenience, we see how the relationship between form and function concerned dwelling and sexual practices.

In their analysis of *The Gentleman's House*, Michael Levenson and Karen Chase define Kerr as 'the evolutionist of domestic life' (2000: 162). The architect does indeed introduce his work with a history of domestic architecture from the Saxons to the Victorians paying careful attention to the progressive internal division of houses and the appearance of specialised rooms: 'the development of the English system [. . .] is its course of progress, in the line thus indicated, from the *Hall* of the Saxon Thane to the *Mansion* of the modern Gentleman' (Kerr 1865: 2). Going further back in time, an article published in 1856 in *The Builder* illustrates a long list of specialised rooms: 'the building contains a large dining-room, working-room, kitchen, baths, and various other conveniences, such as the skittle-alley shed, etc.' (21a). This Darwinian narrative is shared with French architect Eugène Viollet-Le-Duc who, in his *Entretiens sur l'architecture* (1863–1872), starts his theoretical works with a history of dwelling that points at not only the perfection of the latest periods but also at the highest capacity of the white man to develop better homes. In a similar tone, Krafft-Ebing refers to monogamy with the following words: 'die Liebe des Menschen auf höherer Civilisationsstufe nur eine monogamische sein kann' (at a higher level of civilisation, the love of man can only be monogamous) (1894: 4–5). Immersed in the evolutionary and racial thoughts of the nineteenth century, architectural and medical texts present an evolutionist narrative focused on a progressive improvement of man's mores and buildings that leads to perfection. In this context, the aim was to show how Victorian and bourgeois ways of living were expressions of high civilisation.

This strict pattern of division, specialisation and usage is what makes possible the connection between domestic architecture and perversion. Architecture's rigorous classification of rooms sets up the conditions for perversity, in other words, for a transgression of prescriptiveness and a misuse of space. Room specialisation is expressed through architectural boundaries (walls, doors and to some extent windows) that shape spaces. Such an approach to domestic architecture is crucial to understand the significance that shifts in internal distribution will have in the decades to follow, and their connections to perversity. The prescriptive assumptions around which middle-class domesticity was established in England, France, Germany and Austria establish the context in which architectural innovations, which we will see in the following chapters, took place. The polemics surrounding such innovations were related to their potentiality in modifying sexual culture.

In *The Gentleman's House*, Kerr did not simply write a descriptive manual for the architect with objective instructions regarding measures, distribution or decoration but a prescriptive and normative guide for the dwellers on how to inhabit and use each room. Even if Kerr's book seems focused on standard instructions rather than on subjective opinions, the presentation of a descriptive text in a prescriptive form shows how it aimed at naturalising prescriptiveness. Kerr's work was widely received, and the architect gained customers through its dissemination (Girouard 1979: 17–18). Franklin mentions how Kerr's work became a model to follow in the design of mid-Victorian country houses, especially with regard to its systematic planning design (1981: 1). Not only did Kerr become a renowned architect in England but he was also influential abroad. Kerr's work arrived in France via consolidated Second Empire architects, such as César Daly, known as one of the most influential architects of the time together with Viollet-Le-Duc, whose work had also been known in England during the 1850s. Daly, who was also the founder and general editor of the French leading architecture magazine

Revue générale de l'architecture et des travaux publics (1840–1888), constantly shows his admiration of English architecture: serials such as 'Maison d'habitation de Londres' appeared in two issues in 1855. The mutual influences between English and French architecture have been noted by many scholars, such as Sharon Marcus and Donald J. Olsen, who both argue how English and French architects stressed privacy and domesticity in their designs (Marcus 1999: 160; Olsen 1986: 119). Michelle Perrot notes how British domesticity became a model in France after the revolution (1999: 16), while in Austria, Hermann Muthesius' *Das englische Haus* (1905) testifies to the importance nineteenth-century English architecture had in early twentieth-century Vienna (Long 2002: 33). Finally, Mordaunt J. Crook suggests Viollet-Le-Duc's impact on Kerr by noting a shift in architectural leadership from Ruskin to Viollet-Le-Duc in England in 1854 (1987: 71). The *Revue* also shows awareness of contemporary English architecture by making references to the British architectural journal *The Builder* (Steltler 1856: 216–17).

Although *Psychopathia Sexualis* was preceded by works such as Ambroise Tardieu's *Étude médico-légal sur les attentats aux moeurs* (1857) – closer to the publication of *Madame Bovary* and *The Gentleman's House* – it was, like Kerr's work, a representative text of the medico-sexual culture of the time. In fact, Krafft-Ebing's work is a receptacle of previous medical studies especially with regard to the exploration of sodomy and paedophilia. But *Psychopathia Sexualis* was the first structured study on pathological and normative sexualities that aimed at the knowledge and regulation of sexuality in itself. In contrast to Krafft-Ebing's approach, Tardieu, for example, focused his work on rape, sodomy and paedophilia (1857: 1) within a legal frame, hence contextualising sexual knowledge in legal situations and for legal purposes. Thus, despite the time difference between the publication of *Psychopathia Sexualis* and *Madame Bovary*, I approach the former as a paradigmatic work that illustrates the already existent exploration in Flaubert's text of normative/non-normative sexualities. The structure of *Psychopathia Sexualis* reflects contemporary approaches to classification and contamination that are also represented in Kerr's architectural text and through the character of M. Homais in *Madame Bovary*. The structural and conceptual similarities of the texts illustrate how prescriptiveness was part of a wider cultural pattern.

Adultery and the Subversion of Architectural Prescriptiveness

Like Krafft-Ebing and Kerr, Homais, the pharmacist in *Madame Bovary*, epitomises the Victorian spirit at organising and regulating domestic life. Indeed, it is Homais himself who constructs and supports a rigid way of dwelling based on the strict classification and definition of items as represented in his profession. We know that in his domestic laboratory, Capharnaüm: 'il [. . .] passait seul de longues heures à étiqueter, à transvaser' (he spent long hours by himself, labelling) (Flaubert [1856] 2001: 329). Homais' activity as pharmacist has been analysed in terms of an 'incessant production of prescriptive discourse' (Duffy 2015: 37), and as an 'extreme form [of a] will to "contain" everything and everyone in order that everything and everyone may thus be safely "labelled"' (Tanner 1979: 274). The etymology of the term pharmacist, in French *apothicaire*, comes from the Greek *apotheke*, which denotes both box and shop (Duffy 2015: 54). However, Florence Emptaz focuses on the etymological word *pharmakeia*, 'qui désigne l' "emploi de médicaments ou de poisons"' (which refers to 'the use of medicines or poison') (2001: 9); *pharmakeia* derives from *pharmakon*, 'plante médicinale' (medicinal plant), 'drogue, remède ou posion' (drug, remedy or poison) (Emptaz 2003: 9). A reading of the term pharmacist in light of both *apotheke* and *pharmakon* synthetises Homais' work as being that of organising and administrating remedies/poisons. As Derrida notes, 'pharmacée (*Pharmakeia*) est aussi un nom commun qui signifie l'administration du *pharmakon*, de la drogue: du remède et/ou du poison' (pharmacy [*Pharmakeia*] is also a common name that refers to the administration of a drug: of a remedy and/or of poison) (1972: 78). The paradoxical position of Homais lies in the very nature of his profession, which implies the actual adulteration of substances, on one hand, and of discourses through pharmacy's expansion into other disciplines such as medicine, chemistry or agriculture, on the other (Duffy 2015: 59). Homais' ambivalent position is made apparent through his anxiety when Justin leaves the cabinet door open and, with it, the possibility of someone being poisoned with arsenic: 'souvent je m'épouvante moi-même, lorsque je pense à ma responsabilité!' (I often feel scared when I think of my responsibility!) (Flaubert [1856] 2001: 331). But the concept of poisoning does not only refer to chemical substances. Homais keeps an illustrated book on sexuality in his laboratory that could have ended up in his children's hands due to Justin's carelessness:

– *L'amour . . . conjugal!* dit [Homais] en séparant lentement ces deux mots. Ah! très bien! très bien! très joli! Et des gravures! . . . Ah! c'est trop fort!
[. . .]
—Tu n'as donc pas réfléchi qu'il pouvait, ce livre infâme, tomber entre les mains de mes enfants, mettre l'étincelle dans leur cerveau, ternir la pureté d'Athalie, corrompre Napoléon!

(Flaubert [1856] 2001: 332–3)

– *Conjugal . . . love!* [Homais] said separating slowly those two words. Ah! Very well! Very well! Very nice! And the pictures! . . . Ah! It's too much!
[. . .]
– You didn't think, then, that this infamous book could fall into the hands of my children, spark their imagination, tarnish the purity of Athalie, corrupt Napoleón!)

Arsenic and sexual knowledge become potentially accessible when Justin forgets to lock the door. Both arsenic and a supposed perversion of the subject through inappropriate sexual knowledge signal at Emma Bovary, who, in fact, will kill herself with Homais' arsenic after becoming an adulteress. The poisoning of Emma echoes the sexual contamination involved in her adultery, and highlights the ironic role of Homais as regulator. At the same time, the misuse of an architectural element, in this case, a door that should have been locked, and that organises sexual knowledge within Homais' home, threatens to contaminate the children's innocence. Duffy, among others, argues how the archival aspect of the pharmacist's activity, that of accumulating and labelling items, relates to an accumulation of information, and therefore, to control over the communication of such information (Duffy 2015: 53; Emptaz 2003: 7). Access to sexual knowledge is regulated through domestic architecture by employing devices such as (locked) doors and keys. In this case, the transgression of space could potentially result in a sexual transgression as it represents the loss of innocence, a becoming aware of sexual realities that Homais understands to lead to the corruption of children. This moment of lost domestic order is thus intrinsically related to sexual knowledge, something reinforced by Homais' admiration of French philosopher Jean-Jacques Rousseau (1712–1778), for whom innocence was contaminated by civilisation, i.e., scientific knowledge, highlighting Homais' hypocrisy. Contamination is, thus, intrinsic to the idea of both sexuality and domestic space, and so are adultery and adulteration. The scene in the pharmacist's home reflects Kerr's ideas on the importance of boundaries: 'what passes on either side of the boundary shall be both invisible and inaudible on the other' (1865: 67). This premise is based on the acknowledgement that adulteration, which emerges from mixing substances, uses and spaces, is inherent to domestic space. The cabinet's open door exposes the vulnerability of a boundary, as the following sections show, a recurrent fact in *Madame Bovary*.

Through the figure of Homais, Flaubert's novel reflects the incapacity of prescriptive discourses to enact prescriptiveness, as indeed Emma's adultery epitomises. Moreover, contamination does not only concern spaces and bodies but also the text itself. The Flaubertian novel reflects the permeability between different disciplinary discourses, which are also reflected in Homais' practice, and challenges the literary/non-literary boundary (Duffy 2015: 60). Emma's adultery is the most appalling contradiction of a purist culture, which cannot avoid a constant adulteration of spheres, e.g., noises, smells, the body, spaces, substances and discourses. By regulating the use of domestic architecture and sexuality, architects and doctors set up the conditions for their transgression.

Windows and the enactment of illicit desires

Windows are liminal architectural elements, and it was precisely this boundary position that concerned architects well until the 1880s. Daly published his seminal work, *L'Architecture privée au XIXe siècle sous Napoleon III* (1864), exactly the same year as *The Gentleman's House*. In *L'Architecture privée*, Daly points to the basic function of windows:

> Qu'est-ce qu'une fenêtre? [. . .]; – c'est une baie destinée à laisser passer la lumière du jour sans donner accès à la pluie, à la neige et parfois au soleil; – un moyen de ventiler une salle, d'en épurer l'atmosphère, d'en laisser réchapper l'air vicié, sans donner entrée aux rhumes et aux rhumatismes. (1864: I, 9)

> (What is a window? [. . .]; – it is a frame intended to let daylight in without giving access to rain, snow and sometimes sun; – a way to

ventilate a room, to purify the atmosphere, to let out the stale air, without giving way to colds and rheumatism.)

Daly's introduction to the definition of windows already shows the window's own contradictions: 'laisser réchapper l'air vicié, sans donner entrée aux rhumes et aux rhumatismes' (to let out the stale air, without giving way to colds and rheumatism) (1864: I, 9). Indeed, Daly warns against the undesirable effects the window can cause in the dweller's health at the same time as acknowledging the important function of windows. But illness was not the only potential result of a misuse of windows; a lack of privacy was an even greater concern for the architect: '[la fenêtre est] une ouverture qui permet de communiquer avec l'extérieur, mais qui ne doit pas devenir, pour les lovelurs [sic] et les indiscrets, un moyen de se glisser dans l'intérieur' ([the window is] an aperture to communicate with the outside, but which should not become, for prying eyes, a means of slipping inside) (1864: I, 9). Windows are, thus, framed within a constant dialectical movement between too much and too little aperture that needs to be regulated. In other words, the ways in which windows can be used in excess, hence, misused, vary only in degree; they are always a centimetre away from their irreplaceable function. Windows exemplify the ways in which the regulations concerning architectural elements were conceptually close to understandings of normal sexuality in Krafft-Ebing, who understood perversion as normality in excess: 'sexual abnormalities, according to Krafft-Ebing, were not opposed to but rather intensifications of normal forms of sexuality' (Cryle and Stephens 2017: 270). Normal and abnormal uses of windows followed the same cognitive pattern: too much aperture, or too much light would be an excess of air and light, and an opportunity for the voyeurs to spy into the sacred boundaries of the home. The description of the normative use of windows appears in this instance as the only way to regulate their proper function, mediating between the normal use of windows and the unavoidable threat to domestic privacy they pose.

As in Kerr's case, the enactment of privacy was one of architecture's goals for Daly. There is, however, quite a different attitude towards windows in Kerr, who does not seem to focus on their potential danger for privacy as his French contemporary does. But Kerr still shows the search for a balance in carefully defining the placement of windows in the house:

Adultery and the Subversion of Architectural Prescriptiveness

> The *Windows* ought, as a rule, to occupy one side [. . .], rather than one end. A room lighted from the end alone cannot be so cheerful as it might be, especially if looking Northward; it will also be comparatively close; and when daylight is waning it will become unpleasantly dark in one part, whilst sufficiently illuminated in another. (Kerr 1865: 92)

Kerr's concern with windows seems focused on the moderation of light rather than the internal/external boundary and its relation to privacy. But the normative use of the window also appears in relation to its use in excess; in this case, the excess of light on one side of the room would cause its absence on the other. Kerr's approach to windows illustrates, as in Daly, that the window contains in itself the possibilities of both the normal and abnormal, i.e., light and darkness, echoing Krafft-Ebing's approaches to normality. The architect and, we assume, the dweller, need to accept, and negotiate with this fact. But, at the same time, windows make constantly present the possibilities of transgression in the domestic sphere. In *Madame Bovary*, the window, rather than being a tool for voyeurism – in contrast to what we will see in *La Curée* – is represented as a subversive element as it highlights Emma's agency and desire to change her life. If in *The Return of the Native*, Mrs Yeobright, Eustacia's mother-in-law, is represented behind the window, while she turns her gaze to the interior, Emma does look at the other side of the window: 'assise dans son fauteuil, près de la fenêtre, elle voyait passer les gens du village sur le trottoir' (seated in her armchair, near the window, she looked at the villagers passing by on the sidewalk) (Flaubert [1856] 2001: 156). While Mrs Yeobright is represented as part of the domestic interior by the fact that her gaze is turned to the inside, Emma's gaze is addressed towards the outside. The window works as a means of representing Emma as being desirous of something beyond the interior, and by analogy, beyond herself. For Emma, the window is a reminder that domestic space is her own cage. But in looking through it, she initiates a transgression towards the outside. In this context, Andrea Del Lungo has noted how Emma's gaze unsettles traditional representations of female positions at the window:

> La posture d'Emma se révèle capitale, dans la mesure où elle change radicalement l'image de la femme à la fenêtre, jusqu'alors perçue en tant qu'*objet* du regard masculin [. . .]. Avec *Madame Bovary*, un tel

paradigme historique se renverse: la femme devient *sujet* d'un regard incessamment tourné vers le monde extérieur. (2014: 431)

(Emma's posture is crucial, as it radically changes the image of the woman at the window, perceived until then as the object of the male gaze [...]. With *Madame Bovary*, this historical paradigm is reversed: the woman becomes the subject of a gaze incessantly turned towards the outside world.)

Inherent to architecture are the possibilities of usage it offers, impossible to avoid. If *Madame Bovary* captured the transgressive potentialities of the window, so did Hardy's work, although English architects did not place the focus on the window's capacity to alter the domestic imaginary. Kerr was not alone in his naïve approach to windows. An article published in 1856 in *The Builder* echoes Kerr's functional approach in reference to the corridors of a house in Cardiff: 'the whole is lighted by means of six large skylight windows' (21a). No more explanation was given about windows, showing, apparently, no concern. English architects seemed less prompt at noting how windows can turn the interior into a more vulnerable reality, being an object of curiosity to others. Nonetheless, *The Return of the Native* explores the anxieties around the window. After Eustacia has married Clym, their house's window, half open without clear purpose – it is a winter night – facilitates the contact between the lovers, i.e., Eustacia and Wildeve:

> Wildeve, after looking over Eustacia's garden gate for some little time [...] was tempted [...] to advance towards the window which was not quite closed, the blind being only partly drawn down. He could see into the room, and Eustacia was sitting there alone. Wildeve contemplated her for a minute, and then retreating into the heath beat the ferns lightly, whereupon moths flew out alarmed. Securing one he returned to the window, and holding the moth to the chink opened his hand. The moth made towards the candle upon Eustacia's table. (Hardy [1878] 2008: 260)

In the above passage, Wildeve's illicit desire towards Eustacia is negotiated around the aperture of the window, which finally facilitates the communication with Eustacia. Wildeve first encounters a reversible architectural element, the garden gate, which works as invitation to penetrate the garden: a space which though belonging to the house, is still outside its architectural boundaries. The window, 'not quite closed' (260), suggests the trespass of the interior space by allowing Wildeve a better view of Eustacia in the room, inviting him to go in. The fact that the window is partly open also suggests Eustacia's failure at using windows as prescribed in architecture. Such misuse of the window contextualises the communication between lovers. Thus, the window does not let light through but misplaced desire, that of Wildeve for Eustacia. This contrasts with traditional representations of the domestic ideal, where women such as Mrs Yeobright, who is depicted 'sitting by the window as usual' (Hardy [1878] 2008: 206), do not actively use the window as a tool for transgression. Instead, the window is used as a prescriptive source of light that empowers the aesthetic motif of women at home. This establishes a correlation between the misuse of architectural elements and Eustacia's failure at regulating her own sexuality according to its normative use – we will see this correlation again in Fontane's *L'Adultera* (1882).

In the scene of Wildeve by the window, the focus is placed on the window as an instrument to bring the exterior home, exposing the vulnerability of marriage. By representing the window as leading to adultery, the text complements, as well as complicates, Kerr's limited approach to windows. In fact, if Kerr uses the term perversity with regard to the misuse of rooms, *The Return of the Native* enlarges this possibility by including boundary elements in the enactment of non-normative sexuality, something, however, Daly does suggest. It seems paradoxical that Kerr did not include liminal elements such as doors and windows in his explanation of architectural perversity, as they are placed in a more crucial position.

Madame Bovary presents a very similar window scene involving Rodolphe before he actually becomes Emma's first lover. As at the Yeobrights' house, the Bovarys totally fail to keep the domestic haven safe from intrusions. While first, Rodolphe, like Wildeve with Eustacia, keeps his distance from Emma's house, he will eventually penetrate it. Following a similar pattern to that seen above in *The Return of the Native*, Rodolphe tells Emma: 'toutes les nuits, je me relevais, j'arrivais jusqu'ici, je regardais votre maison [. . .], les arbres du jardin qui se balançaient à votre fenêtre, et une petite lampe, une lueur, qui brillait à travers les carreaux' (every night I would get up, come here, look at your house [. . .] the trees in your garden swinging by your window, and a little lamp, a light, shining through the panes) (Flaubert [1856] 2001: 225). Though in a more romantic narrative and adding the subjectivity of speaking in first person as well as emphasising his perseverance, 'toutes les nuits' (every night) (225), the scene Rodolphe describes presents, as in Hardy's text, a window – Emma's – and the light of a candle amid the darkness of the night. Like Wildeve, Rodolphe looks at Emma's window; however, he waits for nights in the same place without daring any contact with her, or so he claims. This fact empowers the mythological aspect of home, which remains a sanctuary in the imagination of the lover, and that gives Rodolphe's forthcoming transgression greater impact.

In both texts, the window works in an ambivalent way: on one hand, it seems to create a distance by means of its borderline position, hence enclosing domestic life, and empowering its idealisation by highlighting its representational nature. On the other hand, however, the window suggests contact between lovers. For Wildeve, the window invites a direct transgression, and in both cases, the window introduces the stranger's gaze, hence representing what Daly warned against: '[la fenêtre est] une ouverture qui permet de communiquer avec l'extérieur, mais qui ne doit pas devenir, pour les lovelurs [sic] et les indiscrets, un moyen de se glisser dans l'intérieur' ([the window is] an aperture to communicate with the outside, but which should not become, for prying eyes, a means of slipping inside) (1864: I, 9). Daly, however, failed to recognise women's desire. He assumed that it was the subject outside who would feel tempted to look inside, indiscreetly, but did not consider the possibility of looking from the inside to the exterior to be problematic. Eustacia's use of the telescope is representative of this female gaze that looks at the world. In Eustacia's case, looking at is a manifestation of her powerful desire: 'she is [. . .] a creature of an overweening projective desire – often crucially expressed in terms of vision' (Hughes 2004: 240). Indeed, since the beginning of the text, we know that Eustacia looks at the Quiet Inn to spy on Wildeve's movements with her telescope: 'she lifted her left hand, and revealed that it held a closed telescope. This she rapidly extended [. . .] and raising it to her eye directed it exactly towards the light beaming from the inn' (Hardy [1878] 2008: 56). The gaze is, indeed, present in Hardy's works. John Hughes notes 'the complex centrality of observation – of looking and being looked at – in Hardy's fiction and imagination' (2004:

229). Eustacia is represented as an active observer looking for the object of her desire, a motif that we will see in *Traumnovelle* through Albertine's gaze, and that relates to the unsettlement of her household.

The limits domestic architecture poses to female desires start being unsettled through the use of windows by the desirous female gaze. Descriptions of the interior like this found in *Madame Bovary* seem to preclude the threat such desires meant: '[Emma] ne savait pas que, sur la terrasse des maisons, la pluie fait des lacs quand les gouttières sont bouchées, et elle fut ainsi demeurée en sa sécurité, lorsqu'elle découvrit subitement une lézarde dans le mur' (Not realising that, on the terraces of houses, the rain forms puddles when the gutters are blocked, Emma felt safe, when she suddenly discovered a fissure on the wall) (Flaubert [1856] 2001: 160). The fissure in the wall represents the beginning of a falling down of the domestic structure. Placed at the start of the Second Empire and the urban renovations of Paris, *Madame Bovary* exposes a domestic life that we will see represented even closer to its end in Zola's *La Curée*. This 'lézarde' (fissure), which echoes Deleuze's idea of a 'fêlure' (crack) in the Rougon Macquart family in 'Zola et la fêlure', is found in the house but it also represents Emma's body as it literally opens for her lovers. The female gaze represents women's own desires, which far from being readdressed into legitimate relationships step outside the domestic boundaries. Following this argument, the next section will look more deeply at Eustacia's gaze as a means of subverting domestic architecture.

Compactness and extension: negotiating sexuality and architectural limits

Compactness, 'the concretion of the rooms so as to economise space and outlay' (Kerr 1865: 75), is one of the features Kerr attributes to the gentleman's house. Looking at the historical evolution of dwelling, Kerr states, 'respecting also improved *arrangement* [. . .], compactness may have become better understood than in the Elizabethan time' (1865: 48). Compactness has to do with arrangement but also with privacy, as too much compactness may lead to a loss of privacy: 'however small and compact the house may be, the family must have privacy' (66). Finally, compactness appears in the list which defines the proper house:

The test of A GENTLEMAN'S HOUSE [...]:
Privacy.	Salubrity.
Comfort.	Aspect and prospect.
Convenience.	Cheerfulness.
Spaciousness.	Elegance.
Compactness.	Importance.
Light and air.	Ornament.

(67)

Paradoxically, spaciousness is listed alongside compactness. Both these qualities should find a balance in order to enact privacy while avoiding a waste of space. The concept of compactness is thus difficult to execute as it might impede, or handicap, privacy, which is one of the most important aims of domestic architecture. In line with normative domesticity, compactness is also present in Blooms-End; but Eustacia subverts the quality of compactness as it allows her actively to look around: '[Clym] for whom she had predetermined to nourish a passion went into the small room, and across it to the further extremity' (Hardy [1878] 2008: 139). The interior of Blooms-End is further described as a mysterious web of corridors and rooms, where Eustacia tries to identify Clym:

> The mummers [...] were seated on a bench, one end of which extended into the small apartment, or pantry, for want of space in the outer room. Eustacia [...] had chosen the innermost seat, which thus commanded a view of the interior of the pantry as well as the room containing the guests. When Clym passed down the pantry her eyes followed him in the gloom which prevailed there. At the remote end was a door which, just as he was about to open it for himself, was opened by somebody within, and light streamed forth. (Hardy [1878] 2008: 139–40)

The complexity of spatial structure at Blooms-End is illustrated through the mapping of Eustacia's desire onto space, which is signposted by Clym's movement. Blooms-End's architectural network appears to be more entangled than that seen through representations of Mrs Yeobright. From Eustacia's perspective, the compactness of Blooms-End is represented as an almost claustrophobic house with small rooms and a lack of space. While such an outlook illustrates the disagreement between Eustacia herself and normative domesticity, it also allows Eustacia to take advantage of the norm of compactness to accomplish her goal. Thus, compactness prepares the setting for subversion by facilitating the movement of the gaze through consecutive spaces. Eustacia is able to see the interior of the next room, where the guests gather, and turns this architectural virtue into a domestic vulnerability, a paradox, which is part of the complexity Blooms-End gains through Eustacia's view. Eustacia's position gives her a command of the scene, and she is able to see Clym going through a door at the other end that is mysteriously opened by someone else: Eustacia has a glimpse of Blooms-End's secrets, which distorts its ideal image.

The concept of compactness in *The Return of the Native* also works as metaphor for the female body and sexual expression. In fact, we know that Eustacia 'had been existing in a suppressed estate, and not in one of languor or stagnation' (Hardy [1878] 2008: 56). Compactness relates to the normativity of domestic space and sexuality: architectural compactness can be seen as the material representation of a suppression of emotions and desires. Jean-Louis Cabanès has explored the aesthetics of expansion and contraction in Flaubert in relation to space and desire, and argues that in *Madame Bovary*, 'l'espace du désir semble illimité' (the space of desire seems to have no limit) (2013: 45). However, we have seen how the Bovarys' house puts limits on such desire. It is precisely Emma's tension against such limits that makes her desire appear as an expansion of her being and sexuality that tends to erase domestic boundaries, as we have seen with Emma looking through the window.

For Emma, compactness is alienation, an experience highlighted by Charles's profession. Emma's life constantly relates to Charles's patients, and she needs to adapt her use of space to that of her husband. Charles's cabinet constitutes his private space, and it takes over the rest of the house where the patients can be heard all over the place: 'l'odeur des roux pénétrait à travers la muraille, pendant les consultations, de même que l'on entendait de la cuisine, les malades tousser dans le cabinet' (during the consultations, the smell of butter penetrated through the wall, just like one could hear patients coughing in the consulting room from the kitchen) (Flaubert [1856] 2001: 81). The house, however, is adequate for Charles as he can receive his patients. The Bovarys' house already presents what Kerr would define as a crucial part of the gentleman's house: 'the *private room* of the gentleman, in which he conducts his affairs' (1865: 121). M. Homais congratulates the newcomers for their choice of house: 'vous vous trouverez [...] jouir d'une des maisons les plus confortables d'Yonville. Ce qu'elle a principalement de commode pour un médecin, c'est une porte sur l'*Allée*, qui permet d'entrer et de sortir sans être vu' (you will find yourself [...] enjoying one of the most comfortable homes in Yonville. What is more convenient for a doctor is a door to the lane through which you can enter and exit the house without being seen) (Flaubert [1856] 2001: 139–40). Echoing Homais, Kerr advises that the cabinet first be 'accessible from a secondary Entrance [...]. The purpose is to admit all sorts of persons on business as directly as possible to this room, without interfering with the Thoroughfares of the family' (1865: 121). Charles's independence is thus assured, and he is able to establish an apparent complicit relationship with the house where he is free to be involved in any kind of activity as well as exit the house without being seen.

However, this compactness will become a tool for deriding the very norms of domesticity and architecture when Rodolphe, entering the Bovarys' house without being noticed by Charles, professes his love for Emma and attempts once more to seduce her: 'Rodolphe, insensiblement, se laissa glisser du tabouret jusqu'à terre; mais on entendit un bruit de sabots dans la cuisine, et la porte de la salle, il s'en aperçut, n'était pas fermée' (Rodolphe, imperceptibly, slipped from the stool to the floor, but one could heard the sound of clogs in the kitchen, and the living room door, he noticed, was not closed) (Flaubert [1856] 2001: 225). If the text suggests that Emma feels invaded by the noises of Charles's patients, the noises coming from the kitchen when Rodolphe is attempting adultery parody Charles's authority and the supposed convenience of the house. Rodolphe's declaration takes place in what Kerr identifies as the parlour-dining room or family parlour (1865: 100), amid the dangers of being seen or heard due to the house's compactness and the open door. Rodolphe's declaration of love in Emma's parlour-dining room seems a mockery of Kerr's precious sense of convenience:

> The pleasures of residence are dependent upon convenience of plan [and] to some masterpiece of arrangement wherein the skill of the architect has provided at every point against those collisions of interests and sympathies which even the little affairs of a household will engender. (1865: 72)

The love scene between Rodolphe and Emma of which Charles remains ignorant is evidence that the house's design is intended to support the authority of the paterfamilias. The family parlour, which Kerr defines as 'homely' (1865: 100), is the very centre of family life, 'used as a family sitting-room; sometimes for both day and evening [. . .]; and sometimes for the evening alone, – at least in winter, when Paterfamilias, having done his day's work and dines, refuses to move any more from his favourite easy chair' (Kerr 1865: 99). Charles's house is indeed a place where interests clash, and where the prescriptiveness of domestic architecture is exposed by illustrating contradictory practices of space.

In *Madame Bovary* and *The Return of the Native*, illicit desires take advantage of the very same architectural principles which aim at enacting normative dwelling practices. This generates a tension between the expansion of such desires and the architecture of domestic space. In this context, Emma and Eustacia present the particularity of engaging with sexual desires which do not conform to the normative idea of domestic convenience and subvert traditional approaches to female sexuality. The architectural representations of the Bovarys' house in Tostes and Blooms-End turn the quality of compactness into a complex tool for subversion: compactness exposes female alienation, but it also empowers women and derides domesticity.

Although Eustacia does take advantage of the structure of Blooms-End, the latter is meant to represent a successful realisation of the domestic ideal: 'inside is Paradise [. . .]. Songs and old tales are drawn from the occupants by the comfortable heat' (Hardy [1878] 2008: 134). Thomasin, who grows up in Blooms-End, is representative of its domesticity as she embodies the civilising role of women: 'help me to keep [my husband] home in the evenings' (259), she says to Mrs Yeobright. From the beginning of the text, Thomasin's concern after her fiancé Wildeve breaks his word to marry her – 'do I look like a lost woman?' (Hardy [1878] 2008: 111) – turns her into an example of sexual domestication in Victorian literature, recalling what Nancy Armstrong defines as 'the premise that [. . .] desire if it is not so domesticated, constitutes the gravest danger' (1987: 6). Not only Thomasin's own reputation but also that of Wildeve is what Thomasin saves in making sure that they finally marry. Wildeve, in love with Eustacia but unable to marry her, needs to readdress his desire in a legitimate way through marriage, and Thomasin appears as the exemplary woman that strives to regulate Wildeve's desires and domestic position. Echoing Krafft-Ebing, who places all the weight of civilisation on the regulation of female sexuality, 'if [a woman] is normally developed mentally, and well bred, her sexual desire is small' (13), and Féré, 'on ne conteste pas que la chasteté de la femme soit la condition de la civilisation' (we do not dispute that the chastity of women is the condition for civilisation) (1899: 31), Thomasin embodies this ideal. Domesticity was articulated at the intersection of normative uses of architecture and sexuality. Thomasin is, indeed, 'the bearer of moral norms and socializer of men, [with] techniques for regulating desire' (Armstrong 1987: 89). Like Mrs Yeobright, Thomasin becomes the angel of the house to safeguard the household and lead its members in the right direction.

Doors and the regulation of sexuality

Like windows, doors are borderline elements that regulate the entrance of the foreign. However, architects did not seem to be as concerned with doors as they were with windows. In fact, doors did not clearly menace the rigid structure of domestic space by simulating the erasure of walls. This would have distorted the cataloguing purposes of architects, naming and defining each room and its usages with extreme precision. In architectural discourses, doors seem to be described in purely functional terms. A closer analysis of ways in which doors are conceived as part of the wider architectural system, however, will illustrate their significance in regulating notions of sexual contamination. Thus, Kerr departs from the importance of doors in the organisation of the plan:

> The relations of the rooms to each other are in fact the relation of their doors; and accordingly, every one can call to mind instances where these Thoroughfares and this relation of doors are so contrived that one appears to understand their system instinctively, and others, on the contrary, where one is always at a loss. (1865: 155)

Doors, Kerr states, establish spatial relationships, communicating and separating rooms. In doing so, however, they also represent a map of emotional, affective and intimate relationships. Stressing the importance of doors in configuring a referential system in which the user should not feel lost, Kerr is implying an intui-

Adultery and the Subversion of Architectural Prescriptiveness 41

tive (and cultural) knowledge of what is on the other side of the door, of which doors lead to which rooms based on their situation in the house. But it is also awareness of how things work in the domestic sphere, emotionally and in terms of privacy and affectivity. Order is very important here, and this order is both architectural and emotional. In social terms, doors also articulate the boundary between classes: 'the family constitute one community: the servants another. Whatever may be their mutual regard and confidence as dwellers under the same roof, each class is entitled to shut its door upon the other and be alone' (1865: 68). Understanding the importance of doors in establishing order is crucial to imagine how domestic space can be potentially violated around a misuse of doors. In a scene where Wildeve visits Eustacia, who is already married to Clym, after they have danced together, and showing his renewed interest in her, doors are used to show the increasing degree of transgression of the domestic space that happens according to the degree of intimacy to which each door relates: going from one door to another and starting from the main door towards more intimate parts of the house, Wildeve crosses spaces of privacy and intimacy: '[Eustacia and Wildeve] had been standing in the entry. Closing the front door and turning the key as before, she threw open the door of the adjoining room and asked him to walk in' (Hardy [1878] 2008: 271). Although main doors do not appear in Kerr's passage, they have an important role in literary representations of home, as Hardy's novel represents. Being an architectural element that allows or denies passage, doors are represented with symbolic significance in relation to (sexual) contamination. Indeed, Wildeve does not stop in the dining room but is pushed into the next room, which architecturally signifies a deeper level of intimacy: 'Wildeve entered, the room appearing to be empty; but as soon as he had advanced a few steps he started. On the hearth-rug lay Clym asleep' (Hardy [1878] 2008: 271). The presence of the unconscious and defenceless husband increases the sense of vulnerability in which the household is placed. Wildeve also declares his intentions to Eustacia in a way that recalls Emma and Rodolphe in the Bovarys' parlour. Taking a more intimate tone, Wildeve suggests his feelings for Eustacia:

> It is easier to say you will sing than to do it, though if I could I would encourage you in your attempt. But as life means nothing to me

without one thing which is now impossible you will forgive me for not being able to encourage you. (Hardy [1878] 2008: 273)

These words, pronounced at the door of Clym's room, alter the experience of domestic intimacy: the intimate words of the lover are said by the intimate space of the husband's room. There is a reversal of values here regarding the moral connotations attributed to the intimate and private spaces of the home. Wildeve, as well as Rodolphe, takes advantage of the space he is in to express his desire and thus subverts the norms that rule the household and, more particularly, the use of intimate spaces.

Once inside the house, the lovers hear the knock on the door and see Mrs Yeobright through the window: 'how can I open the door to her when she wishes to see not me, but her son? I won't open the door' (274), says Eustacia to Wildeve. Clym's main door articulates notions of purity and contamination by contrasting Eustacia's attitude towards her mother-in-law and her lover. While, as we have seen, the house's window and door are open for Wildeve, the experience is very different for Mrs Yeobright, who, in attempting reconciliation with her son after his marriage with Eustacia, will find the door closed. Eustacia introduces Wildeve at home, locking him inside and, eventually, Mrs Yeobright outside. This fact illustrates a reversal of values: the potential lover enters the house, while the mother-in-law is banned from it. Family bonds are spatially broken and deregulated by the position of the characters around the front door and Eustacia's misuse of the conventions of hospitality. The door, whose function is that of negotiating, and regulating, between the inside and the outside, is used to introduce the outsider inside instead of the insider – the family member, hence contaminating the interior. This ultimately leads to Mrs Yeobright's death on her exhausting way back to Blooms-End, a very illustrative way of representing how Eustacia's desire weakens and dissolves the family.

The hesitation of the lovers to enter the house, 'standing in the entry' (Hardy [1878] 2008: 271), relates to notions of the threshold that we also find in *Madame Bovary*. Emma transgresses domestic space by stepping out and leaving home in order to meet her lovers. In this context, the door's threshold acquires particular importance in the case of Emma: '[Emma] sortit, en essuyant ses pieds sur le seuil' ([Emma] went out, wiping her feet on the threshold) (Flaubert [1856] 2001: 152). The threshold is the place which

Adultery and the Subversion of Architectural Prescriptiveness 43

finally will define Emma as her sexuality will be articulated around notions of inside and outside space both in terms of the body and the house. Emma will cross the main door as many times as she wishes, thus mocking again Charles's supposed control of boundary elements, as we have seen in M. Homais' words: 'ce qu'elle a principalement de commode pour un médecin, c'est une porte sur l'*Allée*, qui permet d'entrer et de sortir sans être vu' (what is more convenient for a doctor is a door to the lane through which you can enter and exit the house without being seen) (Flaubert [1856] 2001: 139–40). Emma will take certain control, if not of the interior of the house then of the door, as she will be the one entering and leaving the house for her own purposes. In the same way, she will take control of her own body. However, the opposite happens to Charles: his incapacity to control circulation through the main door aligns with his incapacity to control Emma's body. However, interior doors in *Madame Bovary* appear as potential handicaps. When Rodolphe declares his love to Emma, 'on entendit un bruit de sabots dans la cuisine, et la porte de la salle, il s'en aperçut, n'était pas fermée' (one could hear the sound of clogs in the kitchen, and the living room door, he noticed, was not closed) (Flaubert [1856] 2001: 225). In contrast to the confidence Eustacia shows in throwing open the door, Emma and Rodolphe seem exposed by a lack of agency. In fact, the open door of the Bovarys' living room in a moment precluding adultery echoes Emma's experience of her domestic space in which she is constantly out of control. In Tostes, for example, the ghostly reminder of Charles's late wife makes Emma feel a stranger in her new home:

> Emma monta dans les chambres. La première n'était point meublée; mais la seconde, qui était la chambre conjugale, avait un lit d'acajou dans une alcôve à draperie rouge. Une boîte en coquillages décorait la commode; et, sur le secrétaire, près de la fenêtre, il y avait, dans une carafe, un bouquet de fleurs d'oranger [. . .]. C'était un bouquet de mariée, le bouquet de l'autre! (Flaubert [1856] 2001: 82)

> (Emma went up to the dormitories. The first one was unfurnished, but in the second one, the conjugal room, there was a mahogany bed in an alcove with red drapery. A shell box decorated the chest of drawers; and, on the writing desk, near the window, there was, in a jug, a bouquet of orange blossom [. . .]. It was a bridal bouquet, the other's bouquet!)

Charles's deceased wife is made present through the objects she possessed in life and that brings about a feeling of estrangement in Emma. The presence of the other through a semiology of her objects reflects Laurent Adert's concept of *Autre* (the Other) in Flaubert's narrative: a creaturely or non-personal subject that represents the social discourse, and annihilates every subjective and personal voice (1996: 12). The first house of the Bovarys is also filled with Charles's objects, which represent his profession, and, again, exclude Emma:

> De la cheminée resplendissait une pendule à tête d'Hippocrate [. . .]. De l'autre coté du corridor était le cabinet de Charles, petite pièce de six pas de large environ, avec une table, trois chaises et un fauteuil de bureau. Les tomes du *Dictionnaire des sciences médicales*, non coupés, mais dont la brochure avait souffert dans toutes les ventes successives par où ils avaient passé, garnissaient presque à eux seuls les six rayons d'une bibliothèque en bois de sapin. (Flaubert [1856] 2001: 81)

> (From the fireplace shone a clock with the head of a Hippocrates [. . .]. Across the hall was Charles's study, a small room about six feet wide, with a table, three chairs, and an office chair. The volumes of the *Dictionary of Medical Sciences*, uncut, but whose binding had suffered in all the successive sales they had gone through, decorated practically by themselves the six shelves of a fir wood bookcase.)

Emma's new home is indeed filled by Charles and his first wife, and Charles's cabinet takes over the rest of the space where smells and noises coming from the cabinet can be perceived. Emma is left with no room: she has neither a room of her own nor the feeling of a personal space in the house. Instead, Emma is trapped in a house which is not experienced as hers, and which she cannot change: 'dans cette petite salle au rez-de-chaussée, avec le poêle qui fumait, la porte qui criait, les murs qui suintaient, les pavés humides; toute l'amertume de l'existence lui semblait servie sur son assiette' (in that little room on the ground floor, with the smoking stove, the screaming door, the oozing walls, the damp paving stones; all the bitterness of existence seemed to be served on her plate) (Flaubert [1856] 2001: 120). In this context, Emma is locked within the home and references to doors also work as a means to increase the sense of imprisonment: 'elle remontait, fermait la porte, étalait les charbons, et, défaillant à la chaleur du foyer, sentait l'ennui plus lourd qui retombait sur elle' (she went upstairs, closed the door, spread the coals, and, yielding to the heat of the hearth, the heaviest boredom fell on her) (Flaubert [1856] 2001: 119). Emma succumbs to domesticity and fails, initially, at subverting the domestic space like Eustacia does. In fact, it is Rodolphe who we see initiating adultery and misusing rooms.

In *Madame Bovary* and *The Return of the Native*, open doors signpost sexual transgression, and potentially, the contamination of the household, the family name and the bloodline by conceiving an illicit heir. By opposing privacy, an open door is imagined as an exposure of family life, and permeates normativity with a certain fluidity in contrast to its static appearance. In the last chapter we will see how a decrease in the number of doors in modernist Vienna highlights the sense of sexual fluidity and circulation.

The law in architecture

In Reynaud's view, architecture is the expression of a law: '[l'ordre] tend à prouver que rien n'y a été remis au hasard [dans nous constructions], que toutes choses y sont été justement disposées; c'est la manifestation d'une loi' ([order] tends to prove that [in our constructions] nothing has been put there at random, that all things have been rightly arranged there; it is the manifestation of a law) (1867: 3). In *Madame Bovary*, the whole town of Yonville is signposted by the importance of the law: 'la maison du notaire [était] la plus belle du pays' (the solicitor's house [was] the most beautiful one in town) (Flaubert [1856] 2001: 126). The solicitor's house is the first one being described when the Bovarys enter Yonville for the first time – his profession is associated with the beauty of his house. The beauty of architectural law, and of law itself, is also found in Homais' home: 'ce qui attire le plus les yeux, c'est [. . .] la pharmacie de M. Homais!' (M. Homais' pharmacy [. . .] is what is most alluring!) (Flaubert [1856] 2001: 127). Yonville's town hall, 'construite *sur les dessins d'un architecte de Paris*' (built *according to the designs of a Parisian architect*) and presenting 'une manière de temple grec' (a kind of Greek temple) (Flaubert [1856] 2001: 127), with 'les balances de la justice' (the scales of justice) (127), epitomises the presence of the law at the same time as introducing an implicit critique of the use of historicist style. Viollet-Le-Duc's views on Second Empire architecture in Paris, which we will use extensively in the following chapter, make a direct reference to the employment of classic forms: 'à voir et pratique la plupart de nos édifices publics, ne croirait-on pas que la population de la France est placée sous la domination de conquérants?' (Seeing most of our public buildings, would not one believe that the French population is under the domination of conquerors?) (1863: 657). The architect believed that designs inspired by Roman and Greek models failed to aesthetically express the needs of the contemporary citizen. Flaubert's text reflects Viollet-Le-Duc's theoretical approaches on historical architecture that alienates the subject. The architectural reading of Emma Bovary presents her as a modern woman that will become the scapegoat of a society ruled by obsolete laws expressed in obsolete architecture. In light of this, Emma's death appears ultimately as architecture's failure to shape a different sexual discourse and way of living. In fact, the desires and sexualities of Emma, and also of Eustacia, do not find an appropriate architecture: they cannot inhabit an architecture that aims at a normativisation, a regulation of their subjectivities. Therefore, the misuse of domestic space responds to their sexual nature; it implies a deformation of architectural forms that allows the survival of a form of desire not shaped by the architecture of the house. Not to do so would eventually mean the deformation of Emma and Eustacia as desiring subjects. In this context, Jane Thomas defines the relationship between Hardy's heroines and their homes as 'transformative [of their] regulatory practices' (2013: 40). Indeed, this transformation of domestic and sexual regulations takes place since the very first expression of non-normative sexuality is represented in both novels. This fact potentially opens the path towards a new sexual and domestic discourse, as well as towards a new architecture that takes into consideration women's subjectivities. In Chapter Five, we will see how Viennese architect Adolf Loos designed houses which enact different sexual practices and empower the female gaze. The clash between women's unsettling desires and the spaces they inhabit anticipates the disassociation between the conceptualisation of home, as imagined reality, and the new sexual approaches, which started constituting modern sexuality.

*

This chapter has illustrated the extent to which architectural discourses adopted and shaped medical terms and paradigms, which implied a unique and correct way of using domestic architecture. We have seen how this resulted in the formulation of prescriptive dwelling practices which aimed at preventing the so-called misuse of space. Such misuse consisted in using domestic spaces, or any kind of architectural element, for different purposes than those for which the spaces were designed. The strong regulation of domestic architecture was based on the idea that spatial misuse could lead to perversity, as Kerr clearly states. Opposing perversity, architecture should enact the idea of privacy, which was an essential part of the domestic ideal. In light of this opposition, perversity seemed to include ideas of contamination and adulteration, as we have seen illustrated by analysing the character of M. Homais through his profession in *Madame Bovary*.

By contextualising the analysis of *Madame Bovary* and *The Return of the Native* in light of the above theoretical and cultural framework, this chapter has illustrated the ways in which representations of dwelling practices and the use of spaces go against prescriptive uses in both texts. This finds a correlation with the misuse of the sexual body, in this case, focalised on adultery and a strong female sexuality which resists the prescriptiveness of domesticity established through architectural and medical discourses. Thus, the texts of Flaubert and Hardy represent sexuality as a tool of subversion of normative architecture, which, at the same time, provokes a sexual alienation that seems to lead to sexual subversion.

By exploring a clash between non-regulated sexuality and domestic architecture, this chapter has introduced the ways in which literature imagined the problematic relationship between dwellings and sexual cultures. In *Madame Bovary* and *The Return of the Native*, architecture conforms to architectural discourses of the time; however, architecture is constantly put into question and exposed by the emphasis on the sexual alienation of the heroines and the reality of spatial practices: the actual lived space complicates the enactment of 'qualities' such as privacy. In light of architectural discourses, the practical flaws of a normative architecture both lead and allow the female characters to find a way to subvert normative sexual practices.

Notes

1 See Wolfreys (2009) and Beatty (2004).
2 More information is available at: https://www.architecture.com/image-library/RIBApix/image-information/poster/tour-devrault-royal-abbey-of-fontevraud/posterid/RIBA27627.html (last accessed February 3rd 2022).

2

Sexual Accessibility and Exhibitionism: Glass in *La Curée*

In Zola's *La Curée* (1872), Maxime, son of real estate businessman Aristide Saccard, commits incest with his stepmother Renée Saccard inside the 'cage de verre' (glass cage) (Zola [1872] 1981: 220), the hothouse in the Saccards' residence that epitomises glass architecture. The hothouse, 'a material imprint of [. . .] modernity in [its] characteristic glass and iron construction' (Tanner 2015: 117), becomes a locus of un-domesticated sexuality when Renée and Maxime commit incest. The location of a sexual perversion in an emblematic representation of modern architecture adds to the anxieties around glass in private residences and exemplifies how glass was actively shaping the sexual imagination. In *La Curée*, the 'cage de verre' (glass cage) reimagines notions of boundaries, perversity, natural sexuality, and the public and the private spheres in Second-Empire Paris, the cradle of European urbanism in the second half of the century, as well as the birth of modern Paris.

Napoleon III had in mind a massive renovation of the city according to principles of hygiene and security. Georges-Eugène Haussmann, Prefect of the Department of the Seine in 1853, received the mandate to execute the Emperor's plans whereby he opened up narrow and unhealthy streets to avoid barricades, improved canals and railway networks, and created public green spaces, among other renovations (Harvey 2006: 107). Haussmann accomplished the Emperor's political plans by approaching Paris as a totality where its different parts were interconnected (Harvey 2006: 111). While the Emperor aimed at 'the expulsion of "dangerous classes" and insalubrious housing and industry from the city centre', this project of urban reform led to 'improv[ing] the capacity for the circulation of goods and people' (Harvey 2006: 112).

Although Haussmann's design responded to processes that started with anteriority, such as 'housing investment and residential segregation' (Harvey 2006: 113), notions of circulation conformed to ideas of house moving and echoed the movement of a speculative real estate market that started in the late nineteenth century. In this urban context, Zola locates the Saccards' newly built residence in *La Curée*. Located in Parc Monceau, the hôtel Saccard emerges as a symbol of social, political and economic modernity in which Aristide Saccard makes his fortune in the real estate market. Modernity is stained by corruption both in the public and private spheres, two realities that in *La Curée* appear merged into each other through the novel's engagement with architectural usages of glass. Thus, notions of corrupted domesticity align with a brutal real estate market, to which the Saccards contribute, turning home into a commodity and an object of consumption.

In the Second Empire, Daly's design of an architectural type for new private residences would establish a norm and reproduce a certain aesthetic uniformity all through the city (Pinon 2002: 87). Standardisation and normativisation were at the heart of the new Parisian domestic designs: '[en] l'hôtel privé modern, il y a des règles [...] qui s'imposent à toutes les catégories d'habitations; elles se rapportent principalement à la distribution intérieure' (in the modern mansion, there are rules [...] which apply to all categories of accommodation; they mainly have to do with the interior distribution) (1864: I, 13). Daly proceeds with a detailed explanation of such interior distribution, which should include '[un] étage de caves [...] où se trouve la cuisine avec toutes ses dépendances' (on one floor the cellar [...] with the kitchen and all its adjacent rooms) (I, 15), '[le] rez-de-chaussé' (the ground floor) containing 'les pieces de reception: salles à manger, galleries d'apparat, salons, salles de jeu, etc.' (the reception rooms: the dining rooms, the art galleries, the salons, the gaming rooms, etc.) (I, 15), above this, 'l'appartement de la famille' (the family apartment) (I, 15), and finally, 'au second étage, les chambres destinées aux amis et aux visiteurs étrangers ou à une partie des gens de la maison' (on the second floor, the guest rooms for friends or foreign visitors or for part of the household) (I, 15). On the back side of the hôtel, 'écuries, remises, selleries, vacherie et logements des domestiques' (stables, sheds, a saddlery, a cowshed and the servants' quarters) (I, 15). Although there is no extensive description of the façades, Daly's plans included the detailed outlook of the hôtel privé.

The architecture of the hôtel Saccard belongs to the aesthetic pattern promoted by l'École des Beaux Arts, which was characterised by its inclusion of old styles, thereby giving form to a strong historicism during the Second Empire. At the same time, architectural discussions were taking place among architects such as Eugène Viollet-Le-Duc, who dedicated a whole work to modern architecture and opposed Second Empire historicism (1875). One of Viollet-Le-Duc's main criticisms was the disassociation between architectural form and purpose. According to the architect, buildings should be designed and built in order to satisfy a purpose, a function: 'donner aux matériaux la fonction et la puissance relatives à l'objet, les formes exprimant le plus exactement et cette fonction et cette puissance – c'est là un des points les plus importants de la composition' (to give materials the required function and power according to the object they shape; forms expressing most exactly this function and power – this is one of the most important aspects of design) (1868: 466).[1] Viollet-Le-Duc claimed Second-Empire architecture to be misleading and deceitful due to, precisely, the disharmony between form and purpose. On the other side of the spectrum, the distinguished architect César Daly worked with Haussmann and published an extensive work dedicated to the private residences built under Napoleon III (1864). However, Daly's concern with privacy, seen in the previous chapter, is problematised by Zola's representation of the hôtel Saccard where the material of glass takes over the building's structure and is significantly present in the interior. In contrast to *Madame Bovary*, *La Curée* criticises the openness new buildings evoke through glass, and the practices of exhibitionism and voyeurism they invite, challenging architectural limits and the sense of enclosure they construct. In this context, I will analyse how Zola imagined the ways in which new architectures could not only impact on sexual culture but also modify the idea of home as an enclosed recipient and its association to the enclosure of the female body. The main consequence of an increased use of glass was the blur of boundaries between the inside and the outside that challenged architectural prescriptiveness and its regulative purposes. *La Curée* depicts new private residences that lack all the regulatory elements to enact domestic convenience. In the hôtel Saccard, space is represented as having the opposite impact on sexual desire to that seen in *Madame Bovary*: if in Flaubert's text Emma's desire and sexuality are not accommodated within the regulatory space they inhabit, in *La Curée*, architecture empowers illicit desires, such as incest and adultery. The deregulation of normative sexual practices in the domestic space is imagined in strict relation to an opening of the interior by architectural means, and particularly the use of glass. *La Curée* explores anxieties regarding new architectures of Second-Empire Paris that might precisely go against the domestic prescriptiveness articulated by architects such as César Daly and Robert Kerr. In this chapter, I will primarily focus on the ways in which *La Curée* represents the openness of a theorised enclosure due to an increasing inclusion of glass in private residences, and how this reverberates through sexual boundaries, and the female body.

Susie S. Hennessy (2015) dedicates part of a chapter to the analysis of many of the scenes from *La Curée* that will also appear here. However, her approach to the text is based on a purely historical analysis that places Zola's text alongside interior magazines of the time in order to show Zola's awareness of domestic fashion. This is an approach Hennessy shares with Anca I. Lasc (2015: 47–58). Both authors conclude that domestic scenes in *La Curée* support the fact that in the late nineteenth century women were absolutely attached and assimilated to their homes. These analyses, rich in historical data, differ from mine as I present a historic-cultural approach that aims at illustrating the correlation between architectural innovations and the emergence of new understandings of home and sexuality. Regarding representations of domestic space in *La Curée*, Hennessy argues how women express themselves through the interiors they create as home in the nineteenth century, and that this was seen as an extension of women's selves. My analysis, however, focuses on domestic space as a cultural agent that modifies ways of living rather than being seen as merely the subject's choice and object of decoration. This approach is in line with contemporary architectural theory, as explored by Tschumi, who theorises architecture as a shifting entity, i.e., as something in permanent change, and as 'becoming the action itself' (Spurr 2012: 326). In the context of this chapter, architecture shows its agency in modifying the meaning of home, including ideas of womanhood and sexuality, as envisaged in the domestic ideal.

Reimagining the private/public dichotomy

For Daly, home is *'le vêtement de la famille. Elle est en effet destinée à lui servir d'enveloppe'* (the family's space of seclusion. It is indeed intended to serve as an envelope) (Daly 1864: I, 10). However, Daly's concerns with privacy and his involvement with the renovations of Paris appear paradoxical in light of *La Curée*. In fact, the hôtel Saccard is located in one of the new renovated areas; and, problematically, the residence is imagined to have a negative impact on privacy that goes against Daly's own prescriptiveness. Engaging with the increased number of windows in the new *hôtels privés*, the Saccards' residence is described with 'des glaces si larges et si claires qu'elles semblaient, comme les glaces des grands magasins modernes, mises là pour étaler au-dehors le faste intérieur' (mirrors so large and bright they resemble shop windows in modern department stores, only there to display the splendour of the interior) (Zola [1872] 1981: 53). Daly does, in fact, recommend the social rooms of the hôtel to display the family's wealth in contrast to the more discreet and intimate parts of the house – a contrast aimed at reflecting the separation between private and public spheres:

> L'une est tout entière consacrée à l'intimité, aux devoirs et aux affections de la famille, et elle réclame des dispositions architecturales qui garantissent la liberté et le secret de la vie privée; l'autre est mêlée au monde extérieur [...], et ce second coté, pour ainsi dire public, de notre existence, comporte plus de luxe et d'éclat que le premier. (1864: I, 15)
>
> (One is entirely devoted to the intimacy, duties and affections of the family, and it calls for architectural arrangements which guarantee the freedom and secrecy of private life; the other is mingled with the outside world [...], and this second aspect, so to speak, of our existence, has more luxury and sparkle than the former.)

This separation of the private and the public is key to a reading of Zola's text as it is precisely such a division which is constantly problematised, a problematisation articulated around the novel's engagement with glass. First of all, the windows of the façade in the Saccards' residence work as a means to spread out the interior into the exterior. The use of glass invites exhibitionism and voyeurism rather than ensuring its prescriptive uses such as light access, or ventilation, as Daly states in his definition of windows: 'laisser passer la lumière du jour sans donner accès à la pluie, à la neige et parfois au soleil; – un moyen de ventiler une salle, d'en épurer l'atmosphère' (let daylight go through avoiding the rain, snow and sometimes the sun; a way to ventilate a room, to purify the atmosphere) (1864: I, 9). Secondly, in the Saccards' residence this exhibitionism does not only involve the more social rooms of the house but also its most intimate apartments: 'c'était la maison suspecte du plaisir mondain, du plaisir impudent qui élargit les fenêtres pour mettre les passants dans la confidence des alcôves' (it was the house of wordly and impudent pleasure, which widens the windows to let passers-by in the confidence of the alcoves) (Zola [1872] 1981; 165). Finally, taking on another form, glass also follows from the wide windows in the façade to Renée's apartments: 'on disait: "Le cabinet de toilette de la belle madame Saccard", comme on dit: "La galerie des glaces, à Versailles"' (one said: 'the bathroom of the beautiful Madame Saccard', like one says: 'The Hall of Mirrors in Versailles') (Zola [1872] 1981: 209). Besides mirrors, 'la table de toilette, les verres, les vases' (the dressing table, the glasses, the vases) and 'l'armoire à glace' (the mirror wardrobe) (210) are all objects made of glass. Glass reflects and duplicates domestic space, highlighting the sense of a lack of boundaries and the impossibility of containing the interior within its architectural limits. Art historian Henri Havard notes how mirrors simulate apertures into the exterior: 'deux glaces posées en face l'une de l'autre [. . .] ouvrant à l'œil d'infinies perspectives. Au milieu d'une muraille qui enferme notre esprit, la glace simule une fenêtre donnant sur une pièce voisine' (two mirrors placed opposite each other [. . .] opening endless perspectives. In the middle of a wall that encloses our mind, glass simulates a window overlooking a neighbouring room) (1884: 303). Havard warns against an excess of glass that can turn the room into an uninhabitable space (1884: 303): an uninhabitability that may come from an erasure of all sense of enclosure, thus, relating the excess of glass to the loss of privacy and the lack of boundaries.

The luxury of Renée's rooms suggests that, in fact, they have been created in order to be exhibited. But they also add an interesting aspect by echoing eighteenth-century aristocratic tastes. In this context, La Curée engages with late nineteenth-century critiques of Rococo design by comparing Renée's cabinet de toilette to the hall of mirrors at Versailles. Like many of his contemporaries, such as the Goncourt brothers and art historian Paul Mantz, Havard was very critical of eighteenth-century aristocratic fashions:

> Ainsi, sans pousser les choses à l'excès, sans aller jusqu'à la somptuosité débordante d'une Pompadour, dont le cabinet était tapissé de laques anciens de la plus rare qualité, sans avoir une garniture de toilette aussi richement travaillé que celle de la Dauphine, garniture que la beauté seule du travail sauva de la destruction, ou encore une toilette d'or massif comme celle dont Mme Dubarry tirait vanité. (1884: 428–9)

> (Thus, without being excessive, without going as far as the overflowing sumptuousness of a Pompadour, whose cabinet was lined with gold lacquers of the rarest quality, without having a toilet as richly decorated as that of the Dauphine, decorations which only the beauty of the work saves from destruction, or a toilet of solid gold like the one of which Mme Dubarry felt so proud.)

The association between Renée's cabinet and Versailles not only introduces late nineteenth-century approaches to pre-revolutionary designs, but it also associates Renée with the excesses of Marie-Antoinette. According to many nineteenth-century moralists, eighteenth-century interior design was based on an excess of forms epitomised in the Rococo style. This excess and the use of materials such as gold were considered in the last decades of the nineteenth century as expressions of a sort of moral indulgence and vice. Leora Auslander explains this reception of pre-revolutionary monarchies in the late nineteenth century: 'in the eyes of the late nineteenth century [...] [the] late eighteenth century [was] the period of corrupt, effeminate kings', outlining the 'effeminacy of Louis XV and especially Louis XVI' (1996: 287). This seems clearly the opinion of Mantz who, in 1883, published an article for the *Revue des arts decoratifs*, 'Les Meubles du XVIIIe Siècle' (Eighteenth-Century Furniture), commenting how in the eighteenth century 'l'excentrique était toléré, applaudi peut-etre' (eccentricity was tolerated, maybe even celebrated), which testified 'dans les ames françaises un commencement de folie' (the beginning of madness in the French souls) (1883: 319). The Goncourt brothers defined life in Versailles during the Louis XV kingdom as 'une civilisation [...] à son terme dernier et excessif, [...] un monde [qui] est dans le plein épanouissement d'une corruption exquise' (a civilisation

[. . .] in its final stages and excessive, [. . .] a world where an exquisite corruption was fully blossoming) (1883: 38). The excessive use of mirrors, as found in the hall of mirrors in Versailles, illustrates a fashion found in palaces of the epoch, as well as in libertine literature such as that of the Marquis de Sade, in whose texts mirrors work as a means to replicate pleasure through the infinite repetition of the image. Georgina Downey and Mark Taylor have noted how in Vivant Denon's *Point de lendemain* (1777), 'mirror-covered walls transformed the interior into "a vast cage of reflective glass"', and use other expressions such as 'cage of seduction', or 'hall of mirrors.' (2015: 21). The introduction of libertine motives in *La Curée* points at the inclusion of the erotic within the architectural standardisation of Daly's designs, pointing at a normalisation of lifestyles that are reminiscent of eighteenth-century libertinage.

The blur of boundaries between the domestic interior and the outside continues through the public importance of Renée's cabinet. Public intimacy is architecturally represented in 'la merveille de l'appartement [de Renée], la pièce dont parlait tout Paris, c'était le cabinet de toilette' (the wonder of Renée's apartments, the room all Paris talked about, was the bathroom) (Zola [1872] 1981: 209). By placing the cabinet in the centre of gossip, this place acquires an importance that antedates, for example, the Sezessionstil in Austria represented by Otto Wagner. We will see in the final chapter the significance of Wagner's change in moving the focus from the representational apartments, i.e., mostly the dining room and salon, to the bathroom and bedroom, which became representative of a new architecture in 1898 (Haiko 1984: 28). The imagined accessibility of Renée's cabinet to 'tout Paris' (all Paris) not only antedates turn of the century design fashions but it also conforms to Amy C. Kulper's discussion of the bourgeois public sphere and the public appropriation of the private realm in Victor Horta's Hôtel Tassel (1892–1893): 'the *salon* [. . .] extending the horizon of domesticity beyond the confines of the individual dwelling' (2009: 122). Kulper's analysis of the boundaries between public and private realms very well represents Zola's description of the hôtel Saccard. This throws new light onto Zola's proto-modernism, already discussed by Harrow (2010), and the formation of a new domestic and private culture, represented in *La Curée*, that will emerge with force at the turn of the century. Thus, with almost fifteen years of difference, *La*

Curée explores what Havard articulates in his book, namely, the dangers of an immoderate use of glass in domestic space. The anxieties around the newly used material appeared in different discourses for a period of approximately thirty years until Art Nouveau reacted to the exposure of the interior at the turn of the century – although we will see in Chapter Five how this interior had already absorbed new values. An increasing use of glass will follow well into the present time, where the polemics surrounding the inside/outside dialectics continue. We will recover this topic in the discussion of *Traumnovelle* in light of Sennett's *The Fall of the Public Man* in order to see how the private sphere becomes absolute when the private starts being incorporated into the public domain, modifying the sense of domestic and sexual intimacy.

The descriptions of Renée in her cabinet de toilette add a sense of eroticism to the construction of a public intimacy: 'c'était une grande nudité. Quand Renée sortait du bain, son corps blond n'ajoutait qu'un peu de rose à toute cette chair rose de la pièce' (it was great nudity. When Renée emerged from the bath, her fair body added only a little pink to all that flesh colour in the room) (Zola [1872] 1981: 210). The sensual engagement of Renée with her apartment represents an eroticisation of the space that is constantly highlighted by confusing spatial and bodily boundaries: 'cette baignoire rose, ces tables et ces cuvettes roses, cette mousseline du plafond et des murs, sous laquelle on croyait voir couler un sang rose, prenaient des rondeurs de chair, des rondeurs d'épaules et de seins' (this pink bath, these pink tables and basins, this muslin ceiling and walls under which one believed to see pink blood flowing, took on the roundness of flesh, shoulders and breasts) (Zola [1872] 1981: 210). Recovering the eighteenth-century libertine tradition, Cryle's definition of the relationship between furniture and the body in libertine literature applies also to Renée and her cabinet: 'the relation between the body and furniture is not one of postural constraint but of euphoric osmosis' (2002: 46). Reading Renée's representations in her cabinet in light of libertine literature provides a different conclusion than that argued, for example, by Hennessy in her discussions on Zola:

> This phenomenon of conflating woman and the interior is apparent in *La Curée* [. . .]. From the elaborate gowns that transform her appearance and personality to the satin and lace-festooned bedroom in which

she adopts varying personae, Renée epitomizes the power of metaphor to define and confine woman within the home. (2015: 6)

Very interestingly, the image of the woman-as-home, while referring to traditional nineteenth-century motifs, is also used to introduce the libertine tradition in the new bourgeois homes, and this is what Hennessy's feminist criticism fails to account for. This ambivalent use of the image, libertine and prude at once, is what articulates a shift in sexual and domestic culture that is implicit in *La Curée*. In a very different situation than that of Emma Bovary, Renée is not – taking Cryle's words – under 'constraint' but in 'euphoric osmosis' with her space. That such space is her cabinet carries a load of erotic connotations that place Renée's domestic experience within a libertine context. This combination articulates a new erotic intimacy that we will see in its apogee in *Traumnovelle*. In the case of Renée's cabinet, the juxtaposition of a nineteenth-century cultural identification between home and woman to re-appropriations of libertine literature permeates domesticity and womanhood with new significance. Commenting on this same scene, Harrow argues how 'the eroticization of fabric and furnishing is part of the generalized inscription of the erotic in the folds and swathes of voluptuous drapery and in the sensual morphology of furniture' (2000: 448). Harrow, however, reads this erotic atmosphere as a 'lack of transparency, [. . .] the obfuscation of values, [. . .] the mingling of conviviality and voluptuousness, material luxury and moral licentiousness' (2000: 448). But in fact, while the lack of transparency works as a moral metaphor, literal transparency conforms to this – taking Harrow's terms – 'moral licentiousness' (2000: 448). Renée's material luxury participates in debauchery, precisely, when it is entangled in processes of exhibitionism and ostentation. These belong to the same architectural project of the Saccard residence whereby transparency is represented as literal.

Renée's cabinet de toilette has been discussed in connection to more common nineteenth-century approaches that take into account the veiling of the female body. Takaï, for example, argues a supposed inaccessibility of both women and their cabinets: 'comme la crinoline volumineuse et les sous-vêtements si richement variés éloignent excessivement la nudité féminine du regard, le *cabinet de toilette* où se dissimule tout le secret du corps naturel des femmes devient le lieu inaccessible aux autres' (as the voluminous crinoline and underwear excessively protect nudity from the gaze, the bathroom, where the reality of the female body is kept secret, becomes an inaccessible place) (2013: 341). But in the context of this chapter, Renée's piece is part of a project of domestic exhibitionism, which, in fact, highlights the cabinet's public accessibility through gossip. Though Takaï argues that Renée's cabinet de toilette is architecturally placed away from the public gaze – following the advice of conduct books – it nonetheless is part of the public space of the city when it is talked about, contrasting with Havard's definition of the cabinet as inaccessible (1884: 425). Speech and the discussion of private spaces as a means to unsettle the private/public boundary have been noted by Henri Lafon with regard to the eighteenth-century private garden: 'ainsi par l'exhibition et la discussion, le privé s'offre au public, devient dans une certaine mesure public, et le public est investi par le privé' (thus, through display and discussion, the private opens itself to the public, it becomes to a certain extent public, while the public acquires private features) (1989: 68). Renée's cabinet, however, adds a sense of aggressiveness to this public appropriation Lafon describes. In fact, the cabinet is not meant to be exhibited in the same way that a garden is, and it does not obviously offer itself to public talk. Instead, the cabinet is rather dispossessed of its own privacy by becoming publicly targeted. The accessibility speech gives to Renée's cabinet de toilette appears in concordance with the accessibility of her body when, at the end of the novel, Renée dresses up for the performance of the 'tableaux vivants' (living pictures):

> Devant les énormités de sa vie, le sang de son père, ce sang bourgeois, qui la tourmentait aux heures de crise, cria en elle, se révolta. Elle qui avait toujours tremblé à la pensée de l'enfer, elle aurait du vivre au fond de la sévérité noire de l'hôtel Béraud. Qui donc l'avait mise nue? (Zola [1872] 1981: 311)

> (Seeing the atrocities of her life, her father's blood, that bourgeois blood, which tormented her in times of crisis, cried out inside her. She, who had always feared the thought of hell, should have stayed in the depths of the severity of the Béraud Hotel. Who, then, had stripped her naked?)

The exhibitionism of her body echoes the transparency of the residency she inhabits. The body turns into a more visual and accessible reality, as the interior of the hôtel does, and Renée's abrupt awareness of her vulnerability echoes the violent appropriation of an intimate space (the cabinet). Her body also becomes violently appropriated by the gaze of the others. This relationship between the accessibility of both the cabinet and Renée's body brings out a crucial topic in architectural discourses as well as political and social ones. In the first case, the form-function relationship in architecture that revolves around notions of perversity becomes paramount. In light of Viollet-Le-Duc's architectural theory, the ways in which the hôtel Saccard constructs the experience of home appears as a result of a wider political, i.e., imperial, and aesthetic context. The politically-motivated organisation of Paris under Haussmann responds to the strong aesthetic historicism promoted by L'École des Beaux Arts, the most important artistic institution in France, including the Académie Royale d'Architecture. Secondly, Nao Takaï interestingly analyses the progressive uncovering of the naked body during the Second Empire. Takaï identifies a series of legitimate spaces where the female body was exhibited, one of them being the 'tableaux vivants' (living pictures) at private residences. This activity was carried out even by the emperors, which leads Takaï to conclude that 'l'exhibition de la nudité féminine était un projet d'État sous le Second Empire' (the exhibition of the naked female body was part of a state project of the Second Empire) (2013: 128). While Andrea Del Lungo notes how the nineteenth century produced 'le régime de transparence' (the regime of transparency) (2014: 399) by expanding the use of windows in Parisian private residences, *La Curée* explores architectural transparency further by permeating notions of female representation and sexuality. Thus, the salon's wide windows relate not only to Renée's body but also to its mise en scène in the 'tableaux vivants' (living pictures) she performs in the same salon. Takaï suggests Haussmann's urban project and female nakedness to be part of the same renovation of Paris through the figure of Hupel de la Noue, préfet de la Seine, who prepares the 'tableaux' (pictures) in *La Curée*, and 'Haussmann, le préfet de la Seine, qui a exécuté les grands travaux de Paris' (Haussmann, prefect of the Seine, who executed the great works of Paris) (128). While Takaï's argument sheds light on the relationship between urbanism and sexuality articulated around the exhibition of the female body, a closer reading of domestic architecture in *La Curée* illustrates the entangled relationship between architecture and sexual culture.

Domestic and sexual exhibitionism is one of the consequences of Haussmannian architecture.

The domestic visibility represented in *La Curée* is in line with Diana Periton's analysis of Maxime du Camp's (1822–1894) work on the city of Paris, *Paris, ses organes, ses fonctions, sa vie* (*Paris, its organs, its functions and its life*) (1869–1875), where the city is approached as an organic totality, 'le grand corps de Paris' (Paris's great body) (du Camp 1875: 1), from urban structures to the different professions, where 'the whole is always kept in view' (Periton 2009: 20). This approach to the city of Paris as a body is encountered also in Daly, who in his 1864 work *L'Architecture privée au XIXe siècle sous Napoleon III* defines Paris as 'la grande cité dans l'*ensemble* de son économie architecturale, en considérant la ville entière comme un seul monument dont toutes les parties fussent solidaires' (the great city within the whole of its architectural economy, considering the entire city as a single monument in which all parts are united) (6). This approach contradicts what Sharon Marcus defines as the urban project of Haussmann's Paris, the aims of which were 'the interiorization of Paris, the creation of enclosed, private spaces through both physical and discursive means' (1999: 138), hence protecting domestic space from the outside world. However, in *La Curée*, the political project Marcus claims to have envisaged during the Second Empire appears paradoxical. While Daly – as imperial architect – seems, indeed, to construct a discursive privacy, Zola's text illustrates a domestic experience that negates architectural discourses. Rather, mobility and fluidity were characteristics of Second Empire society, whose 'boundaries in all areas become blurred or are transgressed' (Duffy 2005: 125), something which will increase at the turn of the century. An 1894 article in *La grande dame*, for example, states how 'dans un pareil milieu, nécessairement mobile et ondoyant, les usages mondains ont beaucoup perdu de leur régularité, voire de leur fixité, et qu'ils se transforment perpétuellement' (in such an environment, inevitably mobile and flexible, worldly customs have greatly lost their normativity, even their stability, and they are constantly changing) (361). Indeed, some scholars have noted the high permeability of class and sexuality that defined the period. In his 2003 edition of *Nana*, Auguste Dezalay notes 'le mélange' (the mixture) of social classes found in private salons (footnote 3, 89), something that is also represented in Colette's *Claudine en ménage* (1902). In his introduction to Baronne Staffe's guidebook *Usages du monde* (1891), Frédéric Rouvillois notes the importance and multiplication of conduct books due to 'les frontières incertaines de la bourgeoisie' (the uncertain boundaries of the bourgeoisie) (2007: 17), which created the need for regulation and distinction. The use of glass in domestic space is part of this progressive vulnerability and openness of boundaries in the social milieu. At the same time, this need for regulation recalls the anxieties around contamination in a context in which it becomes impossible to avoid it.

Architectural cultures

The hôtel Saccard embodies the antithesis of Viollet-Le-Duc's approaches to architectural form in relation to the building's function. For Viollet-Le-Duc, private dwellings should be based on simplicity, and designed according to the functional needs of the structure. An example of this was a hôtel privé Viollet-Le-Duc himself designed in Paris, which he describes as follows: 'les façades sont élevées en pierre et briques, et d'une grande simplicité. Toute la décoration consiste dans la disposition des baies qui sont percées en raison des besoins intérieurs' (the façades are built in stone and brick, with great simplicity. All decoration consists in the arrangement of the bays which are pierced due to interior needs) (1877: 3). The emphasis on stone and the structure's simplicity aligns with the description of the villa de Tamaris, home to the Comtesse de Puiseux, published in an 1894 article in the French magazine *La Grande Dame: Revue de l'élégance et des arts*. Villa de Tamaris was characterised by the presence of almost unnoticeable windows (3), which comes to stress the Countess as a model of femininity and motherhood: 'sa vie est celle d'une mère de famille dévouée à tous ses devoirs, désireuse de rester ignorée' (her life is that of a mother, devoted to all her duties, longing to remain ignored) (1). In opposition to glass and its association with the unveiling of the female body, in the villa de Tamaris, the opacity of domestic space relates to the invisibility of the body at the same time that architecture enacts privacy and intimacy. Havard echoes this same idea of 'emmurailler' (enclosing) the interior: 'surtout de ne pas les [fenêtres] placer où elles ne doivent point être, car elles semblent supprimer la muraille' (especially not placing [the windows] where they should not be, because they seem to take over the wall) (1884: 303). The 'virtues' of the Comtesse de Tamaris shape a particular model of womanhood in the domestic sphere, itself representative of a type of domestic culture. This female ideal continued to be advocated, for example, by late nineteenth-century moralists such as Jules Simon whose book *La femme du vingtième siècle* advocates for a revival of what was considered the original sense of domesticity: 'mon but [...] est de revenir en arrière, et de faire la femme de XXe siècle sur le modèle de la femme du XVIIe. Cette femme-là était, avant tout, une femme d'intérieur' (my objective [...] is to go back to take as a model for the woman of the twentieth century that of the seventeenth century. That woman was, above all, a domestic woman) (1892: 2). This 'femme d'intérieur' (domestic woman) contributes to a myth of femininity which is supported by the architecture she inhabits, altogether articulating the domestic ideal. We will see how Huysmans placed this ideal in seventeenth-century Netherlands, to which Simon might be referring.

In *La Curée*, stone is a prominent material in hôtel Béraud, located at Ile Saint-Louis, Renée's childhood home and a common location for the old bourgeoisie. Renée's experience of the architecture and materials found in the hôtel Béraud stands out for its contrasts with her mise en scène in the Saccards' residence:

> Lorsqu'elle [Renée] arriva, la cour de l'hôtel Béraud la glaça, de son humidité morne de cloître [...], elle monta le large escalier de pierre, où ses petites bottes à hauts talons sonnaient terriblement [...]. Elle tremblait en traversant l'enfilade austère des vastes pièces, où les personnages vagues des tapisseries semblaient surpris par ce flot de jupes passant au milieu du demi-jour de leur solitude. (Zola [1872] 1981: 233)

> (When she [Renée] arrived, the courtyard of the Béraud Hotel, with its dreary cloistered humidity, made her feel frozen [...], she went up the wide staircase of stone, where her little high-heeled boots made a terrifying noise [...]. She trembled as she crossed the austere row of vast rooms, where the vague figures of the tapestries seemed surprised by this flood of skirts passing through the half-light of their solitude.)

The representation of the hôtel Béraud is centred around Renée's experience of gravity, which is evoked through the qualities of stone buildings: humidity, noise, austerity, the house's association to a 'cloître' (cloister), and the series of uncanny portraits on the walls construct a very different domestic atmosphere than that found in the hôtel Saccard. The hôtel Béraud represents what Daly refers to as the 'hôtel aristocratique', which embodies a regime based on inheritance and blood, and in opposition to the modern bourgeois ways of production and superiority based on effort and capitalist ethics:

> Le principe de l'aristocratie ancienne était le sang et la tradition; l'inégalité moderne est née de la richesse, qui représente essentiellement les économies du travail. L'hôtel aristocratique, signé des armoiries de la famille, en personnifiait la supériorité d'origine et la vie d'apparat; tandis que de nos jours [...] l'hôtel est pour le financier, le commerçant et l'industriel plutôt encore un moyen de bien-être. (1864: I, 13–14)

> (The ancient aristocracy was based on blood and tradition; modern inequality arises from wealth, which represents a system of work. The aristocratic home, with the family coat of arms, represented its given superiority and ceremonial life; while nowadays [...] the mansion is for the investor, the merchant and the industrialist a means of well-being.)

While Daly points at the relationship between domestic architecture and modes of production, linking the Saccards' residence to Aristide's profession, each of these architectural models also differs in relation to the set of qualities it is associated with. In the hôtel Béraud stone constructs home as a site for family history, roots, and its transmission among generations. As David Spurr notes, 'If the building materials of stone, wood, and earth or brick carry the symbolic charge of hearth and fatherland, then an entirely new set of values is implied in the new materials of steel, glass, and reinforced concrete' (2012: 59). The increasing incorporation of glass in the façade of private residences consequently removes stone, and incorporates new domestic values, which in *La Curée* stand for pretence, ostentation or exhibitionism but that we will see transformed into honesty and freedom in Fontane's *L'Adultera* (1882). In this context, the Saccard residence challenges the domestic culture of the old bourgeoisie that is imagined to disappear under an excess of glass. The final exhibition of Renée's body in the tableaux vivants is nothing but the summit of this domestic architecture of the Second Empire: a body constructed through a modified experience of intimacy incorporated by the material of glass that relates also to a new type of woman.

Viollet-Le-Duc and Zola share their strong criticism of Second Empire architecture, which, in the case of Zola, also represents an immoral society. Zola's depiction of the hôtel Saccard suggests his alignment with Viollet-Le-Duc's views rather than with those of Daly. The Saccards' residence resembling 'grands magasins' echoes Viollet-Le-Duc's concerns with the violation of the form-purpose principle. However, while Zola's text is critical of an architecture that cannot materialise privacy and isolation, this same architecture leads to, and is an expression of, a new idea of home. This new construction of the domestic differs from the domestic ideal articulated through several discourses during the nineteenth century, and places the emphasis on performativity, initiating, thus, the deconstruction of bourgeois domesticity as a natural reality:

> Entre les œils-de-bœuf des mansardes, qui s'ouvraient dans un fouillis incroyable de fruits et de feuillages, s'épanouissent les pièces capitales de cette décoration étonnante [. . .]. Le toit, chargé de ces ornements, surmonté encore de galeries de plomb découpées, de deux paratonnerres et de quatre énormes cheminées symétriques, sculptées comme le reste, semblait être le bouquet de ce feu d'artifice architectural. (Zola [1872] 1981: 52–3)

> (Among the ox-eye windows of the attics, which opened into an incredible jumble of fruits and foliage, flourished the central pieces of this astonishing decoration [. . .]. The roof, full of these ornaments, still surmounted by split lead galleries, two lighting rods and four enormous symmetrical chimneys, sculpted like the rest, seemed to be the bouquet of this architectural display.)

The exuberant façade of the hôtel Saccard emanates theatricality, inviting the passer-by to stop and look at the majestic building, its outside as much as its inside. The specific reference to department stores when windows are described as 'glaces des grands magasins modernes' (shop windows of modern department stores) (Zola [1872] 1981: 53), while preserving the sense of stage, evokes newness and eroticism. In fact, shopping in the new department stores of the late nineteenth century has been defined as a sexualised activity (Wilson 2013: 150), an idea already articulated in Zola's *Au Bonheur des Dames* (1883). But department stores also establish a clearer link to economic transactions, thus referring to the context in which the marriage between Aristide Saccard and Renée Béraud takes place. Indeed, Aristide agrees to marry Renée for a sum when she falls pregnant following a rape; at the same time, economic transactions represent Aristide's profession in the real estate market. Finally, within the context of Zola's work, the relationship between the theatre and commerce recalls the figure of Nana that permeates the notion of home with a sense of prostitution; and, as Masha Belenky notes referring to the scene between Renée and Maxime in the café Riche, 'the difference between proper bourgeois lady and prostitute' blurs (2013: 35). However, Belenky does not discuss the text's engagement with windows and the ways in which these generate confusion between different kinds of stereotyped women, or between the home and the public world. But it is precisely the shattering of boundaries between the private and the public spheres that breaks down the distinction between public and domestic sexuality: in other words, between the prostitute and the bourgeois wife. This domestic and aesthetic modification is focalised in the figure of Renée Saccard, who, due to her old bourgeois origins, embodies the conflictive transformations of home at the end of the nineteenth century. Aude Campmas has defined Zola's text as 'le roman de l'intériorité violée' (the novel about violated interiority) (2013: 181), referring to the accessibility of the domestic interior. However, it should be noted that this violation is particularly focalised on Renée's body by becoming locus of cultural change. We will see how the dissolution of boundaries between bourgeois sexuality and prostitution evolves in *En ménage* and *Traumnovelle*.

Urban nature and sexuality

La Curée belongs to a complex moment when, on one hand, the nature of sexuality and the causes of sexual perversities were being re-examined, and, on the other hand, scientific discussions on animal/human boundaries were taking place. Regarding the first point, Zola's text is placed within a wider discussion on the relationship between nature and sexuality that started introducing the genetic factor into the pathological or perverse. This was seen as a process towards the normalisation, i.e., naturalisation, of different sexualities:

A partir du moment où Westphal a démontré l'existence d'une perversion instinctive plus forte que la volonté et poussant certains individus à réaliser le plaisir sexuel avec d'autres individus du même sexe, il s'est fait une évolution graduelle des idées qui a abouti à un changement absolu. (Féré 1899: 154)

(Since the moment when Westphal proved the existence of an instinctive perversion, stronger than will and prompting certain individuals to achieve sexual pleasure with other individuals of the same sex, there has been a gradual evolution of ideas that resulted in an absolute change.)

Natural instinct becomes a key concept in widening the range of normative sexualities. That is, the acceptance of, in this case, homosexuality, is granted as far as it can be argued in terms of the natural. Nature played, hence, an important role in the definition of the normal, and the location of sexual boundaries. Regarding the boundaries between the human and animal worlds, Fae Brauer notes Zola's knowledge of Darwin's writings which were initially received both in England and France as a threat to the line drawn between the animal and the human worlds: 'not only had [Darwin] abolished the intellectual barrier separating humans from animals, but more perilously, he had blurred the distinction between morality and brute instincts' (2009: 204). Renée's description as a cat while she commits incest with Maxime in the hothouse – '[une] grande chatte accroupie, l'échine allongée, les poignets tendus' (a big squatting feline, her spine extended, her wrists outstretched) (Zola [1872] 1981: 220) – echoes the dissolution of the boundary between the animal and the human, as well as between 'morality and brute instincts'. Echoing eighteenth-century expressions, the term 'cage de verre' (glass cage) (Zola [1872] 1981: 220) describes the hothouse in the garden of the Saccards; a glass construction that shapes a space where normative gender roles and sexuality are absolutely turned upside down: 'Renée était l'homme [. . .]. Maxime subissait. Cet être neutre, blond et joli, frappé dès l'enfance dans sa virilité, devenait, aux bras curieux de la jeune femme, une grande fille' (Renée was the man [. . .]. Maxime was taken. That neutral being, blond and beautiful, struck in his virility from childhood, was becoming, in the curious arms of the young woman, a girl) (Zola [1872] 1981: 217). The practice of space within the hothouse dissolves family and domestic structures as illustrated in the incestuous relationship between Renée and Maxime. The divisions, which we have seen so neatly theorised in architecture and medicine and that articulated normativity, do not hold in a glass structure that unsettles clear distinctions. However, such a structure also represents the place where modern definitions of sexuality are being constructed. On this occasion, glass is associated with nature; thus, the representation of incest in the hothouse problematises the traditional use of nature as a moral referent in medico-sexual discourses. In this sense, *La Curée* antedates Féré's discussions on notions of 'nature' and 'the natural' in relation to evolution and sexual perversity: 'en réalité il n'y a aucune raison pour que les actes sexuels échappent à la responsabilité et les faits montrent qu'ils n'y échappent pas; la nature et la société éliminent les pervertis et favorisent les sobres' (in truth, there is no reason for which sexual acts escape responsibility, and the facts show that they do not; nature and society eliminate the perverts and favour the healthy) (1899: 13). Nature was used as a referent to classify normative sexuality, and in this regard, Féré engages with definitions of the sexual normal by placing it in relation to the natural. An example of this is found in his discussions on Havelock Ellis's approach to masturbation as a normal or natural act:

> Ellis reconnaît que les phénomènes auto-érotiques sont anormaux parce qu'ils s'écartent de la fin naturelle, mai qu'en l'absence de moyens naturels de satisfaction ils sont inévitables [. . .]. Cette manière de comprendre l'auto-érotisme qui amène à considérer la masturbation comme normale me paraît s'applique strictement aux animaux. (1899: 301)

> (Ellis acknowledged that autoerotic phenomena are abnormal because they deviate from the natural end, but that in the absence of natural means of satisfaction they are inevitable [. . .]. This way of understanding autoeroticism, which leads one to consider masturbation as normal, seems to me applicable only to animals.)

Féré understands that Ellis sees masturbation as a replacement during 'l'absence de moyens naturels' (the absence of natural means), which leads Féré to see the potential definition of masturbation as natural, hence normal. He seems, however, to disagree by expressing with irony that masturbation should be seen as normal only in the case of animals – 'considérer la masturbation comme normale me paraît s'applique strictement aux animaux' (to consider masturbation as natural seems to me applicable only to animals). What is interesting in the present context is the use these discourses made of the terms animal, natural and normal to define normative and perverse sexuality. The animalistic description of Renée in the hothouse engages precisely with this terminology. In this sense, *La Curée* suggests an alignment with Féré's difference between natural and animal sexualities. However, Renée's animalistic traits are not placed in a savage nature but, theoretically, in a domesticated one. The (un)domestication of nature goes through an analogical process of (un)domesticating sexuality. Thus, in *La Curée*, the savagery with which incest is described conforms to a nature that is not domesticated anymore but instead goes against common bourgeois approaches to nature, that in Zola's context is part of a corrupted society. The hothouse negates nature as a referent of the normal.

If the hothouse is used to represent discourses of new sexualities, it was also a modern space par excellence. The hothouse assimilates other nineteenth-century constructions of glass for public uses such as the 'expositions universelles' of 1867 or 1878 that have been interpreted as the will to uncover and know all hidden realities (Hamon 1992: 75). But, while Zola's style aimed at showing everything as if through glass, glass also acquires a negative meaning that brings it closer to the railway in Harrow's view, 'at once rational and mythical, [it] is connective and ultimately destructive' (2010: 48). Zola's use of glass 'exposes the tensions crisscrossing the sites of modernity: beauty and horror, power and collapse, energy and implosion' (Harrow 2010: 48), and glass as a modern material does not escape its own paradox. The depictions of the hothouse in *La Curée* add to the text's critical views on Second Empire constructions and the ostentatious attitude of the new bourgeoisie. The savagery relating to glass, especially in the hothouse, adds to Zola's critique of exhibitionistic private spaces that relate to their effects on intimacy and sexuality. Tanner argues how 'popular with Paris's well-to-do during the Second Empire, and particularly during the 1860s, these climate-controlled "winter gardens" were featured in the homes of France's most fashionable citizens' (2015: 117). However, Georg Kohlmaier and Barna von Sartory have noted how the middle classes in England, France and Germany clearly perceived a difference between glass constructions for public and private buildings: 'light-filled rooms with glass façades or roofs were acceptable only in public buildings, which formed places of congregation for transitory movement: stations, covered markets, exhibition halls, and hothouses' (1991: 22), while the interior remained a site of privacy. The sexualisation of the hothouse in *La Curée* represents nature as a category that escapes domestication and exposes the failure of normative structures. Kohlmaier and von Sartory place the creation of private greenhouses in the context of colonisation and industrialisation, and the attempts at recovering a mythical relationship with nature (1991: 12): 'the glasshouse, with its greenery, was [...] a symbol of the Garden of Eden on Earth' (14). The sexual performance in the Saccards' greenhouse, however, expresses an evil rather than paradisiac setting that eradicates any idyllic meaning. In *La Curée*, nature, described as 'cette nature si artistement mondaine [où] les anciens dieux cachaient leurs amours géantes, leurs adultères et leurs incestes divins' (this nature so artistically mundane [where] the ancient gods hide their great loves, their adulteries and their incestuous relationships) (Zola [1872] 1981: 47), points at the incest between Renée and Maxime as well as being strongly contextualised within the Second Empire and the urban works of Paris. In fact, in *La Curée*, the meaning of nature, i.e., gardens and parks, taken within the new Paris does not belong to a wider process of domestication but of corruption. By placing the incest in the hothouse among discussions on natural sexuality, the text allows a different reading than the traditional association between women and nature argued, for example, by Takaï, who notes the role of nature as opposed to the constructed spaces of the home:

> Le caractère artificiel de la chambre se révèle hostile à la jeune femme, tandis que la nature de la serre la libère et horrifie Maxime [...]. L'association de la nature avec les femmes inquiète les hommes, et c'est en contraignant ces dernières sous le règne de l'artifice qu'ils se rassurent. (2013: 337)

(The artificiality of the room appears hostile to the young woman, while the nature of the hothouse sets her free and horrifies Maxime [...]. The association of nature and women disturbs men, and it is the submission of women to the kingdom of artifice that reassures men.)

However, the hothouse conforms to the artificiality of the whole Saccard residence in what Harrow defines as 'Saccard's attempts to "domesticate" the exotic' (2000: 446). The same artificiality found in the rooms of the Saccards is also located in the hothouse, where plants from different parts of the world have been arranged in order to create an architectural effect. The hothouse does not represent the natural world as opposed to the constructed environment; instead, nature is also a structure within the wider structure of the new Paris.

Napoleon III took the idea of creating green spaces from his exile in London between 1848 and 1850. He not only imported the idea of urban parks but also that of 'arbres d'alignement' (rows of trees) to plant alongside the streets for shade and decoration (Willsdon 2003: 108). However, the many critiques the project received were due to what was considered a pompous artifice, and a disregard of the natural forms of the city. One of the old parks affected by such a transformation was in fact the Parc Monceau – location of the hôtel Saccard – that was 'truncated to permit the construction of the long, straight boulevards so hated by those who mourned "old Paris"' (Willsdon 2003: 113). Parc Monceau was an important part of Haussmann's urban renovation of Paris, and in 1861 it became the first new public park created by Haussmann. Parc Monceau was part of a new neighbourhood that mostly hosted the new bourgeoisie, and together with Buttes-Chaumont and Montsouris conformed what Heath M. Schenker defines as an 'emerging map of social and political identities' (1995: 207). Thus, an important linkage between the Saccards and the new Paris of Napoleon III is established not only through domestic architecture but also through its geographical location: Parc Monceau is found at the origins of the urban expression of a new society strongly marked by the formation of a new bourgeoisie, of suspicious morality, that, as represented in *The Rougon-Macquart*, mostly ascended from popular bases. In *La Curée*, Parc Monceau is a scene for the promenades of Renée and Maxime as well as for their secret and incestuous encounters. Promenades were also places located within the urban space promoted by Haussmann's renovations that, as Claire A. P. Willsdon notes, refer 'not to the action of walking, but the spaces where inhabitants of, and visitors to, the new Paris might walk – boulevards, streets, parks and gardens' (2003: 108). Maxime and Renée enjoy incest in concrete places that were recognisable icons of Second Empire Paris. Parc

Monceau, which Zola defined as 'grass and flowers [...] on displays as if in the windows of a shop' (Willsdon 2003: 113), echoes the commercial exhibitionism of the hôtel Saccard.

Haussmann himself defined gardening 'comme une sorte de corollaire de l'Art Architectural' (like a sort of corollary of architectural art) (1985: 174), hence establishing a linkage to domestic architecture, and emphasising the artificiality of nature. In *La Curée*, the visual linkage between the 'petit salon' (small salon) and the hothouse empowers the connection between nature and domestic architecture further: 'et [Maxime et Louise] de rire, se croyant seuls, sans même apercevoir Renée, debout au milieu de la serre, à demi cachée, qui les regardait de loin' (and [Maxime and Louise] laughing, thought they were alone, without noting Renée, standing in the middle of the hothouse, half hidden, observing them from afar) (Zola [1872] 1981: 76). This scene, in which Renée spies Maxime and his fiancée, triggers Renée's first desires towards her stepson before the incest takes place: 'et sous la lumière vive, Renée songeait, en regardant de loin Louise et Maxime. Ce n'était plus la rêverie flottante, la grise tentation du crépuscule, dans les allées fraiches du Bois [...]. Maintenant un désir net, aigu, l'emplissait' (and under the bright light, Renée contemplated, looking from a distance at Louise and Maxime. It was no longer the floating reverie, the grey temptation of twilight, in the cold alleys of the Bois [...]. Now a clear, sharp desire filled her) (79). Renée's desire is suggested to be caused by her tropical surroundings, a voluptuousness inspired by the exotic plants and, particularly, by the erotic smell of the place: 'c'était cette odeur humaine, pénétrante, sensuelle, cette odeur d'amour qui s'échappe le matin de la chambre close de deux jeunes époux' (it was that human smell, penetrating, sensual, that smell of love that escapes in the morning from the closed room of two young spouses) (80). The sexualisation of nature and its evil connotations – 'l'arbuste derrière lequel elle se cachait à demi, était une plante maudite, un Tanghin de Madagascar' (the shrub behind which she was hiding was a cursed plant, a Tanghin from Madagascar) (81) – trigger Renée's sexual desires towards Maxime. Against all nineteenth-century scientific previsions that looked at the hothouse as 'a museum in which the masterpieces of nature were gathered together, listed in a catalogue' (Kohlmaier and von Sartory 1991: 1), nature in the Saccards' hothouse escapes the regulatory aims of the nineteenth century. In fact, 'catalogue' recalls the structures of sexological and architectural works seen in the previous chapter; and, like sexuality and architecture, the natural world in *La Curée* resists domestication.

In the hôtel Saccard, the categories of sexuality and nature signify the opposite of what the bourgeoisie intended. Belenky has noted how Zola 'radically rewrites these social spaces [Parc Monceau, café Riche and the Batignolles omnibus], investing them with a meaning opposite to what Haussmann intended them to signify [social order]' (2013: 28). Belenky argues that parks were made in order to control bourgeois leisure, and accordingly, were imbedded with respectability, especially for mothers, nannies, and children. However, 'the spatial link between the park and the *serre* reinforces the idea of reversibility between the openly immoral space of the hothouse and the ostensibly ordered space of the park' (Belenky 2013: 31). In differentiating between 'the immoral space of the hothouse' and the 'ordered space of the park', Belenky understands that these spaces conformed to two distinct social orders. However, both the Saccards' hothouse and Parc Monceau are built in Second Empire Paris and respond to the same process of urban renovation. As Harrow notes in commenting on another green area, the Bois de Boulogne, 'the Bois represents the annexation of nature to the city and to ideology' (2000: 450). Indeed, in *La Curée* all urban nature is represented as imbued with the same values.

The dissolution of forms

The bodies of Renée and Maxime oppose static definitions of gender and the sexual body by evoking a sense of fluidity and ambiguity: '[Maxime] la [Renée] trouvait originale. Par moments, il n'était plus bien sûr de son sexe' ([Maxime] found her [Renée] original. At times, he was not sure anymore of her sex) (Zola [1872] 1981: 184). For Maxime, Renée appears androgynous and undefined, while Maxime is described as 'hermaphrodite étrange venu à son heure dans une société qui pourrissait' (a strange hermaphrodite who came in due time to a rotting society) ([1872] 1981: 152). Discussions about fluid sexual and gender forms were abundant in the late nineteenth century. In 1877, Texier commented about the new Parisienne's fashion: 'un vêtement qui n'est ni masculin ni féminin, l'uniforme d'un troisième sexe, – cette anatomie monstrueuse, ces gonflements de Vénus Callipyge, ce mensonge perpétuel, cette caricature impudente où l'indécence se noie dans le ridicule, cela la Parisienne?' (a garment which is neither masculine nor feminine, the uniform of a third sex, – this monstrous anatomy, this swelling of Venus Callipyge, this perpetual lie, this impudent caricature where indecency becomes ridicule, is that the Parisienne?) (12). By using the term 'mensonge perpétuel' (perpetual lie), Texier echoes Viollet-Le-Duc's discourse where 'mensonge perpétuel' (perpetual lie) is defined as the disassociation between form and purpose in Haussmannian architecture: 'notre architecture, dite monumentale, est un mensonge perpétuel. Habituellement, dans nos édifices, toute forme apparente est inutile et ne sert que d'ornement' (our so called monumental architecture is a perpetual lie. Usually, in our buildings all apparent form is nothing but useless and only functions as an ornament) (1868: 662). According to Viollet-Le-Duc, architectural form is disassociated from function, an idea that permeates notions of bodily forms in their relation to sexual functions, as Texier suggests. This parallel illustrates how sexual and architectural discourses were guided by the same epistemological structures whereby definition, understood as both meaning and the description of the features and limits, was one of their main outcomes. In fact, both for Viollet-Le-Duc and Simon the meaning of the body and the built space are inseparable from their features and limits; a shift in one reflects a shift in the other. The dissolution of forms is of paramount concern in this context as it is understood to imply a dissolution of someone's being or something's nature.

The first deviation from traditional gender roles between Renée and Maxime is suggested through the role Renée plays regarding Maxime's education: 'l'étrange éducation que la jeune fille donnait à l'enfant; les familiarités qui firent d'eux des camarades; plus tard, l'audace rieuse de leurs confidences; toute cette promiscuité périlleuse finit par les attacher d'un singulier lien' (the strange education that the young woman gave to the boy; the familiarities that made them comrades; the laughing audacity of their confidences; all this perilous promiscuity ended up binding them in a singular bond) (Zola [1872] 1981: 211). Renée embodies the role of the seducer who leads younger women towards debauchery, echoing again libertine literature such as de Laclos's *Les liaisons dangereuses* (1782). At the same time, Féré's statement, 'sous l'influence de l'habitude, les défauts d'éducation entrainent des pervesions qui deviennent tout aussi constitutionnelles que les perversions congénitales' (under the influence of habit, defects in education lead to perversions that become just as constitutional as congenital perversions) (1899: 18), seems to illustrate the sentimental education Renée gives to Maxime, and its impact on Maxime's physiological structure. Such physiological alteration would modify his bodily forms as well as the nature of his being. Maxime, however, is placed, more clearly than Renée is, within a context of family degeneration. Féré, following Krafft-Ebing, describes both hermaphroditism and androgyny as different types of sexual inversion (1899: 169), which Féré defines as 'une des formes les plus caractéristiques de la dissolution du sexe et de la dégénérescence' (one of the most characteristic forms of the dissolution of sex and of degeneration) (171). Féré's work L'instinct sexuel engages with discussions on degeneration, which include the role of heredity in perversions and vices. This contrasted with the focus on the acquired characteristics of abnormal sexuality during the first half of the nineteenth century. Maxime's hermaphroditism is clearly related to late nineteenth-century theories of degeneration:

> Ses [Maxime] cheveux bouclés achevaient de lui donner cet 'air fille' qui enchantait les dames [...]. La race de Rougon s'affinait en lui, devenait délicate et vicieuse. Né d'une mère trop jeune, apportant un singulier mélange, heurté et comme disséminé, des appétits furieux de son père et des abandons, des mollesses de sa mère, il était un produit défectueux [...]. Hermaphrodite étrange venu à son heure dans une société qui pourrissait. (1981: 152)

> (His [Maxime's] curly hair gave him that 'girlish look' that enchanted the ladies [...]. Rougon's race became more perfect in him, delicate and vicious. Born of a too-young mother, acquiring a singular mixture, shocked and as if disseminated, of the furious appetites of his father and of the abandonment, of the softness of his mother, he was a defective product [...]. A strange hermaphrodite who came in due time to a rotting society.)

The progressive loosening of body forms within the Rougon-Macquart family suggests an increased difficulty in distinguishing male and female physiologies. Masculinity is dissolving in Maxime, while it is emerging in Renée. This fluidity of traditional gender characteristics points at a lack of specialisation, i.e., fixation, that, Féré states, 'se manifeste d'abord le plus souvent par la diminution des processus relatifs au choix ou au contrôle' (often is first manifested by a decrease of the processes related to choice or control) (1899: 36). Féré's words imply a weakness in the act of choice produced by the alteration of a specialised physiological function. The physician's approach to definition and specialisation conforms to that of architects such as Kerr, for whom, we have seen, rooms should be clearly defined in terms of function in order to avoid perversities. The idea of mobility and lack of definition, hence of function, is approached by both physician and architect in relation to sexual and architectural perversity, altogether impacting on wider notions of well-defined structures. This aversion towards ambiguity reinforces their respective approaches to sexuality and domesticity as static realities, whereby homogeneous and hegemonic ways of living were created.

Maxime does not only contrast with the static approach of sexual and medical discourses through his body but also through his reckless house moving. He does not have his permanent residence in the hôtel Saccard; instead, he appears with a nomadic life inhabiting many places: 'il menait la vie plus nomade du monde, logeant dans les maisons neuves de son père, choisissant l'étage qui lui plaisait, déménageant tout les mois' (he led the most nomadic life in the world, staying in his father's new houses, choosing the floor he liked, moving every month) (Zola [1872] 1981: 168–9). Maxime embodies the new domestic values of mobility and ephemerality – values that Texier identifies in the new architecture: 'on fait une architecture et un art passagers, pour une société éphémère' (one makes of architecture a temporary art for an ephemeral society) (1877: 39). These concerns were also present, for example, in Germany, where Berlin was experiencing a similar process of estate market speculation and a change in ways of dwelling, as the German architectural journal the *Deutsche Bauzeitung* expressed in 1867: 'Die Folgen der Wanderexistenz von Miethshaus zu Miethshaus, die wir zu führen gewöhnt sind, wirken eingreifender auf unser Empfindungsleben, als wir uns dessen bewusst sind' (the consequences of a wandering existence from rented house to rented house, which we are used to, have a more invasive effect on our emotional life than what we think) (64). In *La Curée*, domestic instability is contextualised in the new capitalism: the concept of home itself is turned into an economic value rather than being rooted within a family history expressing a sense of permanence and static values. Simon's moral claims

Sexual Accessibility and Exhibitionism 77

refer to the ways in which the new economy permeates notions of family: 'toute une nouvelle famille de vols et d'escroqueries est née avec l'importance croissante de la fortune mobilière. On a reculé aussi par les mœurs proprement dites. Le lien familial s'est relâche de toutes façons' (a whole new family of thefts and scams has appeared with the increasing importance of personal fortune. We have also receded in customs. The family bond has loosened in all ways) (1892: 9). Berman notes how a characteristic of the new Parisian urbanisation and capitalist economy is the short duration of the new constructions: 'the pathos of all bourgeois monuments is that their material strength and solidity actually count for nothing and carry no weight at all, that they are blown away [...] by the very forces of capitalist development that they celebrate' (2010: 99). That means that the new Paris is constantly being demolished and rebuilt within a new social dynamic that announces the fragile structures of contemporary western society in terms of relationships and family.

Notions of domestic mobility and ephemerality were considered part of a bohemian lifestyle in the first half of the nineteenth century, as opposed to a bourgeois sense of interior: 'l'habitat bohème s'oppose axiologiquement à l'habitat bourgeois parce qu'il n'est conçu ni dans la stabilité ni dans la durée' (the bohemian habitat is opposed to the bourgeois habitat because it is not conceived for stability or as a long-term residence) (Glinoer 2015: 61–2). Such instability also affected sexuality and the configuration of a permanent household: 'les relations de couple ne sont pas moins précaires toutefois dans la vie de bohème que les changements de logement, de meubles et de café' (couple relations are no less precarious in bohemian life than changes in accommodation, furniture and coffee) (Glinoer 2015: 67). In Maxime we see a voluntary appropriation of non-bourgeois ways of living in the same way that we have seen the re-appropriation of libertine motifs in Renée. Thus, *La Curée* represents a domesticity under construction for new types of bourgeoisies, being permeated by different domestic traditions. We will see in Chapter Four how Huysmans' *En ménage* represents the consolidation of an unstable domestic life both in architectural and sexual terms in the life of a common middle-class citizen.

The constant demolishing and building in the Second Empire made permanent the presence of ruins in a paradoxical relationship to the concepts of newness and the modern the new Paris stood for. Thus, while Haussmann put the emphasis on the new, the sight of ruins became also a landmark of capitalism. In Zola, the ruins are not only found in buildings but also in the biological decay of the Rougon-Macquart family. The analogy between the ruined Paris and the family metaphorically illustrates the strong paradox of the modern, as Berman describes it: 'to be modern is to find ourselves in an environment that promises adventure, power, joy, growth, transformation of ourselves and the world – and, at the same time, that threatens to destroy everything we have, everything we know, everything we are' (2010: 15). Those words reflect Aristide Saccard's situation: while he is involved in speculative construction, and inhabits new buildings, this same new construction bears itself a seed of death and destruction. In Deleuze's words, it is the *fêlure*, not only of the Rougon-Macquart but also of the new economic system. As architecture, sexuality becomes also caught within this circle of demolition and construction, and becomes part of this same paradox. In Zola, sexuality is in fact a means to transmit decay from one generation to the other, in the same way as Saccard builds one building after the other without the intention to improve them in quality (thereby making them subject to the rules of personal profit, to the detriment of the social good). Women, also, become receptacles of new economic values; scholars have noted how Renée is permeated with the values of the new real estate market as Arisitide Saccard approaches her in the same speculative terms: 'Aristide Saccard's exploitation of building opportunities in Paris mirrors his exploitation of his wife Renée' (Foss 2017: 59). The blurring of gender differences and roles has been analysed in relation to the re-organisation of Paris: '[Zola] suggest[s] that the rebuilding of social space in Paris corresponded with a rebuilding of familial and sexual relationships, either through homosexual eroticism or through non-conforming gender identities' (Foss 2017: 66). Medical and architectural discourses could, thus, participate in the mobility of the new economic system; the relationship between sexuality, architecture and economic liberalism could be the object of further research.

*

In *La Curée*, an increment in the use of glass in the private residences of the new bourgeoisie modifies traditional understandings of home and sexuality. Glass is imagined to permeate domesticity with a sense of exhibitionism and an alteration of boundaries, thus turning private space into a more public reality. The loss of domestic privacy reflects on the sexual body, especially that of Renée, and on constructions of sexuality and intimacy, which become permeated with notions of publicity. Thus, while stone ensured privacy and sexual modesty, glass brought mobility, accessibility, and publicity to the domestic domain. For this reason, many moralists perceived a change in the domestic sphere, describing what they called the disappearance of the interior and family life, as for example, in the Goncourt brothers: 'la vie sociale y fait une grande évolution qui commence. Je vois des femmes, des enfants, des ménages, des familles dans ce café. L'intérieur s'en va. La vie retourne à devenir publique' (social life is beginning to undergo a great revolution, I see women, children, households, families in this coffee shop. The interior is fading away. Life becomes public again) ([1860] 1956: 835). Nevertheless, it is important to note that the concept of the interior did not disappear; instead the domesticity of the old bourgeoisie was being replaced by a new architecture that modified ideas of interior space but did not annihilate it altogether. In fact, in the first decades of the twentieth century there would be a strong commitment to articulate a new home, both among architects such as Eileen Gray, and authors such as those of the Bloomsbury Group. In the next chapter, we will see already in the 1880s how glass and new domestic values are beginning to acquire positive connotations in Fontane's *L'Adultera*.

This chapter has also introduced the important concept of mobility regarding domesticity and sexuality. In contrast to the static and homogeneous domestic discourse analysed in the first chapter, here we have seen a dynamic approach to dwelling where house moving destabilises traditional bourgeois domesticity, at the same time that bodily forms blur leading to sexual and gender inversion. Thus, Maxime's androgynous body and his constant house moving reflect a de-formation, a loss of domestic and sexual forms as constructed by normative architectural and sexual discourses. However, mobility will be an important factor in domestic and sexual representations in the following chapters, and the idea of a mobile domestic culture will generate a variety of ways of dwelling and the diversification of domestic discourses, which echo the incessant production of terms in sexology.

Although sexual discourses aimed at regulating sexuality, they also provoked a more tolerant attitude towards the social and legal assimilation of some sexualities considered pathological, especially if they were seen as congenital like inversion. What was perceived as natural, i.e., normal, sexuality, rather than acquired sexual behaviour, was thus an important parameter to measure tolerance towards non-hegemonic sexual forms. Therefore, natural sexuality became less identified with procreation, which had been an important parameter against which to define normal sex. However, in *La Curée* the animalistic representation and association between nature and incestuous adultery create a counter-discourse that places nature in line with undomesticated natural instincts. We have seen how this idea is framed within the wider context of Second Empire Paris and the corruption of society, which expands even into nature. Thus, in *La Curée* nature is invalidated as a moral referent for sexuality, and the association of both realities appears as the impossibility of domesticity and the violation of family boundaries.

In the strong inherited domestic culture of the nineteenth century, the traditional disassociation between form and function pointed at a cultural crisis in ways of living. The new Parisian woman, as Texier calls her, characterised by an ambiguous sexual form, an ambiguity that in *La Curée* extends to Maxime Saccard, is associated with the new architecture by discursive means. Thus, sexual dissolution takes place together with that of the old domesticity, a pillar of which was the transmission of property through the father: that is, the transmission of architectural forms, inseparably from those of the male body. The analysis of Maxime Saccard has illustrated the ways in which theories of degeneration also engage with the dissolution of a domestic patriarchal tradition.

Notes

1   This discussion between architectural form and purpose continues today. Architect Bernard Tschumi is a contemporary defender of the association between form and purpose and against what he calls imagistic architecture, which he defines as based on an image rather than actual purposes. An example of imagistic architecture is Burj Al Arab, Dubai, where a pattern is constantly reproduced.

3

Glass Dwellings and the Dissolution of Adultery in Fontane's *L'Adultera*

Published in Germany eleven years after *La Curée*, *L'Adultera* (1882), mostly located in Berlin, narrates the story of the young Melanie Caparoux, the daughter of a Swiss nobleman, who marries Ezechiel van der Straaten, 'einer der vollgültigsten Finanziers der Hauptstadt' (one of the capital's most important financiers) (Fontane [1882] 1959: 7). Fontane's narrative opens in the apartment of the van der Straatens located in a new area of Berlin under construction. With two daughters, the van der Straatens live in the fictional Grosse Petristrasse, which is supposed to be near the real Petriplatz (Seiler 2011: 36), itself belonging to the area of Spitalmarkt where new apartment buildings were built in the early 1870s (*Deutsche Bauzeitung* 1871: 133). Ezequiel invites Ebenezer, 'ein Volontär, ältester Sohn eines mir befreundeten Frankfurter Hauses' (a volunteer, the eldest son of a friend of mine in Frankfurt) ([1882] 1959: 17), to spend some time in their summer villa in Tiergarten. Ebenezer starts an affair with Melanie and finally marries her. Ezechiel van der Straaten has his profession in common with Aristide Saccard, as well as his passion for increasing his fortune. Melanie resembles Renée Saccard in the connotations of her origins, which in the text evoke the old domestic tradition and *savoir-faire*, a marriage of the old to the new money. The Saccards enjoy a glasshouse within their properties, as the van der Straatens did; although Ezechiel sold the glasshouse to the gardener, the family is free to visit and enjoy the glasshouse near their summer residence in the Tiergarten. We will see, however, how Ezechiel's lack of ownership of the glasshouse relates to his loss of control over Melanie. Paris and Berlin in the novels of Zola and Fontane respectively undergo a process of real estate speculation, which is itself linked to the increasing number of *nouveaux riches*, and the professions of both Ezechiel and Aristide. Although in Paris this speculative transformation of the city had been taking place since the 1860s, in Berlin, according to Rüdiger Görner it did not occur until the 1880s (2001: 13), the period in which *L'Adultera* is set. However, mentions of 'Bauspekulation' (real estate speculation) (1873: 121) appear in the *Deutsche Bauzeitung* in 1873 – the first journal dedicated exclusively to architecture and engineering, first published in 1867, and which continues today.

As in *La Curée*, we will see how windows play a prominent role in *L'Adultera*, as they represent a more open sexual culture conveyed through the visual effect of a lack of boundaries. Glass is also found in the aquarium that the van der Straatens own within their property. The analysis of this object will illustrate Ezechiel's inability to control Melanie's desire and sexuality when the aquarium falls to pieces. In contrast to the paradoxical representations of glass in *La Curée,* in Fontane's text glass signifies a more liberal approach to sexuality and the supposed unbreakable aspect of marriage. However, we will see in more detail how the text is not free from a certain irony towards more progressive ways of living, as the reason behind society's tolerance towards Melanie's new marriage appears ambivalent. Windows, the greenhouse, the aquarium and also a vitrine are significant objects through which new approaches to domesticity, female desire and sexuality are formulated. The aesthetics of glass represent the opening of domestic boundaries and the disempowerment of traditional domestic discourses that allow Melanie to leave her husband and begin a new marriage with her lover. The relationship between glass, notions of modern architecture and new approaches to female adultery can be read in light of an awareness of glass in Berlin in the last decades of the nineteenth century.

Far from the dramatic representation of adultery seen in *Madame Bovary*, Melanie's adultery is represented in a new light precisely because glass permeates the spaces she inhabits. The domestic architecture in *Madame Bovary* and *The Return of the Native* is not particularly rich in glass; instead, windows – and also doors – are limited to their regulative functions in allowing foreign access and creating tensions around notions of domestic contamination expressed in female adultery – contamination not only strictly sexual but also of the household and family line. My reading of *L'Adultera* will show how Fontane's text suggests that the representation of adultery differs according to the architecture it associates with. This is not surprising if we consider that adultery is a prominent domestic topic of the nineteenth century. The main space of the adulteress was the house – as we have seen in the first chapter. Normative space built through structure and materials conforms to certain notions of female sexuality, based on seclusion and enclosure, hence highlighting adultery as a trespassing of confinement. That is to say, the adulteress and adultery are, somehow, defined by architecture, as this conveys sexual law. In *L'Adultera*, instead, the quality of transparency finds an analogy with the human quality of honesty. Thus, this chapter argues that in *L'Adultera* the idea of misplaced desires and sexuality is complicated by notions of self-realisation, implying the acknowledgement of one's sexual desires and true feelings. The representation of female adultery is thus open to sympathy and justification. Honesty is a key value that contrasts with the glass-associated exhibitionism seen, for example, in *La Curée* and that in *L'Adultera* opposes the domestic double standard and embraces a culture of transparency.

More liberal understandings of adultery are not only articulated through the aesthetics of glass but also through an appropriation of the biblical scene of the woman taken in adultery, as represented in Tintoretto's painting *The Woman Taken in Adultery* (1546–1548). Ezechiel gives Melanie a reproduction of Tintoretto's work, from which Fontane's text borrows its title, at the beginning of the narrative. The Italian painting works as anticipation and closure of the actual topic of the text: when, at the end of the narrative, Melanie and Ebenezer come back to Berlin after having married in Italy, Melanie is surprised at the rapidity with which her neighbours assimilate and normalise her situation: 'gewärtige sie nicht, einer Strenge zu begegnen, zu der die Welt in der Regel nur greift, wenn sie's zu *müssen* glaubt, vielleicht einfach in dem Bewußtsein davon, daß, wer in einem Glashause wohnt, nicht mit Steinen werfen soll' (do not expect them to behave with severity, as usually people only do so when it is strictly necessary, perhaps simply because they know that whoever lives in a glass house should not throw stones) (Fontane [1882] 1959: 100). The meaning that can be inferred from the expression 'wer in einem Glashause wohnt, nicht mit Steinen werfen soll' (whoever lives in a glass house, should not throw stones) is supported by Melanie's other words, 'die Welt ist inzwischen fortgeschritten, und jetzt ist alles Vertiko!' (The world has moved forward and now everything is a glass cabinet!) (Fontane [1882] 1959: 119), which I will show formulate the concept of the glass house, or more broadly, glass culture and its repercussions in the domestic sphere. Although the architectural journal the *Deutsche Bauzeitung* does not present any important record in the use of glass in private residences of the late nineteenth century, Melanie's engagement with glass to define her domestic situation reflects an awareness of new architectural and domestic possibilities at the time.

Tintoretto's painting works as closure, not only of *L'Adultera*'s narrative, but also in a wider sense, of adultery as cultural topic. In a glass house the function of liminal elements is far less predominant, as windows disappear. We will see how this aesthetic change suggests a change of sensibility in the 'dwellers' of glass houses: they are the dwellers of modern architecture and as such, they are bearers of modern sexualities. The significance of adultery is represented as belonging to an old domestic tradition. The previous chapter reflected the modifications on ideas of sexuality, intimacy and the sexual body brought out by the use of glass in private residences. In Fontane's text these modifications seem to be in a process of assimilation and seen as engines of modern ways of living. We will see how, ultimately, glass normalises adultery within society, and dissolves it as a topic by dissolving the domestic boundary between inside and outside. I will argue how this overcoming of the topic relates to architectural conceptualisations of culture, in this case, through glass.

The painting *The Woman Taken in Adultery* introduces the importance of images in mediating Ezechiel's and Melanie's expectations and understandings of adultery. For Ezechiel the painting serves as a warning and revelation, as his experience when he first saw the painting highlights: 'als wir letzten Sommer in Venedig waren, und ich dies Bild sah, da stand es auf einmal alles deutlich vor mir' (when we were in Venice last summer and I saw this picture, all was suddenly clear) (Fontane [1882] 1959: 14). Ezechiel wants to be constantly reminded of Melanie's potential to commit adultery, and therefore, he has pursued a copy of the painting, which he plans to hang near his desk – although he will finally put it in the gallery – stamping the household with a scarlet letter. For Melanie, instead, the painting 'ist eigentlich ein gefährliches Bild' (is actually a dangerous picture) (Fontane [1882] 1959:

12); it signifies danger for the household and herself, who seems to feel threatened by its premonitory capacities.

Ezechiel's anxiety about the possibility of Melanie's adultery brings him to make the topic ever-present at home. This anxiety seems in fact to illustrate Ezechiel's inability to have control over his wife and links to his economic situation: Ezechiel purchases not the original Tintoretto but a copy, as he cannot afford the original – in the same way that he sold the greenhouse. This lack of access to the object implies a lack of access to the represented topic, and especially to Melanie. At the same time, it highlights notions of possession that permeated traditional marriages by establishing a relationship between sexual access and transactions as in *La Curée*. Ezechiel's economic limitation actually translates into his inability to control the purity of his possessions, in the same way that he cannot control the purity of his wife. In fact, Ezechiel's need for social improvement leads him to marry Melanie, a foreigner, hence introducing a certain kind of impurity within the German domestic tradition, with which the text engages by presenting reminiscences of Goethe's *Die Wahlverwandtschaften* (*Elective Affinities*) (1809). First of all, both *L'Adultera* and *Die Wahlverwandtschaften* present a lake scene that triggers the forthcoming adultery between Melanie and Ebenezer in the first case, and Eduard and Ottilie in the second case. Secondly, both texts present the inclusion of new members of the household that become the adulterous partners. In *L'Adultera* it is the guest Ebenezer who becomes Melanie's lover. In *Die Wahlverwandtschaften* the two guests, Ottilie and the Captain, become the lovers of Eduard and Charlotte respectively. Thus, *L'Adultera* is placed within the wider German literary tradition of adultery. We will find as well explicit references to Goethe in the work of the German architect Cornelius Gurlitt, who attempted to associate the architectural design of late-nineteenth-century homes with the German tradition.

Melanie's contamination of the German domestic tradition

German architect Richard Lucae (1829–1877), director of the Berliner Bauakademie from 1873 to 1877, advised in 1869 on the moderation of light in rooms through the reduction of windows: 'Die Fenster liegen an der langen Seite des Zimmers und nehmen mit den sich zwischen ihnen bildenden sogenannten Spiegelpfeilern diese ganze Wand ein. Ein solcher Raum wird kaum einen düsteren Eindruck machen können' (The windows are on the long side of the room and, with the so-called mirror pillars between them, take up this entire wall. Such a room will hardly make a gloomy impression) (2). However, Lucae continues: 'aber das Licht läuft im ganzen Zimmer herum und beleuchtet die Gegenstände fast zudringlich' (but the light goes around the whole room and illuminates the objects almost obtrusively) (2-3). Lucae's concern with the obtrusive nature of light echoes French anxieties about the use of glass in private residences. Although not explicitly formulating the potential exhibition of the interior to strangers, as Daly did, Lucae suggests it by referring to light as a dangerous element that might expose the interior and warns against the loss of privacy: the domestic interior needs to remain a place of seclusion.

Lucae's approach to natural light resembles the fear of contamination seen in *Madame Bovary*. In *L'Adultera*, notions of domestic contamination are made intrinsic to the household of the van der Straatens through the foreign origins of Melanie. Before becoming an adulteress, she already adulterates home by belonging to a different domestic tradition than that found in Germany. This national and historical breach precedes any kind of sexual contact and the consequent possibility of contaminating the family lineage. The idea of a domestic tradition passed through family history was present both in French and German architectural discourses as the house was the place par excellence where this cultural inheritance was preserved and continued. French architect Charles Lucas (1838–1905) describes home as the place 'pour y fermer en paix les yeux des grands parents; pour y élever [...] la jeune famille [...]; pour y conserver enfin, à l'ombre du foyer domestique, sous les regards bienveillants des portraits des ancêtres [...] ce culte des nobles et glorieuses traditions' (to peacefully close the eyes of our grandparents; to raise [...] the young family [...]; to preserve, there, finally, by the shade of the domestic hearth, under the benevolent gaze of the portraits of our ancestors [...] the cult of the noble and glorious traditions) (1878: 2). In 1867, the *Deutsche Bauzeitung* published an article echoing this same idea: 'die Geschichte des Hauses ist zu gleicher Zeit die Geschichte der Familie [...], auf unser modernes Leben übergehend, wie dasselbe, trotz der verloren gegangenen Gemütlichkeit der sogenannten alten guten Zeit doch auch wieder einen ungeahnten Reichtum seiner Gestaltung gewonnen habe' (the history of the house is at the same time the history of the family [. . .], passing over to our modern life. The house's form holds an unforeseen richness despite the lost cosiness of the so-called good old days) (H. L. 1867: 63). Fontane's text also engages with similar discourses when Ezechiel, knowing that Melanie wants to leave him, shows his resignation with references to his ancestors:

> Bah, die Nachmittagsprediger der Weltgeschichte machen zuviel davon, und wir sind dumm genug und plappern es ihnen nach. Und immer mit Vergessen allereigenster Herrlichkeit, und immer mit Vergessen, wie's war und ist und sein wird. Oder war es besser in den Tagen meines Paten Ezechiel? (Fontane [1882] 1959: 89)

> (Bah, the preachers of world history are making such a mess of it, and we are stupid enough to repeat it after them. Always about forgetting your very own glory, about forgetting how it was and is and will be. Or was it better in the days of my godfather Ezechiel?)

In this context, Melanie's background already exposes her potential unsuitability to nurture the family history of the van der Straatens. Ezechiel's attitude does not escape a certain irony in regard to his own marriage as well as towards the happiness marriage can provide. This irony could be interpreted as giving place to Fontane's own voice about Prussian nationalism. But it also introduces a distance regarding the domestic ideal, demythologising marriage.

Melanie's foreignness finds complicities with Ebenezer's, of Jewish ancestry, who arriving from a long stay in New York, after having been in Paris and London, brings foreign manners to the household (Fontane [1882] 1959: 17). Ebenezer's foreignness is not only expressed in his background but also in his approaches to domestic culture and the role of women. It is thus that Ebenezer contaminates not only the household through his forthcoming adultery with Melanie, but also the very same representations of the domestic tradition. Ebenezer makes his own the motif of women at the window: 'Ich hasse junge Frauen, die beständig am Fenster passen, "ob er noch nicht kommt"' (I hate young women who always stand by the window to see 'whether he is coming yet') (Fontane [1882] 1959: 114). We have seen in Chapter One the poetics of the window and its importance in creating the domestic imaginary. A common female place, sitting by the window, not only defined women's position in relation to domestic boundaries but also signified women's relationship to such interiors, as we have seen through the attitudes of different women such as Emma Bovary, or Thomasin Yeobright. At the same time, the concept of the 'angel of the house' describes women who, like Thomasin Yeobright, conform to domestic regulations. By criticising traditional representations of women at home, Ebenezer is consequently deconstructing the myth of the 'angel of the house': 'Ich bin nicht der Narr, der von Engeln spricht. Sie war keiner und ist keiner. Gewiß nicht. Aber ein freundlich Menschenbild ist sie, so freundlich, wie nur je eines über diese arme Erde gegangen ist' (I am not a fool that speaks of angels. She was not and is not. Certainly not. But she is a friendly being, as friendly as anyone has ever walked on this poor earth) (Fontane [1882] 1959: 80). Melanie's intelligence, feelings and personality make her more desirable for her lover than her domestic duties as wife and mother. With his words, Ebenezer distracts Melanie from protecting the integrity of the household, and seems to reinforce her foreignness by modifying her traditional role at home. But Ebenezer's preference for a woman away from the window and his disbelief in the 'angel of the house' still suggest an association of Melanie with her position within the domestic space: she is still defined by the place she occupies in the house, therefore, continuing to some extent the image of house as woman and woman as house.

While windows formed an important motif in domestic literature, they also had an architectural role in creating what Lucae calls 'Gemütlichkeit' (cosiness), a combination of both light and shadow: 'wenn die Fenster in der gleichen Wand wie vorhin bleiben, jedoch ganz dicht aneinander gerückt werden, so daß der Raum gewissermassen in eine Lichtregion in der Mitte und in zwei Schattenregionen zu beiden Seiten getheilt wird' (when the windows remain in the same wall as before, but are moved very close to one another, so that the room is, as it were, divided into a region of light in the middle and two regions of shadow on either side) (1869: 3). The position and size of windows are not only important in regard to light and ventilation as seen in the previous chapters, but decisive in creating a homely feeling. 'Gemütlichkeit' adds a personal dimension to the mere and rather technical functionality of windows usually seen in architectural texts. As the creation of 'Gemütlichkeit' depends on the alternation of light and shadow, that is, of transparency and opacity, the juxtaposition of windows and walls without windows becomes a key architectural design. Important in this context is the fact that 'Gemütlichkeit' seemed to be part of the domestic ideal, something that becomes patent when considering the central role of windows in representations of domestic space. The feeling of well-being caused by 'Gemütlichkeit' belongs to the creation of the domestic imaginary that sought to idealise the experience of being at home. Therefore, as the size and number of windows increased, the alternation of transparency and opacity decreased and so did the possibilities of creating 'Gemütlichkeit'. The experience of home would, then, change. Representations of glass houses, for example, did engage with a modified experience of the domestic realm. In *L'adultera*, Melanie's choice of terms usually evokes glass, adding to Ebenezer's distortion of the imaginary that placed women by the window. It is in this sense that Melanie's words at the end of the narrative, after coming back from her honeymoon with Ebenezer, 'die Welt ist inzwischen fortgeschritten, und jetzt ist alles Vertiko!' (the world has moved forward and now everything is a vitrine!) (Fontane [1882] 1959: 119), acquire new significance. Melanie's metaphorical use of 'Vertiko' (vitrine), which she associates with progress, refers to the transparency and freedom of a new cultural and social moment. In fact, Melanie's comparison of the old with the new – 'Entsinnst du dich noch, als du sagtest: "Alles sei jetzt Enquete." Das war damals. Aber die Welt ist inzwischen fortgeschritten, und jetzt ist alles Vertiko!' (Do you remember when you said: 'everything is now an inquiry'? That was then. But the world has moved forward and now everything is a vitrine!) (Fontane [1882] 1959: 119) – suggests a change in ways of living. In a 'Vertiko', glass is absolute, which disempowers discourses about intrusion and contamination as well as traditional understandings of 'Gemütlichkeit' – the latter might now be found somewhere else. This structure aligns with Melanie's body as a foreign construction itself, on the one hand, and with her subversion of traditional domesticity, on the other. In fact, Melanie's suggested distance from the window – she is not represented at it – invites us to read her as subverting the domestic ideal as represented in the daily-life scenes in the van der Straatens' apartment: 'Alles atmete Behagen, am meisten der Hausherr selbst, der, in einen Schaukelstuhl gelehnt und die Morgenzeitung in der Hand, abwechselnd seinen Kaffee und den Subskriptionsballbericht einschlürfte' (Everything breathed comfort, mostly the master of the house himself who, leaning in a rocking chair, with the morning paper in hand, alternately sipped his coffee and the subscription report) ([1882] 1959: 9). We have seen the expression 'master of the house' in Chapter One and its association to an architecture designed for the benefit of man's affairs; in *L'Adultera* such an expression functions as a way to place the beginning of the domestic narrative within the domestic tradition. However, Melanie alters this tradition by failing at closing windows and doors – 'alle Türen und Fenster standen auf' (all doors and windows were open) (Fontane [1882] 1959: 74) – as if finding complicity with light and breaking the limits of domestic space. Hillebrand notes how windows in Fontane's *Vor dem Sturm* (1878) modify the concepts of 'Geborgenheit' (security) and 'Behagen' (comfort) (1971: 257), two key ideas for the relationship of the Bürger to his/her domestic space that Lucae articulates as 'Gemütlichkeit'. In *L'Adultera* 'Geborgenheit' and 'Behagen' are dispossessed of their usual sense of enclosure, as defined, for example, by Walter Benjamin as a shell (2002: 220), or case (221). For Melanie, 'Geborgenheit' and 'Behagen' are found on the other side of the window, from where 'eine balsamische Luft' (a balmy air) comes (Fontane [1882] 1959: 74). Thus, the traditional sense of domesticity for which enclosure and separation were an essential part, and which women were responsible to reproduce, is modified by widely opening all doors and windows: the interior opens towards the outside in a way that suggests the misuse of architectural elements seen in the previous chapters. In sexual terms, this is illustrated by Melanie's withdrawal from her husband to her lover, who is an intruder as much as she is. Interestingly, Melanie's association with light permeates her character with positive connotations that complicate the moral implications of female adultery.

In this sense, the 'Vertiko' suspends the domestic culture in which issues of contamination emerged, seen in Chapter One. Glass implies a different engagement with the topic of contamination, which we have seen related to adultery as well as to the wider epistemological approaches of the nineteenth century. The erasing of visual boundaries between the inside and the outside impacts the perception of clearly defined spatial positions framed by a container/contained relationship. The detailed use of windows defined in architectural discourses, precisely in order to avoid an overwhelming sense of intrusion, played an important role in constructing the domestic ideal. The privacy of domestic life was architecturally expressed through an increasing division of rooms based on the acknowledgement of limits, classification and regulation of the use of space. However, erasing the boundary between the interior and the exterior cancels out the function of regulatory elements, i.e., windows and doors, and the possibility of misusing them. In aesthetic and literary terms, we have seen the importance of misusing regulatory elements according to architectural norms: the misuse of space finds a correlation with adultery in *Madame Bovary*. However, in a glass house natural light cannot be regulated. Conceptually, windows become ubiquitous and seem to progressively disappear, and with them vanish all the poetics of the window: the impossibility of the window as a concept in a glass house handicaps the representation of a domestic culture based on notions of limits, intrusions and the contamination of spheres. What remains, however, is the material of glass, the shape of which will stop being a window and become something else, signifying something different in the process.

In terms of ways of living, this is expressed through the assimilation within the legal and social parameters of Melanie's adultery into marriage, dissolving the act of adultery itself. By turning into marriage, adultery stops being represented as an absolute social evil; instead, it becomes relative as it can be legally integrated. This fluidity in the concept of adultery corresponds to the fluidity 'perversion' will take in psychoanalysis, as we will see in the final chapter, which turns domesticity into a less static and regulated reality.

The hidden/known aesthetics of adultery

In 1888, Cornelius Gurlitt, German art historian and president of the Bund Deutscher Architektur from 1920–1926, published his work *Im Bürgerhaus* (*In the Bourgeois House*), where he advises on the decoration of rooms, colours, the placement of furniture and architectural elements such as doors and windows. By giving clear instructions, Gurlitt aims to evoke a domestic imaginary that he locates in the old bourgeois tradition. Like other architects, whose writings added to the creation and perpetuation of the domestic ideal, Gurlitt's text is not historically specific: 'Wisst ihr noch, ihr Geschwister, wie schön es im Esszimmer nach dem Abendbrot war, wenn Vater uns von den Kämpfen und den Erfolgen seines Lebens erzählte, wenn er die alten Volksweisen sang?' (Do you remember how nice it was when, in the dining room, after supper, our father told us about the struggles and the successes of his life, when he sang the old folk tunes?) (1888: 101). However, the paradox of Gurlitt's account lies in the fact that while praising old times, he criticises their architecture, which he identifies with historicism – a critique that he shares with Viollet-Le-Duc in France, and that is also based on the disjunction between form and purpose: 'jene hunderterlei Dinge, deren Form und Farbe nicht im Mindesten den Zweck verkünden, im Gegentheil ihn möglichst verstecken, gehören nicht in eine kunstgemässes, stilvolles Haus' (those hundreds of things, the shape and colour of which do not in the least announce their purpose, on the contrary, they hide it as much as possible, do not belong in an artful, stylish house) (1888: 45). This results in an ambiguity in Gurlitt's view of the relationship between architecture and domesticity: Gurlitt argues that modern houses are not homely due to their architecture and interior design. However, he criticises the architecture of previous times although such architecture did not impede houses being homely.

This ambiguity is found throughout Gurlitt's work, especially, in regard to doors, windows, mirrors and the regulation of light. Gurlitt's dialectics of light and shadow are held in a permanent tension in which no definite conclusion is reached, hence continuing the anxieties around domestic limits as in the cases of other German and French architects, for instance Lucae, Havard and Daly. On one hand, Gurlitt praises German panel windows and the lighting of the interior as a means to eradicate secretiveness: 'Es entspricht [. . .] unserer ganzen Lebensanschauung, dass Klarheit die uns umgebenden Räume durchdringe, dass keine Ecke finster, dämmerig bleibe, sondern dass überall hin das Auge ungehindert streife' (It corresponds [. . .] with our whole vision of life that clarity permeates the spaces that surround us, that no corner remains dark or dim, but that the eye roams everywhere freely) (1888: 163). Transparency, which Gurlitt seems to associate with honesty, is seen as properly German, and in fact he links it to German culture through the figure of Goethe: 'Der Ruf des sterbenden Goethe "Mehr Licht!" drang in unsere Wohnhäuser' (The call of the dying Goethe 'More light!' penetrated our houses) (1888: 163). On the other hand, however, light seems to raise issues of inconvenience as transparency clashes with notions of domestic privacy, and more importantly, it can unsettle the exterior/interior boundary:

Glass Dwellings and the Dissolution of Adultery 93

Das grosse Fenster verband das Zimmer zu sehr mit der Aussenwelt, die Geschicklichkeit der Menschen, grosse völlig durchsichtige Scheiben zu schaffen, durch diese die Grenze zwischen Zimmer und Aussenwelt für das Auge völlig zu verwischen, wuchs zu sehr, als dass nicht die künstlerische Abgeschlossenheit des Raumes zu schaden kommen musste. (1888: 165)

(The large window connected the room too much with the outside world, the skills of those who created large, completely transparent panes, through which the boundary between the room and the outside world was blurred for the eye, grew too much and the artistic seclusion of the room was damaged.)

The danger of incorporating too much glass in walls is that the interior is connected indiscriminately to the outside. The visual boundary, as Gurlitt mentions, disappears, as we have seen in *La Curée*. With this visual, ultimately conceptual, dissolution of the interior/exterior dialectics, home as an architectural construction becomes progressively replaced by a non-architectural reality: we saw in Chapter One how domestic space conforms to the regulations of architectural prescriptiveness. Erasing the conceptual boundary between the inside and the outside by employing glass modifies the concept of home as generally articulated in the nineteenth century: a privileged and domesticated realm free from the dangers of the public sphere. In this context, Gurlitt's desperate question, 'Warum müht man sich, die Abgrenzung zwischen Innenraum und Aussenwelt zu einer fast unmerklichen zu machen, wenn man nachher sie so augenfällig zu betonen gedenkt?' (Why do you try to make the boundary between the interior and the outside world almost imperceptible and afterwards you intend to emphasise it so conspicuously?) (1888: 167), testifies to the high awareness of glass and the social disregard towards privacy and isolation that concerns the architect. Interestingly, Melanie also engages with notions of honesty and transparency but takes them further. For Melanie, the concept of the glass house articulates her change from one type of domesticity, represented by the social structures that hold her marriage together, to another, which is characterised as being the result of a conscious choice and true feelings. Melanie metaphorically describes the former with the term 'Teppich' (carpet) ([1882] 1959: 119), and the latter with the word 'Vertiko' (vitrine) ([1882] 1959: 119). By using these objects,

Melanie materially expresses her move from the hidden/known dialectics of domesticity to the transparency found in the new concept of the glass house. The affair itself between Melanie and Ebenezer conforms to ideas associated with glass as their mutual love is represented as honest and authentic. Melanie associates freedom with the new poetics, and politics, of glass. The theorisation of a glass culture allows her to free herself from the domestic tradition represented in the image of the carpet. *L'Adultera* represents a situation that Texier identified in France, and that we will see in the next chapter in *En ménage*. Common domestic objects also express an aesthetic change and illustrate the importance of material culture in articulations of new ways of living. The traditional household imagined in the nineteenth century dissolves to give place not only to new discourses, but also to new architectural representations and interior designs.

A foreseen glass culture would potentially introduce a set of new values at home that had not only been articulated in the nineteenth century but also continued well into the twentieth. The importance of Gaston Bachelard's *La poétique de l'espace* (1958), where the domestic imaginary is related to concepts of enclosure, is a paramount example of the strength that traditional formulations of domestic space had and, probably, still have. Melanie's words appear modern even in light of mid twentieth-century works. The Bachelardian home evokes strength, and a sense of protection and refuge, including several references to the image of mother as house and vice-versa. The French philosopher puts in play the dialectics of the inside/outside and of the hidden/visible, just as Gurlitt does through his discussion of windows and light. Shadow spaces are also an important part of Bachelard's poetics, which are the recipient of a whole architectural tradition, and in fact darkness is part of the hidden realities of home. We have seen how Lucae relates these dialectics to 'Gemütlichkeit'. All these values disappear with the concept of the glass house, and one of the most important consequences of this is the potential disassociation of the house from the mother. The images of the house as mother and the mother as house that prevailed in a certain domestic and architectural tradition were based on the understanding of the mother as the locus of security and protection. This idea is suggested in Fontane's text by exploring the reactions of Melanie's daughters to her marriage with Ebenezer:

Melanie hatte sich rasch erhoben und war den verwundert und beinah erschrocken dastehenden Kindern entgegengegangen. Als sie aber sah, daß Lydia einen Schritt zurücktrat, blieb auch *sie* stehen, und ein Gefühl ungeheurer Angst überkam sie [. . .]. Lydia warf ihr einen Blick bitteren Hasses zu, riß das Kind am Achselbande zurück und sagte: 'Wir haben keine Mutter mehr.' (Fontane [1882] 1959: 111)

(Melanie got up quickly and went to meet the children who were standing there in amazement and almost in fear. But when she saw that Lydia took a step back, she too stopped and a feeling of great fear overcame her [. . .]. Lydia gave her a look of bitter hatred, yanked the child back by the armpit and said: 'We have no mother.')

The house as mother, and the mother as house, are two associations that dissolve in the figure of Melanie, as perceived especially by her children when she goes to see them after coming back from her honeymoon with Ebenezer. The representation of Melanie as a bad mother finds a correlation with the kind of domestic architecture Melanie aligns with: glass. The house that cannot provide a sense of isolation and protection from the outside world cannot be related to the womb, nor to the maternal qualities traditionally associated with women as seen in Bachelard and the nineteenth-century authors discussed in the previous chapters. The children's statement 'wir haben keine Mutter mehr' (we have no mother) points to the death of a certain idea of motherhood predominant in the nineteenth century.[1]

Beyond the window

After Ebenezer has declared his love to Melanie, they go back to the Tiergarten Villa, where 'alle Türen und Fenster standen auf' (all doors and windows were open) (Fontane [1882] 1959: 74). The openness of doors and windows once the possibility of adultery becomes more tangible evokes, again, notions of boundaries and (de)regulation. We have previously seen how this passage represents Melanie's failure to regulate space, but her detachment from such regulations also correlates with a new sense of calm and recovered freedom: 'von den Frisch gemähten Wiesen her kam eine balsamische Luft' (a balmy air came from the freshly mown meadows) (Fontane [1882] 1959: 74). Bruno Hillebrand notes the motif of windows in Fontane's narrative as representing a turning point in the lives of the characters: 'etwas wird mitgeteilt, das im Fontaneschen Werk sonst nur latent zugegen ist, absichtlich zurückgehalten und überdeckt: die innere Befindlichkeit des Menschen' (Fontane's work communicates something that is only latently present, deliberately withheld and covered up: the inner state of the human being) (1971: 256). In *L'Adultera* this latent reality is not only Melanie's love for her guest but also the new ways of living which such love represents, in contrast to a rather mainstream domestic discourse. With wide-open windows, the space Melanie inhabits seems to open up in strong opposition to that of Emma Bovary, whose house seems in permanent tension with Emma's sexuality. However, as David Darby notes, both the gazes of Emma and Melanie through the window point at an outside full of promises, in contrast to other Fontane female characters such as Effi Briest and Cécile:

> Melanie's window, from which she views the street from the confines of the Van der Straatens' apartment, is a place where she experiences '[e]twas wie Sehnsucht' [a kind of longing [literally: something like longing]], but this emotion is in the vein more of Emma Bovary at her window than of Effi Briest or Cécile. It is a longing that draws its power not from the irredeemable loss of a better past [. . .], but rather from the aspiration to nebulous freedoms. (2016: 96–7)

The idea of openness is echoed in Hillebrand's interpretation of the window as 'Symbol oder Ausdrucksträger der Hoffnung, der sich eröffnenden Ferne' (a symbol or expression of hope, of the opening distance) (1971: 258). At the van der Straatens', windows and doors lose their regulatory function by evoking a sense of a complete intrusion from the outside surroundings. The total openness of the windows also expresses the continuation between the inside and the outside found in the image of the 'Vertiko'. In John Walker's words, if *Effi Briest* (1898) reflects the concerns of *'ein weites Feld'*, that is, 'the potentially open and unlimited field of [. . .] subjectivity' (2011: 129), in *L'Adultera* we see how this 'weites Feld' materialises through an architectural openness that links the interior to the exterior. Melanie's subjectivity expands from the house's structure to a space free of regulations (the outside), or at least, free from domestic prescriptiveness and her role as Ezechiel's wife. The linkage between what is at each side of the window blurs the differences between the domestic and

Glass Dwellings and the Dissolution of Adultery 97

the un-domestic, and permeates the concept of home with new meaning.

The open doors also suggest the openness of internal limits and the destabilisation of the house's division into specialised rooms. Through open doors, the lack of prescriptiveness created by merging interior and exterior spaces permeates the very inside of the house. By insinuating a connection between all the rooms of the house, the sense of privacy is altered, while the division of spaces according to gender roles is deconstructed. The form-function architectural principle seen in previous chapters as a main rule for architectural prescriptiveness is here challenged. There is, however, a previous moment in the narrative where this same principle is violated. When the van der Straatens host a dinner in the Berlin apartment, 'Wer aber zum ersten Male hier eintrat, der wurde sicherlich durch eine Schönheit überrascht, die gerade darin ihren Grund hatte, daß der als Speisesaal dienende Raum kein eigentlicher Speisesaal war' (But anyone who entered here for the first time was surely surprised by the beauty that was precisely due to the fact that the room that served as the dining room was not actually a dining room) ([1882] 1959: 23). This situation, which it is suggested has been caused by Ezechiel, is an expression of one of his uncommon traits and indicates a certain disorder at the van der Straatens'. Furthermore, at the dinner, 'Alle hatten sich inzwischen placiert, und es grab sich, daß Melanie bei der von ihr getroffenen Anordnung vom Herkömmlichen abgewichen war' (In the meantime, everyone had taken their places, and it was obvious that Melanie had deviated from common practice in the arrangement she had made) ([1882] 1959: 24). Melanie's deviation from domestic order is anticipated in this scene before she meets Ebenezer. The van der Straatens' household is thus peculiarly represented from the beginning, pointing somehow (as well as Tintoretto's painting does) at the forthcoming and more intense deviation of traditional domesticity caused by Melanie's romantic affair.

Ebenezer, the new lover

The aesthetics of glass with which *L'Adultera* engages do not only imply a change in understandings of female sexuality and domesticity, but also in the representation of Ebenezer as a lover. Ebenezer's prominent role in destabilising the household is publicly known, thus illustrating Texier's critique regarding the new place lovers now have. Texier argues that the role of the lover at the end of the nineteenth century consists in providing for the domestic budget (1877: 73), which is not the case in *L'Adultera*, but he still notes a change from the secrecy to the publicity of adultery reflected in Fontane's novel:

> L'adultère assis près du foyer domestique, installé dans la chambre conjugale, régularisé en quelque sorte. Que lui manque-t-il? Il a la connivence ou l'aveuglement du mari, la tolérance du monde qui sourit, – il a l'estime des fournisseurs. On le salue dans la rue, dans le salon; on le saluerait même dans l'alcôve. (1877: 74)

> (Adultery, sitting near the domestic hearth, settled in the marital room, in a way, regularised. What is it missing? It has the connivance or blindness of the husband, the tolerance of the world that smiles at it – it has the respect of the suppliers. We greet it in the street, in the living room; we would even greet it in the alcove.)

Texier's words contrast with historian Michelle Perrot and the ways in which she describes nineteenth-century domesticity: 'la règle élémentaire de l'esprit de famille, la défense de son honneur passent pourtant par la sauvegarde de ces secrets partagés qui la cimentent et l'opposent à l'extérieur comme une forteresse' (the fundamental rule of the family, its honour, consists in keeping those shared secrets which protect it and oppose it to the outside like a fortress) (1999: 243). The aesthetic opposition that we have seen expressed through the objects of the carpet and the vitrine illustrate the opposing theorisations of two domestic cultures: while the former highlights privacy and secretiveness, the latter emphasises transparency. Such transparency, while understood as hypocrisy in light of Texier's words, translates into honesty and fairness in *L'Adultera*, showing the many ways in which the new tendency found different responses. While Ebenezer appears as the object of Melanie's true feelings and desire, and as a more suitable match for her personality, Ezechiel is represented as an inappropriate husband and inferior in manners to Melanie, who is constantly feeling embarrassed by her husband's comments, as she explains to Ebenezer:

> Das ist ja, wie sie wissen, oder wenigstens seit *heute* wissen müssen, der Ton unseres Hauses. Ein bißchen spitz, ein bißchen zweideutig

und immer unpassend. Ich befleißige mich der Ausdrucksweise meines Mannes. Aber freilich, ich bleibe hinter ihm zurück. Er ist eben unerreichbar und weiß so wundervoll alles zu treffen, was kränkt und bloßstellt und beschämt. (Fontane [1882] 1959: 60)

(As you know, or at least must have known since today, this is the tone of our house. A little pointed, a little ambiguous and always inappropriate. I use my husband's language. But of course, I stay behind. He is just unreachable and knows how to hit everything that offends, exposes and embarrasses so wonderfully.)

Ezechiel's attitude and personality as head of the household and Melanie's husband is a more important fact than Melanie's status as wife.[2] That is, Melanie's true being and honesty appear more important than being faithful to her social roles as wife and mother. In this situation, the lover's role turns into a positive force: he is not a deceiver but someone who points at, and encourages, the right path to follow, in this case, Melanie's true self. This representation of the lover is further supported by representing Ezechiel as partly responsible for his wife's affair. When Ezechiel announces to Melanie the coming visit of Ebenezer, 'wir werden einen Besuch empfangen, oder vielmehr einen Gast, oder [. . .] einen Dauergast [. . .]. Einen neuen Hausgenossen!' (We will receive a visitor, or rather a guest, or [. . .] a permanent guest [. . .]. A new housemate!) (Fontane [1882] 1959: 17), Melanie shows her discomfort: 'schon das Wort, das sich sonst nirgends findet, kann einen ängstlich machen' (even the word that is found nowhere else can frighten you) (17). Melanie, who seems aware of the potential danger the situation may lead to, exposes her husband's imprudence and highlights Ezechiel's unsuitability for the role of 'master of the house'. At the same time, however, Ezechiel links the narrative of his marriage to *Die Wahlverwandtschaften*, where the inclusion of people in the household disrupts domestic life. Following my discussion on Melanie's contamination of the German tradition, it is Ezechiel who, in fact, causes this Goethesque situation, linking Melanie's adultery to German representations of adultery. Far from placing the weight of adultery on the wife, its cause is instead complicated by simultaneously involving husband and wife, bringing co-responsibility to marriage.

While embedded in the German literary tradition, the domestic situation in which Melanie meets Ebenezer echoes Texier's remarks on the state of the relationship of husband-wife-lover in France. In 1877, Texier used the expression 'ménage à trois' to describe how having a lover had become a common fact, to the extent that the lover was part of the household. The process of regularisation this involves is illustrated in Fontane's text through the marriage between Melanie and Ebenezer – 'l'adultère s'est embourgeoisé' (adultery is bourgeois) (1877: 83), complains Texier, criticising lax attitudes towards marriage. Texier's critique of new domestic forms and attitudes towards domesticity are also echoed through the narrator of *L'Adultera*. In fact, *L'Adultera*'s last chapter represents society's inconsistent judgements: '[diesen Äußerungen] bedeutete[n] [Ezechiel] nichts. Er hatte sich selbst zu skeptisch und unerbittlich durchforscht, als daß er über die Wandlungen in dem Geschmacke der Gesellschaft, über ihr Götzenschaffen und Götzenstürzen auch nur einen Augenblick erstaunt gewesen wäre' ([these words] meant nothing to [Ezechiel]. He had examined himself too sceptically and relentlessly to be for a moment astonished at the changes in society's tastes, at its idol-making and idolatry) ([1882] 1959: 122). In light of this passage, society's quick absorption of the new marriage between Melanie and Ebenezer does not reject an ironic reading. In fact, on one hand, society's tolerant attitude could be seen as a capacity to accommodate moral disruption provided certain forms of nicety are preserved. On the other hand, the novel could present a situation that the public would unlikely accept in reality, thus highlighting bourgeois hypocrisy. The feminist implications in *L'Adultera* are merged with the representation of a morally inconsistent society, stopping Fontane's text from being a parable of female emancipation. Thus, while glass does articulate a domestic change, the narrator's attitude seems sceptical about the reasons behind new domestic possibilities.

Recovering the earthly paradise in the greenhouse

Nature in Berlin, as in Paris, was also part of the new economy: '[dass] in Berlin schon fast die meisten Gärten ähnlicher Art der Bauspekulation zum Opfer gefallen sind, nicht hoch genug geschätzt werden kann' (in Berlin most of the gardens of a similar kind have fallen victim to building speculation and cannot be valued highly enough) (*Deutsche Bauzeitung* 1873: 121). Public gardens were being built in London and Paris, and Berlin was also undertaking reforms to become a green city. The summer residence of the van der Straatens at the Tiergarten engages with this green project. In this urban context, the Tiergarten residence and the Saccards' hôtel share their respective newness: both constructions were modern domestic residences at the time. Darby defines the area as the 'fashionable Tiergarten district' (2016: 96) and, as in the case of Renée and Maxime, the greenhouse is a site of romance for Melanie and Ebenezer, where the latter declares his love to Melanie: 'er [. . .] kniete nieder und hielt sie fest, und sie flüsterten Worte, so heiß und so süß wie die Luft, die sie atmeten' (he [. . .] knelt down and held her, and they whispered words as warm and sweet as the air they breathed) (Fontane [1882] 1959: 73). We have seen the cultural implications of the greenhouse in the previous chapter: 'the very lushness of the vegetation, the dimness of the shadows, the warm heavy-scented air, and the twisting, turning paths were ideal for romance. Proposals of marriage [. . .] were thought appropriately made in the conservatory' (Woods and Warren 1988: 165). Thus, *L'Adultera* also engages with this romantic tradition; however, as in *La Curée*, the greenhouse scene between the lovers presents its own cultural significance. By resembling the architecture in Tintoretto's work, the greenhouse in *L'Adultera* engages with wider cultural and religious implications. The greenhouse – a 'mächtige Glasbau wölbte such über ihnen' (mighty glass building [which] arched over them) (Fontane [1882] 1959: 72) – seems to be a glass representation of the architecture present in Tintoretto's work, where arches and columns with a view on nature host the scene of the adulteress about to be stoned. The religious connotations of the greenhouse in *L'Adultera* are also highlighted by the space's resemblance to church architecture. The greenhouse is indeed further defined as presenting 'langen und niedrigen Backsteinöfen hin, den bloß mannsbreiten Mittelgang hinauf, bis an die Stelle, wo dieser Mittelgang in das große Palmenhaus einmündete' (long and low brick stoves, up the man-width centre aisle to the place where this centre aisle led into the large palm house) (Fontane [1882] 1959: 72). The stoves and the narrow aisle under an arched structure are reminiscent of a temple. Finally, there is 'eine Wendeltreppe schlängelte sich hinauf, erst bis in die Kuppel und dann um diese selbst herum und in einer der hohen Emporen des Langschiffes weiter' (a spiral staircase, first into the dome and then around it and into one of the high galleries of the main nave) (Fontane [1882] 1959: 72). Thus, the first explicit act of adultery between Melanie and Ebenezer takes place in an architecture permeated with religious significance. As in the architecture represented in *The Woman Taken in Adultery*, where the arching structure opens into nature, the greenhouse seems the 'Eingang eines Tropenwaldes' (entrance to a tropical forest) (Fontane [1882] 1959: 72). Through the architectural similarities between both representations, the biblical meaning made present through the incorporation of Tintoretto's scene in Fontane's text is modified by Melanie's engagement with glass: Melanie's expression, 'wer in einem Glashause wohnt, nicht mit Steinen werfen soll' (those who lives in a glass house, should not throw stones) (Fontane [1882] 1959: 119), recovers the biblical passage represented above and modifies its narrative by re-imagining its architecture. By linking the greenhouse to Tintoretto's painting, the former plays an important role in defining the coming of a less restricted domestic culture.

By placing the greenhouse in the Tiergarten residence, modern and fashionable design practices again characterise the spaces where new sexual attitudes and ways of living are defined. In contrast to *La Curée*, the greenhouse in *L'Adultera* recovers the sense of earthly paradise at the same time that it transforms the meaning of non-normative sexuality. We have seen how *La Curée* reflects the impossibility of domesticating nature in a corrupted society that leads to the sexual – almost evil – animalism of the lovers in the Saccards' hothouse; hence re-inverting the historical tradition that associated the greenhouse with paradisiacal representations. However, in *L'Adultera*, adultery, far from being associated with ideas of brutalism and, even less, incest, restores a certain paradisiacal sense to the greenhouse, which is now the locus of happiness for the lovers. By hosting a love scene, which will lead to the configuration of a new and licit household, the text re-appropriates notions of domesticity and the natural, incorporating a disregard towards wider social structures by highlighting the importance of one's own feelings. Following the traditional romantic motif of the greenhouse previously mentioned, *L'Adultera* articulates a new domestic story that opens up the possibility of a happy ending by going through adultery and divorce.

The greenhouse in *L'Adultera* also symbolises a new relationship to nature – different from that illustrated in *La Curée* – one that contrasts with domestic space as constructed reality. Katrin Scheidig has noted how in Fontane, 'der Mensch verhalte sich innerhalb des Kulturraumes domestiziert und gesellschaftskonform, im Naturraum dagegen seiner Natürlichkeit entsprechend eher triebhaft' (Humans behave in conformity with society within the space of culture, whereas in nature they tend to be instinctual in accordance with their naturalness) (2012: 16). This 'Natürlichkeit', as represented in the relationship between Melanie and Ebenezer, opposes traditional domestic structures. Unlike in Zola's text, nature in the greenhouse does not partake of the values of the family residence but creates an autonomous space that frames a new romance permeated with positive connotations. In fact, the greenhouse is not owned by Ezechiel anymore; this means that it is not related to the actual domestic space. Melanie can enjoy the greenhouse more at ease, and her husband's loss of wealth seems to empower her. Free from Ezechiel's control, the greenhouse becomes autonomous and conforms to Melanie's desires. Melanie, who Ezechiel also loses, sees the possibilities of a new future in a glass structure that architecturally represents the glass culture. Thus, in *L'Adultera*, resisting traditional domesticity does not find the negative implications represented in *La Curée*. Instead, a traditional and alienating domestic life for Melanie opposes the possibility of a new one that she desires and chooses.

The broken aquarium and the modern woman

Among the domestic amenities in the Tiergarten Villa there is an aquarium, which Ezechiel defines as that 'erbärmlichen Glaskastensammlung' (miserable glass collection) (Fontane [1882] 1959: 66). When Melanie is about to take Ebenezer on a tour around the house, where the aquarium and the greenhouse conform the most exotic and interesting sites, Ezechiel recalls his appalling experience when on a previous occasion the aquarium's glass broke: 'Nicht mehr und nicht weniger als einen Ausbruch, Eruption [...]. Steht unser ganzer Aquariumflur nicht nur handhoch unter Wasser, sondern auch alle Schrecken der Tiefe zappeln um uns her' (Nothing more and nothing less than an eruption, an explosion [...]. Our whole aquarium corridor was not only underwater, but also the horrors of the deep were wriggling around us) (Fontane [1882] 1959: 66). The aquarium is another glass structure that, like the greenhouse in *La Curée*, unsuccessfully sets up limits to nature. The aquarium's inability to contain life inside it echoes Ezechiel's own impotence to retain Melanie as his wife:

Ich sage dir, es geht vorüber, Lanni. Glaube mir, ich kenne die Frauen. Ihr könnt das Einerlei nicht ertragen, auch nicht das Einerlei des Glücks. Und am verhaßtesten ist euch das eigentliche, das höchste Glück, das Ruhe bedeutet. Ihr seid auf die Unruhe gestellt [. . .]. Ihr wollt gar nicht ruhen. Es soll euch immer was kribbeln und zwicken, und ihr habt den überspannt sinnlichen oder meinetwegen auch den heroischen Zug, daß ihr dem Schmerz die süße Seite abzugewinnen wißt. (Fontane [1882] 1959: 86–7)

(I tell you it will pass, Lanni. Believe me, I know women. You cannot endure monotony, not even the monotony of happiness. And what you hate the most is the actual, great happiness, that is, rest. You dwell in the unrest [. . .]. You do not want to rest at all. There should always be something to tingle and pinch, and you have an acute sensuality or, if you like, the heroic ability to take pleasure from pain.)

Ezechiel's frustration at not being able to retain Melanie, '[Ich] will dich behalten' (I will keep you) ([1882] 1959: 89), is anticipated in his recollection of the aquarium's explosion. It takes place in the presence of Ebenezer before he and Melanie walk through the greenhouse and declare their feelings for each other. Ezechiel cannot control the domestication of nature and womanhood just as he cannot own the greenhouse anymore. In opposition to Renée Saccard, who is part of her husband's increasing wealth in the real estate market (Foss 2017: 59), Melanie's independence seems to benefit from Ezechiel's decreasing fortune.

Ezechiel points at Melanie's excessive sensuality as one of the triggers of the dissolution of the household. Like the aquarium's content, Melanie's sensuality cannot be placed within a disciplinary structure. In fact, all the monsters of the deep, everything that was supposed to be underneath, or echoing Teixier, 'sous le manteaux de la cheminée' (under the mantelpiece), rise to the surface in an explosion that inundates domestic space. This image antedates the coming discourse of psychoanalysis, where all the uncanny ghosts haunting home are uncovered and become articulated. Part of Ezechiel's dreadful experience consists in seeing what should be covered, and the image of the oceanic monsters rising to the surface of domestic space symbolises his fears about the expression of Melanie's sexuality.

The monsters of the deep stand for all the realities that domestic and sexual discourses did not express, and for which there was no architectural form: they are the un-formed. In Denis Hollier's words, discourses 'excluent l'informe comme innommable' (exclude the formless as unspeakable) (1974: 64). However, the sudden visibility of the 'innomable' (unspeakable) appears as a reality that deforms the structure of domestic space (although eventually it will re-form again). In other words, if domesticity was based in a series of concepts and ideas – in enclosure, protection from the outside, the angel of the house, the moral sphere, the invisibility of sexuality, the master of the house etc. – then the inclusion within domestic discourse of disruptive elements buried until then, necessarily modifies the domestic imaginary and what home represented for the middle classes. Essential to this change are the questions of woman and her roles as wife and mother, as they were at the time inseparable from the construction of traditional domestic discourses.

Bender notes how in Fontane's texts 'le liquide peut signifier la force élémentaire du désir [. . .]. Le motif représente également [. . .] la liquéfaction de l'ordre social, et plus généralement la possibilité de franchir une limite d'apparence infranchissable' (liquid can signify the elementary force of desire [. . .]. The motif also represents [. . .] the dissolution of social order, and more generally the possibility of crossing a seemingly insurmountable limit) (2010: 484).[3] In *L'Adultera* the scene in the lake also represents water's relationship to desire. While it is in the greenhouse where Melanie and Ebenezer explicitly profess their love for each other, their boat trip is the first opportunity at intimacy. Although not in an open way, Melanie becomes aware of her feelings for Ebenezer in the boat:

[Ebenezer] nahm ihre Hand und fühlte, daß sie fieberte. Die Sterne aber funkelten und spiegelten sich und tanzten um sie hier, und das Boot schaukelte leis und trieb im Strom, und in Melanies Herzen erklang es immer lauter: wohin trieben wir? (Fontane [1882] 1959: 60–61)

([Ebenezer] took her hand and felt that it was feverish. The stars, however, twinkled and reflected and danced around them, and the boat rocked softly and drifted in the current, and in Melanie's heart it sounded louder and louder: where are we drifting?)

The question 'wohin trieben wir?' (where are we drifting?) has a literal and metaphorical meaning: while Melanie, in the boat, is wondering about the form her friendship with Ebenezer will eventually take, the boy rowing the boat suddenly realises that he has slightly lost the way: 'Und sieh, es war, als ob der Bootsjunge von derselben Frage beunruhigt worden wäre, denn er sprang plötzlich auf und sah sich um [. . .], daß sie weit über die rechte stelle hinaus waren' (And see, it was as if the boat boy had been worried about the same question, because he suddenly jumped up and looked around [. . .] they were far away from the right place) (Fontane [1882] 1959: 61). In this scene feelings are mapped out in space through the idea of direction. Melanie's feelings seem to drift far away from the shore, and thus, from home into an unknown area. This motif is also found in Goethe's *Die Wahlverwandtschaften*, where a boat trip on the lake triggers the adulterous feelings of Eduard for Ottilie.

Water characterises Melanie in an even stronger way. Isabel Nottinger notes the ambiguous adaptation of the Melusine-Mythos in Fontane's *Der Stechlin*, where Melusine von Barby-Ghiberti is identified with the element of water, and represents the new woman (2003: 146). The Melusine-Mythos, however, is not represented in a negative light but Fontane instead makes the figure of the new woman more morally complex; in Nottinger's words she embodies both the femme fatale and femme fragile (2003: 147–8). The representation of a fragile and sexually self-assertive woman modifies the evil connotations attached to the new woman at the turn of the century, showing her human side. This union of fragility and assertiveness is also embodied in Melanie, as we can see in the experience of her own vulnerability in relation to Ezechiel's inappropriate behaviour, her feelings for Ebenezer, and her love for her children. However, Nottinger denies the Melusine-Mythos in Melanie as she is able to find a third way out from the oscillation between femme fatale and femme fragile (2003: 149). In fact, Melanie does not yet fully represent the new woman, though she certainly points at it. Melanie presents a certain newness in challenging the traditional female role as mother, and searching for new ways of living.

In sexual terms, Melanie reinterprets her definition as adulteress. In this sense, the woman Melanie becomes is illustrated by her new reading of Tintoretto's painting when she receives a miniature of the painting from Ebenezer (Fontane [1882] 1959: 124). Referring to the adulteress represented in the miniature, Melanie tells Ezechiel: 'Sieh, Ezel, sie hat geweint. Aber ist es nicht, als begriffe sie kaum

Glass Dwellings and the Dissolution of Adultery 107

ihre Schuld?' (See, Ezel, she cried. But does not it look like she barely understood her guilt?) (124). In freeing female adultery from guilt, Melanie changes her first interpretation of the painting at the beginning of the text, 'es ist eigentlich ein gefährliches Bild' (it is actually a dangerous picture) (Fontane [1882] 1959: 12). The presence of the painting at the opening and closure of the narrative invites reflection on Melanie's experience; it constructs what Patricia Howe calls a 'self-reflective text' (2001: 141). Melanie's reflection finds analogies with glass and water in their reflective and mirroring characteristics, empowering further the association between modern architecture and Melanie's approach to sexuality.

In a wider architectural and social context, the aquarium not only has a symbolic meaning, illustrating Melanie as a new kind of woman, but was also considered a construction belonging to the new Berlin. The *Deutsche Bauzeitung* published an article on aquariums in 1873 under the section 'Berliner Neubauten':

> Dem Bauwesen unserer Zeit ist neuerdings eine Reihe von Aufgaben als speziell moderne und eigenartige gestellt worden, in denen sich als Grundcharakter das Bestreben kundgiebt, auf Anregung der in so hohem Grade populär gewordenen Naturkunde die verschiedenen Bildungen der Natur in einem künstlerischen Rahmen zu vereinigen [. . .]. Bisher waren es vorzugsweise Anlagen für die Betrachtung und Schaustellung der Thierwelt und für das Leben der Wassertiefe. (121)

> (The building industry of our time has recently received a series of tasks that are particularly modern and peculiar, based on the endeavour to unite various natural formations in an artistic framework at the suggestion of natural history, which has become so popular [. . .]. So far it has mainly consisted of facilities for viewing and exhibiting the animal world and life in the depths of water.)

The above passage shows how the aquarium configured an artificial structure that aimed at controlling and regulating nature in order to be accessible to the public. This tension between artificial constructions and the natural world is represented in *L'Adultera* through an association of the female condition with the very same nature man domesticates. But in Fontane's text, this tension is brought to its limits and finally breaks out, indicating the end of a particular relationship of man to nature that at the same time affects his relationship to female sexuality.

The aesthetic effect of glass not only modifies the concepts of domesticity and sexuality, but also translates into architectural language emergent approaches to those realities and the new psychoanalytical discourse that will construct them. The qualities of glass function as metaphor for the practice of the psychoanalyst, who deciphers (that is, articulates) through linguistic form what is in the depths of the human mind. Although psychoanalysis is not a straightforward practice, relying on coding and interpretation, it aims at bringing to light the realities dwelling in the unconscious. Thus, psychoanalysis somehow was representative of the new quality of transparency, which would eventually become a value, and impact on notions of marriage, feelings and sexuality.

*

Opposing the architects' concerns with keeping domestic space partly in shadow and protected from the outside, *L'Adultera* further develops the idea of an increasing dissolution of architectural boundaries through glass. However, the representation of glass does not consist, as in *La Curée*, in imagining its impact on new private residences but in its theoretical potentialities and the formulation of new ways of living. This chapter has shown how *L'Adultera* locates such potentialities within the domestic realm in a way that empowers Melanie by breaking with traditional domesticity. Inherent to the glass culture is the dissolution of notions of sexual contamination: the imperceptible boundary between inside and outside suggests a merging of private and public spheres that alters ideas of female reclusion. Thus, *L'Adultera* formulates the concept of the glass-dwelling as a space free from sexual regulations which, by being associated with ideas of transparency and honesty, acquires positive connotations. Honesty is in fact one of the leading qualities in the organisation of contemporary private life. And in *L'Adultera* honesty is an essential part of a new representation of womanhood in Melanie, being characterised by a search to fulfil her true being and act according to her feelings. We have seen how these characteristics appear in analogy with those of glass. There is, therefore, a modification of the traditional model of woman articulated around the aesthetics of glass.

In this new framework, notions of bourgeois sexuality are also modified. In the following chapter we will see how, in blurring the boundary between public and private spaces, the strict opposition between private and public sexualities, i.e., marriage and prostitution, is also blurred. In this context, notions of domestication and un-domestication, or normative and non-normative sexuality, become central to discussions on domesticity. This means that bourgeois sexuality will be in need of redefinition in order to identify, again, the proper and improper use of the body, and create new limits. By doing so, domestic culture becomes more inclusive as it embraces different forms. This also impacts on the importance of nineteenth-century marriage: framed within a strong domestic culture, the different spaces of the house were designed for families according to age, gender and class in order to facilitate privacy and isolation as seen in Chapter One. We have seen how ideas of contamination were strictly related to domestic structures. In the merging of the private and the public, contamination and adultery lose their importance: adultery stops being a domestic topic to become, as we will see even clearer in the next two chapters, a mere event.

The domestic tradition that created the topic of adultery was architecturally formulated around the dialectics of the hidden/visible, as we have seen described in several architectural texts instructing on the position of windows, and facilitating the creation of lights and shadows. Those architectural practices engaged with issues of contamination, of which adultery emerged as its primordial literary expression. In the glass culture, adultery cannot be articulated through architectural aesthetics anymore. The conflating of interior and exterior space makes difficult the creation of a perceptible boundary, and the fusion of spheres cancels out the sense of a regulated space. With this modification in architectural aesthetics, literature engages with a new dwelling culture. Architecture in *L'Adultera* expresses a new approach to sexual and domestic culture, where glass constructions do not respond to exhibitionists' longings, as found in *La Curée*, and expressed by Texier's words: 'la femme se transformait en meuble de montre et de parade' (the woman was becoming a piece of furniture for showing) (1877: 40). Instead, glass conforms the space of a new, self-assertive woman as represented in Melanie, who overcomes her association with household possessions.

The new architecture of Berlin, such as that found in the Tiergarten area, is also the location for the exploration of a transition between ways of living. Berlin's urban modernity frames the disintegration of the van der Straatens' household, while new domestic fashions, such as a domestic aquarium, have been analysed as representing the emergence of new theorisations of domestic life, such as psychoanalysis. We have seen how the aquarium links to other glass representations, such as open windows and the greenhouse, which show a resistance to traditional domestic structures and their normativity by failing to set limits on Melanie's sexual desires. Female sexuality overcomes traditional domestic structures while showing the need for new dwelling cultures. This fact will be prominent in the following two chapters, which show a higher empowerment of female sexuality, leading to a redefinition of domestic space marked by the introduction of the erotic.

Notes

1. Although focused on nineteenth-century France, Elisabeth Badinter's *L'Amour en plus* (1980) is a good analytical example of the construction of motherhood for political and social purposes.
2. Wolfgang Matz analyses the role and responsibility of the husband in adulterous novels in *Die Kunst des Ehebruchs: Emma, Anna, Effi und ihre Männer* (2014).
3. Note that in light of Bender's argument, liquids in Fontane antedate Zygmunt Bauman's analysis in *Liquid Modernity* (2000).

4

Domestic and Sexual Circulation in Huysmans' *En ménage*

Huysmans' *En ménage* (1881) tells the story of André, a middle-class married man who lives in an apartment in Paris with his wife Berthe. After finding Berthe with her lover, André separates from his wife, a situation that leads him to a constant change of home and sexual partners. This sense of permanent motion breaks with the static definitions of home articulated by the domestic ideal. In this context, *En ménage* represents a dissolution of normative sexual practices that finds a correlation with a constant change of homes. Sexuality and domesticity are permeated with mobility as every change of partner is signposted by a change of domestic space. This situation is ambiguously experienced by André, whose life becomes defined by a lack of stability and a constant need to find a proper place to live, and a woman. However, he does not altogether reject his new freedom either. André experiences the contradiction of longing for a more traditional way of living constituted by a household, a wife and a servant, while at the same time he conforms to an emerging cultural view based on the deconstruction of the domestic ideal. We will see how this paradox permeates Huysmans' text with a certain cynicism regarding changes in domestic culture. From a male perspective, *En ménage* represents the pleasures and the challenges of a lifestyle where the household becomes de-regularised by the introduction of divorce and more liberal relationships. We have seen how Maxime Saccard willingly changes places and women without any intention of settling down until his official engagement with Louise. However, André is trapped in the configuration of a new way of living and organisation of family life he himself has not fully chosen but has encountered: while for

Maxime this dynamic approach to domestic space and sexuality is an alternative to a settled bourgeois life, André belongs to a period when this dynamism starts constituting the norm, and becoming, eventually, more generalised. This seeming lack of choice makes it necessary for André to introduce an element of cultural negotiation.

Important for the approach this chapter takes to analysing *En ménage* is the intertextual relationship between the novel and Huysmans' essays on seventeenth-century Dutch art. Huysmans wrote several essays on seventeenth-century Dutch painting in which he praises the technique and the topics of artists such as Frans Hals, Pierre de Hooch and Rembrandt, among others. For the writer, the seventeenth-century Netherlands is 'la joyeuse et pittoresque Hollande!' (the happy and picturesque Holland!) (1877: 76), and in Huysmans' imaginary the Netherlands is still representative of the domestic ideal: 'les Pays-Bas évoquent dans l'imaginaire de l'écrivant un pays de bonheur car lié à la vie "clémente" d'autre fois' (the Low Countries evoke in the writer's imagination a country of happiness as it is linked to the "lenient" life of other times) (Smeets 2009: 9). Describing Pierre de Hooch's characters, Huysmans states, 'ce sont de braves bourgeois, d'honnêtes ménagères, des enfants pas bruyants' (they are brave bourgeois, honest housewives, quiet children) (1875: 47). For this reason, domestic representations in Huysmans have been traditionally read in light of the artistic tradition of the Dutch Golden Age, which has led scholars to highlight the nostalgic aspect of Huysmans' work.[1] In contrast to the secure and peaceful domestic spaces represented in Dutch painting, Paris in the 1880s appears deprived of a place called home, and a site where the turmoil of public life is taking over the private sphere. By opposing static notions of domestic space, movement challenges the domestic ideal. Thus, in the first section of the present chapter we will see how *En ménage* deconstructs the representation of the domestic ideal in Paris, an ideal still present in the last decades of the century. Architects such as the Frenchman Charles Lucas (1838–1905) defined home in 1878 as the place

> pour y fermer en paix les yeux des grands parents; pour y élever [. . .] la jeune famille [. . .]; pour y conserver enfin, à l'ombre du foyer domestique, sous les regards bienveillants des portraits des ancêtres [. . .] ce culte des nobles et glorieuses traditions. (2)

(to peacefully close the eyes of our grandparents; to raise [...] the young family [...]; to preserve there, finally, by the shade of the domestic hearth, under the benevolent gaze of the portraits of our ancestors [...] the cult of the noble and glorious traditions.)

In *En ménage*, however, there is no place for such discourses. Instead, we encounter a quite different reality that invites us to turn Huysmans' work into a critique of a society that does not strive towards materialising the domestic ideal.

Domestic architecture in Paris after the period of Haussmann, and until the emergence of Art Nouveau, remained static and free from any major innovations. Monique Eleb states how architecture between 1880 and 1900 'n'est cependant pas marquée [...] par des changements de mentalité qui révolutionneraient la distribution des appartements bourgeois. Au premier abord, les principes d'organisation des plans présentés par César Daly [...] sont encore observés' (is not characterised [...] by changes in mentality that would revolutionise the distribution of bourgeois apartments. At first glance, the organisational principles of the plans created by César Daly [...] are still observed) (1995: 6). However, it is as well a period of freedom in which architects built in a strongly eclectic way, choosing their favourite styles. *La Revue générale de l'architecture*, for example, dedicates an article to the eclectic styles of domestic architecture in 1882: '[il y a] conséquence également avantageuse de l'éclectisme moderne: la diversité de formes, la variété de caractère supprimant aujourd'hui toute monotonie dans l'aspect architectural des nouveaux quartiers' (the consequences of modern eclecticism are the diversity of forms, the variety of character which, nowadays, eliminates any monotony in the architecture of the new districts) (Rivoalen 1882: 112–14). Such 'monotonie' makes reference to the private residences built under Haussmann. Architect Julien Guadet also refers to Haussman's urban reform in similar terms: 'on a taxé ces compositions monumentales de monotonie, et on a cru que le désordre et l'imprévoyance engendreraient le pittoresque, tandis qu'en même temps on enfermait plus que jamais toute recherche artistique dans des réglementations' (monotony characterised these monumental compositions, and many believed that disorder and improvidence would engender the picturesque; at the same time, all artistic research was limited more than ever by regulations) (1901: 228). In the post-Haussmannian period many architects raised their voices against the regular and uniform forms of the Second Empire (Eleb 1995: 10). However, although domestic architecture did not undergo important changes, the way in which home is represented in Huysmans' work illustrates a change in the organisation of private life. One way in which *En ménage* deconstructs the domestic ideal consists not in what is represented, but in how. While the apartment buildings might follow a Second-Empire structure, they are embedded with movement, circulation and dynamism. By engaging with architectural elements used for communication, such as a building's stairways or corridors, *En ménage* conveys a sense of instability and permeability. This same mobility characterises the relationship of the main character André with home. Although longing for a space that embodies the domestic ideal, André is incapable of putting it into practice. Instead, he constantly moves home and modifies his interiors' layouts as if trapped in a repetitious compulsion. In this way, the narrative represents a domestic experience based on instability and ephemerality.

In *En ménage* we find neither a critique of cultural changes as in *La Curée*, nor an ironic-romantic version as in *L'Adultera*, but an openly comic representation of them. The comic aspect of Huysmans' text stems from all the challenges its characters encounter as well as from the paradoxes this new way of living entails. Thus, conversations between André and his close friend, Cyprien, about women, home and the compatibility of relationships and one's personal freedom are the main topics in the text. Expressions of modern architecture, such as the Hippodrome (1863), are also discussed. Those architectural references conform to discourses on new ways of living and the new woman, which in *En ménage* are characterised by being economically independent and having a public presence and active life outside of the home. Hence, I will argue that *En ménage* represents new aesthetic values themselves associated with new ways of living.

Of particular interest is the fact that domestic life is critically portrayed from two male points of view. In contrast to all the novels seen in the previous chapters, where the problematics about the theory and practice of domesticity were articulated through female experiences, *En ménage* places the crisis of domesticity in men. This belongs to a wider literary context which explored the crisis of masculinity in the late nineteenth century. For example, Guy de Maupassant's *Bel-Ami* (1885) portrays a change in gender roles, as Nicholas White also notes on *The Family in Crisis in Late*

Nineteenth-Century French Fiction (1999: 83–4). Maupassant's work presents Madeleine Forestier, who helps her husband to win his powerful position in the journalistic world, as an independent, assertive and attractive woman. Madeleine not only shows her intellectual superiority to her husband, but also breaks social conventions in marrying a younger man of more humble origins after the death of her husband. The representation of masculinity in crisis can be read in light of legal and cultural issues concerning marriage, divorce, the importance of feminism and the progressive autonomy women won in the 1880s in France. Significantly, divorce had been a very popular social issue in France from the late 1870s and was reintroduced by the Naquet Law in 1884 (Pedersen 2004: 15). With the beginning of the Third Republic (1870–1940), feminist organisations grew stronger and multiplied. The main concerns of these organisations in the 1870s and 1880s were marriage and divorce legislation, and women's rights. The periodical *Le Droit des femmes* was founded in 1869, and the 'Association pour le droit des femmes' (Association for Women's Rights) was constituted in 1870 (Pedersen 2004: 23). Regarding marriage, feminism criticised the legislation on the property rights of women, and the surrender of women's legal identities to their husbands (Pedersen 2004: 23). The 'Association pour le droit des femmes' played an important role in reintroducing divorce in the Naquet Law. Marriage and divorce became main topics in the fin de siècle, and the expression 'crisis of marriage' was widely used (Pedersen 2004: 45). Regarding economic autonomy, a French law in 1881 allowed women to have their own savings accounts (Phillips 1988: 595). Besides this, the number of women employed in administrative jobs increased in the early 1890s (Zidjeman et al. 2014: 551). In this social context, in *En ménage* men are represented as rather vulnerable subjects in terms of domestic authority, and as potential victims, while women take more power and control over their sexuality and domestic affairs.

En ménage shows male discussions on domestic life that nineteenth-century literature traditionally located in women: opposite views on domesticity, as seen for example in Thomasin and Eustacia Vye in *The Return of the Native*, are found in André and Cyprien. Thus, the tensions surrounding the theory and practice of the domestic ideal are placed on men. We find an example at the very beginning of the text, where André is represented living according to the domestic ideal, which Cyprien mocks:

—Rester, pendant deux heures, dans un coin, regarder des pantins qui sautent, salir des gants et poisser des verres, se tenir constamment sur ses gardes, s'échapper, lorsqu'à l'affût du gibier dansant, la maîtresse de maison braconne au hasard des pièces, si tu appelles cela, malgré l'habitude que tu en peux avoir depuis que l'on t'a marié, des choses agréables, eh bien! tu n'es pas difficile.

André haussa les épaules et, crachant le jus de tabac qui lui poivrait la bouche, dit simplement:

—Peuh, on s'y fait! (Huysmans [1881] 2009: 39)

(—Stay, for two hours, in a corner, watch jumping puppets, dirty gloves and used glasses, be constantly on guard and ready to escape when, looking for prey, the hostess searches the rooms at random; if these are for you, despite being used to it after getting married, pleasant things, well! You are easy.

André shrugged his shoulders and, spitting out the tobacco juice which peppered his mouth, said simply:

—Bah, let's get used to it!)

In the scene above, André seems obliged to appear condescending in order to justify his domestic life. André's experience is very different from that of Charles Bovary, who finds all the complacencies of his domestic life in the typical representations that conformed to the domestic imaginary (Flaubert [1856] 2001: 167). André, instead, seems the male version of a mocked and resented Emma Bovary, who we have seen spending hours by the window (Flaubert [1856] 2001: 156). Far from being a state of bliss, in *En ménage* marriage usually becomes a boring monotony. Thus, the polemics of domesticity open the text, and introduce a series of discussions about the place and nature of marriage at the end of the century.

Deconstructing the representations of the interior

The representation of the domestic ideal in *En ménage* appears in a contradictory way, echoing the difference between lived and theorised domesticity experienced in the long nineteenth century, and that has been analysed by many scholars especially regarding Victorian England.[2] While on one hand, after his separation from Berthe, André shows a constant nostalgia for the traditional way of living and his old married days, on the other hand, these feelings are intertwined with episodes of disgust and rejection towards such a way of living. The transition from one state to the other depends on whether domesticity appears as a representation or a lived event. In the first case, the image-like experience of home life is particularly felt when, in moments of solitude, André imagines domestic life, or when wandering the streets of Paris, he gazes at the scenes behind the windows. On these occasions, the interior is turned into a representation that epitomises happiness. However, when André remembers his actual domestic experience, home turns into a quite different reality. From feeling 'le regret de la vie familiale perdue, le désir fou de revoir Berthe' (regret for the lost family life, the mad desire to see Berthe again) (Huysmans [1881] 2009: 144), to experiencing disgust at the bourgeois interior formed by the Désableau, Berthe's family:

> André avait la nouvelle vision de la famille invariablement occupée de la sorte: madame Désableau regardant entre deux aiguillées voler les mouches et faisant, avec des clins d'yeux, de silencieuses recommandations à sa fille de ne pas troubler, en bougeant, le travail du père; Berthe cousant [. . .]. Désableau en arrêt devant une phrase, hésitant pendant des heures entre un mot et un autre [. . .]. Un dégout profond lui [à André] venait. (Huysmans [1881] 2009: 145)

> (André had a vision of the family occupied in this way: Madame Désableau was watching the flies fly between two spouts, while she winked silently and recommended to her daughter not to move and disturb her father's work; Berthe was sewing [. . .]. Desableau stopped in front of a sentence, hesitating for hours between one word and another [. . .]. A deep disgust came to him [André].)

The scene André remembers conforms to a traditional representation of domestic life that paradoxically stands in opposition to his longings. This contradiction could be read as a desire for another type of family organisation, and for another representation of domestic life. However, the pursuit of comfort and well-being persists in a traditional understanding of domesticity. In fact, in another scene, when André moves into a new apartment on his own, his first concern is to hire his old housekeeper Mélanie to ensure that domestic duties are covered:

> Le feu et la lampe allumés, les vêtements brossés et recousus, le diner prêt à l'heure et mangé, les pieds dans mes pantoufles, je vais donc

avoir tout cela à des égards en plus pour mes trente-cinq francs par mois; je suis sauvé! (Huysmans [1881] 2009: 76)

(The fire and the lamp on, the clothes washed and sewn, dinner ready on time and eaten, my feet in my slippers, I'm going to have all this for my thirty-five francs a month; I'm saved!)

Patrick Bergeron describes a cultural tension between being and not being bourgeois: 'la question est épineuse pour ces bourgeois anti-bourgeois et ces romanciers anti-romanesques de s'aménager un régime de vie viable et de tolérer les vicissitudes du quotidien' (it is a thorny question for these bourgeois anti-bourgeois and these anti-romantic novelists to develop a viable regime of life and tolerate the vicissitudes of everyday life) (2009: 113). But this tension, which I prefer to call a contradiction, is framed within the context of the domestic ideal and its literary representations. André is a character who still identifies himself with traditional domesticity, suggesting man's incapacity to configure a single household and reproducing the idea that woman is a condition to materialise the concept of home. But the fact that such need comes from a representation of domesticity, rather than from André's actual experience, illustrates the power of images in defining expectations, creating discourses and establishing normative ways of living. André is trapped in the space between discourse and experience and cannot decide on either of them.

Architect Charles Rice theorises this situation through the concept of 'doubleness' (2007: 2), which refers to the space between discourse and experience of the domestic interior: 'this image-based sense [...] encompasses a reverie or imaginal picture like Baudelaire's, one which could transform an existing spatial interior into something other. Significantly, doubleness involves the interdependence between image and space, with neither sense being primary' (Rice 2007: 2). Rice's words do indeed accurately echo André's situation as he dreams of his life within an interior, which is in fact all image-based. Besides, André's contradictory feelings towards domestic life illustrate what Rice defines as the power of the represented interior: 'with the historical emergence of the interior, desire and control appear as two sides of the same coin: desiring an interior means submitting to its mechanisms of control' (2007: 37). In fact, André does not succeed in putting in practice another interior other than that shaped by traditional domestic discourses, involving the presence of a woman and the practice of gender activities – a reality that seems to be absolutely embedded in his own imaginary. In Jérôme Solal's words, 'l'homme huysmansien rêve de clôture, de confort, de contrôle d'un intérieur' (the Huysmansian man dreams of enclosure, comfort, control of the interior) (2009: 122). This remains a dream never to be realised as it is André who is subjected to the tyranny of space and its specific laws. Besides, Rice's analysis of the image-based interior is significant for Huysmans' work in relation to Dutch domestic painting. Heidi de Mare comments on how, in the nineteenth century, when concepts of domesticity and privacy were consolidated, the Dutch Golden Age was perceived as the epitome of domestic life:

> The all-embracing concept of domesticity proves to be a creation not of the seventeenth century but of the nineteenth century. It was during this latter period that domestic, bourgeois family life became a nucleus around which the nation was formed [...]. These sentiments were then projected into the past and applied to seventeenth-century paintings, books, and houses [...]. Thus was born the wide-ranging, homogenous concept of domesticity. (2006: 14)

As an art critic, Huysmans' admiration of Dutch domesticity reflects a social construction of notions of home that permeated the nineteenth century, and that *En ménage* embodies in André. However, André's frustrating experience of a domestic life that does not respond to its formulated discourse and representations works as a way to deconstruct this same domestic imaginary that the character embodies. The tension between imagined and lived spaces persists for the whole text, and in fact constitutes one of its main topics. The clear illustration of the contradictions between real and imagined domesticity, and the separation between both, deconstructs and exposes the ensemble of discourses and representations that articulated the domestic ideal. André is an example of what Walter Benjamin calls the 'phantasmagoria of the interior' (2002: 9), as Huysmans' character inhabits an image that he tries but fails constantly to materialise through the layout of his interiors. André becomes a ridiculous figure, a victim of his own naiveté and imagination that mistakes reality for its representations.

Le ménage à l'envers

When André finds his wife with a lover at home, André is depicted as an extremely functional husband concerned with keeping up appearances and diminishing the negative social and emotional impacts of the encounter. Adultery does not constitute drama but, instead, is represented in its plainness, or as an annoying coincidence to be quickly solved. In this context, André's words to his wife's lover show his impassive attitude:

> Vous cherchez une carte de visite, dit André, on ne la trouve jamais lorsqu'on en a besoin, c'est comme un fait exprès. Mais, peu importe, votre nom de famille m'est indifférent; quant à votre prénom, ma femme doit le connaître, et, au cas où elle ignorerait votre adresse, vous pourrez la lui envoyer demain, pour qu'elle aille vous rejoindre si bon lui semble. Maintenant, prenez votre chapeau et partons. (Huysmans [1881] 2009: 46)

> (You're looking for a business card, says André, you never find it when you need it, it's like on purpose. But whatever your last name is, it is irrelevant to me. As for your first name, my wife must know it, and in case she doesn't know your address, you can send it to her tomorrow, so that she can join you if she sees fit. Now take your hat and let's go.)

The above scene captures the banality of adultery, as it stops being a literary topic and becomes a mere domestic event in the narrative. As Robert E. Ziegler describes it, '*En Ménage* is [. . .] a cynical and bleak chronicle of stultifying domesticity' (1993: 18). Indeed, for André the adulterous episode seems another aspect of the tediousness of marriage and domestic life. Thus, surprisingly, André's domestic experience establishes an association with that of Emma Bovary for whom adultery happens to become as tedious as marriage itself: 'Emma retrouvait dans l'adultère toutes les platitudes du mariage' (Emma found in adultery all the platitudes of marriage) (Flaubert [1856] 2001: 379). Berthe presents a similarly Bovaresque experience in her marriage expectations: 'dans le mariage, elle voyait la revanche de sa vie monotone et plate, elle voyait un avenir de courses enragées à travers les théâtres et les bals, tout un horizon de diners et de visites' (she saw in marriage the revenge of her monotonous and boring life, she saw a future of rapturous races through theatres and balls, a whole horizon of dinners and visits) (Huysmans [1881] 2009: 85). Similar to that of Emma is also Berthe's experience of adultery: 'la terre promise qu'elle avait entrevue lui échappait encore. Les voluptés tremblantes de l'adultère ne la soulevèrent point. Devant l'amant comme devant le mari, l'émoi des sens avorta' (the promised land she had glimpsed was still eluding her. The trembling pleasures of adultery did not satisfy her. In front of her lover as in front of her husband, sensuality and emotions disappeared) (Huysmans [1881] 2009: 96). The similarities of Berthe and André with the character of Emma Bovary show how tediousness and routine have become the characteristics of domestic life for both men and women. From *Madame Bovary* to *En ménage*, the monotony of marriage turns from a dramatic representation to a cynical and comic one. And while in *L'Adultera* we have seen the banality of adultery, there is still place for happiness, which may be found in a new relationship. In contrast, *En ménage* presents the mundane aspects of adultery and of any kind of relationship, hence leading towards an absolute demythologisation of domesticity and romance.

André's reaction towards Berthe and her lover also shows a matter of fact attitude towards female adultery, which reflects its assimilation and seeming naturalness. This view is supported by the fact that adultery is only a casual event of the narrative, and one whose importance will dissolve while other topics will emerge with more strength. In this context, Solal notes that adultery in *En ménage* takes place at the beginning of the narrative, and he analyses how this position in the text affects the topic itself: 'le début par l'adultère marque aussi la fin de l'adultère. *En ménage*, c'est l'envers du couple' (beginning with adultery also signifies the end of adultery. *En ménage* is the couple in reverse) (2009: 608). This spatialisation of adultery within the narrative is mapped into the architectural representation of André's apartment: the order of representation goes from the back – from the most intimate spaces – to the frontal, semi-public rooms. In other words, the reader knows the bedroom of André and Berthe before accessing the living room, something which opposes the common norm found in architectural and decoration texts of the time: 'la chambre, il ne faut pas l'oublier, est, avant tout, l'asile des actions mystérieuses, des grands et des petits secrets; le refuge des souvenirs. C'est dans le logis, un véritable sanctuaire' (it should not be forgotten that the bedroom is, above all, the refuge of mysterious actions, big and small secrets; the refuge of memories. The house is a true sanctuary) (Havard 1884: 400). The apartment is thus presented and represented *à l'envers* (in reverse). This literary representation of architecture gives a public significance to intimate domestic spaces, contributing to their demythologisation. The lack of intimacy in André's bedroom illustrates what Solal identifies as something characteristic of Huysmans' work:

> Les concepts de dehors et de dedans étant par essence indissociable, la tension vers le repos intérieur [. . .] est tout à tour contrariée et relancée: il n'est point de dehors sans la ressource envisageable d'un refuge qui constitue le contrepoids (et le contrepoison), il n'est point de dedans sans la tentation d'une sortie, sans le risque d'une expulsion. Constamment assujettie à son envers, la quête de l'intériorité semble condamnée à l'échec. (2009: 121)

> (The concepts of outside and inside are in essence inseparable, the tension towards inner rest [. . .] is in turn thwarted and revived: there is no outside without the resource of a refuge which constitutes the counterweight (and the antidote), there is no inside without the temptation of going out, without the risk of expulsion. Constantly subject to its reverse, the quest for interiority seems condemned to fail.)

In fact, the lack of opposition between the private and public spheres handicaps the experience of the interior. André's bedroom has become a public space, not only for its order of representation but also for the introduction of a third party – the lover. This fact echoes other bedrooms in French literature, such as Nana's, which customers queue to access (Zola [1880] 2003: 74). Placed within the French literary tradition of the second half of the nineteenth century, André's domestic space becomes permeated with notions of publicity, the erotic and prostitution. In *En ménage*, the bedroom is now a space that constructs an alternative narrative to that of privacy and exclusivity. In this case, it is the representation of architecture that constructs a concept of domesticity based in a modified sense of privacy: such representation places the focus on the intimate parts of the house, and thus turns the sexual life of marriage into a more accessible reality. Moreover, this accessibility exposes the domestic ideal. If we take as a reference Huysmans' engagement with representations of domestic spaces in seventeenth-century Dutch paintings, we will note how the interior is not made completely accessible. In Pierre de Hooch's *Interior* (1658–60), for example, we find semi-accessible spaces; this semi-publicity plays with notions of the veiled and unveiled, evoking a certain degree of mystery and secrecy that sustains the mythical aspect of home life. The semi-hidden room at the back of the painting contributes to a sense of privacy and exclusivity that is accompanied by an overall sense of peace, enclosure and protection, all of them values that are missing in Huysmans' bedroom scene. In this painting, we find again a woman represented in profile and concentrated on her domestic labour as in the case of Thomasin and her aunt in *The Return of the Native*. Thus, the way in which the interior is represented also involves a certain portrayal of female characters, all together contributing to the image of the domestic ideal.

The spatial connotations of 'l'envers' (the reverse) are also represented in sexual and gender relationships. A sense of gender inversion distils from the importance given to the husband instead of the adulteress in the scene of adultery. In Huysmans' bedroom scene, the focus is not as much on Berthe's own experience of adultery or her reaction to André's finding out, but on André's attitude to the situation. This places the husband as the central subject of the domestic narrative, and supports the idea that *En ménage* is not a text on adultery, as the characters involved in the act take a secondary place in the narrative. This inverts traditional representations of domestic novels like, for example, *Madame Bovary*. The gender inversion is also expressed through André's representation as a social victim and the object of people's talk, which ironically turn him into a weak and perfidious husband:

> [La concierge] révéla des détails inattendus sur la femme d'André [. . .]. Elle avait un amant, ou l'avait entrevu, la nuit, alors qu'André le reconduisait, en l'éclairant. Sans nul doute ils étaient tous de connivence, l'amant était le fils d'un capitaliste, il entretenait le mari et la femme. André était un fainéant et un sagouin, un homme sans profession, un journaliste, un flâneur qui trafiquait des femmes. (Huysmans [1881] 2009: 122)

> ([The concierge] revealed unexpected details about André's wife [. . .]. She had a lover, or had seen him, at night, while André was leading him back, enlightening him. No doubt they were all in complicity, the lover was the son of a capitalist, he supported husband and wife. André was a slacker, a man without profession, a journalist, a flâneur who trafficked women.)

The above passage presents André's lack of authority over his domestic affairs and wife, as well showing people's lack of respect towards him due to the way in which he has dealt with his wife's adultery. We have already seen in *L'Adultera* a certain lack of control on the husband's side but in *En ménage* this is stressed when André becomes an object of ridicule. Although Berthe herself experiences fear of social rejection, her actions seem to be socially undermined while all the shame falls on her husband. André finds himself dispossessed of any act of recognition, and he is even humiliated by his wife. This links to Emmanuel Godo's analysis on André's masculinity, which Godo defines as modern: '[André n'est] doué non plus des attributs traditionnels de la virilité, comme le courage, la volonté ou l'honneur, mais de ceux de la condition moderne de l'homme, insatisfaction chronique, impuissance, sens suraigu de la compromission' ([André is] no longer endowed with the traditional attributes of virility, such as courage, will or honour, but with those of the modern condition, that is, chronic dissatisfaction, helplessness, an acute sense of compromise) (2007: 72). André's unsatisfaction is represented in domestic terms when, after his separation, 'commença pour [André] une longue pérégrination à la recherche des locaux vides' (a long peregrination in search of empty places starts for [André]) (Huysmans [1881] 2009: 56). The idea of domestic peregrination reflects with irony the sacred dimension the domestic space had during the nineteenth century and for André himself. Forced to leave home, André is not represented as the master of the house and head of the household but rather as a marginalised figure who pays for his wife's infidelity, and risks becoming homeless.

In relation to *La Curée*, where we have seen a gender and sexual inversion in the relationship between Renée and Maxime, 'l'envers' (the reverse) in Huysmans' text appears in a generalised and imposed form. That is, while the scenes depicting Renée and Maxime in the greenhouse emphasise the performativity of the roles temporarily acquired, André seems unable to behave otherwise in front of Berthe's adultery and society. André finds himself led by the circumstances, which push him to involuntary and permanent changes of address in order to find a place he can call home.

Ephemeral homes and transient women

After André's separation from Berthe, Cyprien instructs his friend on emotional and sexual mobility: 'dans la vie, on n'a rien à soi. On loge ses affections dans des meublés, jamais dans une chambre qui vous appartienne! Dame, oui [. . .], c'est dur; on voudrait avoir son petit lopin de bonheur et en être seul propriétaire!' (In life, you own nothing. We lodge our affections in rented apartments, never in a room that belongs to you! Women, yes [. . .], it's hard; we would like to have our little piece of happiness and be its only owner!) (Huysmans [1881] 2009: 52). Cyprien's strong association between home and women is shown by his use of the words 'en être seul propriétaire' (to be its only owner), which refer to both 'chambre' (room) and 'dame' (woman). Thus, sexual, emotional and domestic mobility are interdependent realities: home is not a stable possession anymore, neither is a woman. Sexuality and emotions are still architecturally imagined although it is not through the representation of a solid house, as is the case with Bachelard's phenomenology, but the ephemerality of rented and furnished places. This representation of sexuality and women in architectural terms shows the strong association between the house and the female body present in the nineteenth century that *En ménage* inherits and modifies at the same time.

While Cyprien's words, 'on n'a rien à soi' (one owns nothing) (52), express the lack of stability in property ownership and refer to sexual and emotional transience in modern relationships, they also point at the debilitation of a strong patriarchal domesticity. Cyprien shows a matter of fact attitude that suggests a more general and common situation than that found, for example, in Ezel's attitude when Melanie leaves home in *L'Adultera*. Indeed, in Fontane's text there is still a certain ambivalence regarding male authority, but Cyprien is giving André instructions on how to manage the situation as it is, in fact, unavoidable: 'on loge ses affections dans des meublés, jamais dans une chambre qui vous appartienne!' (We lodge our affections in rented apartments, never in a room that belongs to you!). Cyprien's use of the third person suggests he is expressing general norms with which one needs to be familiar.

In regard to Cyprien's statement about the disassociation between feelings and possessions, André is trapped again in the space between imagination and facts. While André does what

Cyprien recommends – lodging one's affections in rented places, he imagines that he owns those places through the relationship he establishes with them: he aims at making permanent every new place he moves into and, therefore, he reorganises the layout accordingly. Henri Havard's book editor illustrates the paradox of aiming at stabilising the unstable when referring to Havard's rules for furnishing the house: 'l'orthographe du mobilier se trouve définitivement fixée' (the grammar of furniture has finally been fixed) (1884: VII). Havard aims at creating a norm in interior decoration, as his book's title shows, engaging with the word grammar – *L'Art dans la maison (grammaire de l'ameublement)*, a title that reflects what could be both a contradictory and a changing cultural moment in which we see an attempt at conciliating mobility and stability. Moreover, Havard's aim in writing *L'Art dans la maison* is to find a solution to the bad taste that he sees as a consequence of an increased number of moves:

> Est-il encore d'autres raisons à cette aberration du goût? – Certes, et peut-être de plus concluants. La première de ces raisons est que le mobilier a perdu le caractère de durée qu'il avait autrefois. Il serait bien imprudent, en effet, d'exiger de lui une perpétuité qui n'existe plus dans nos mœurs. A chaque génération [...] les meubles sont partagés, dispersés, donnés ou vendus et l'on fait maison nette [...]. Dans les grandes villes, se caractère limité s'accentue par la multiplicité des déménagements. (1884: 5)
>
> (Are there still other reasons for this aberration of taste? Certainly, and they are maybe even more conclusive. The first of these reasons is that furniture has lost the durability it once had. It would be very imprudent, indeed, to demand of it perpetuity, which no longer exists in our customs. Each generation [...] shares, disperses, gives and sells furniture, and we clean the house [...]. In large cities, this fact is accentuated by the many moves.)

Behind the apparent concern on taste, Havard's text shows uneasiness regarding a sense of mobility that seems to be embedded in a new way of living, hence Havard's attempt at creating a fixed rule. André constitutes another piece in this whole puzzle of domestic life, as he finds himself reorganising all his different domestic interiors as well as his own interiority. Thus, the word 'réorganisation' is common in the text from the moment

André leaves his first home: '[André] méditait une réorganisation d'intérieur, s'ingéniait à éviter d'avance les misères que se ruent dans les logements sans femme' ([André] was thinking about a reorganisation of the interior striving to avoid in advance the miseries that fill a house without a woman) (Huysmans [1881] 2009: 54). This need for reorganising domestic space avoiding an unpleasant interior without the presence of a woman shows André trapped again in a domestic nostalgia. In order to survive the new situation he is in, he will first try to reconstruct his place with Berthe by reproducing its layout and hiring his old housekeeper, Mélanie:

> Après les angoisses du déménagement effectué comme d'habitude par des maçons aux trois quarts ivres, les difficultés à caser les meubles sans contrarier le jeu des fenêtres et des portes, les batailles contre la brique des murs qui repoussait et tordait les clous, les fatigantes recherches, à quatre pattes, dans le tas des volumes vidés en bloc sur le parquet, André [. . .] était enfin parvenu à organiser son intérieur. (Huysmans [1881] 2009: 105)

> (After the anguish of house moving which, as usual, had been carried out by half-drunk masons; after the difficulties to make the furniture fit with windows and doors, the battles against the brick of walls, which pushed back and twisted the nails, the tiresome searching, on all fours, among the pile of volumes emptied *en bloc* on the parquet floor, André [. . .] had finally managed to organise his interior.)

The above passage captures André's physical and emotional efforts to relocate from one place to another. The difficulties, struggles and fatigue of André in placing his old 'meubles' (furniture) in a new 'immeuble' (house) illustrate again the attempt at conciliating the mobile with the stable. André's old furniture represents this longing for continuity, which is ironically placed in what is called the 'meuble', while the 'immeuble' becomes transient in André's experience. The difference should be noted between 'de meublé' (furnished apartment), mentioned by Cyprien, and the unfurnished places André moves into every time: André's only way to fight domestic instability is to keep his old furniture with him. Moreover, the unfurnished rented place allows it to be called 'immeuble' as opposed to 'meublé'. A 'meublé' would in fact cancel any illusion of stability in André.

Thus, in his attempts to turn a rented place into a permanent home, André will again reproduce his emotions in the new apartment, which eventually becomes as cosy as his previous one: 'dérangé et un peu offusqué tout d'abord par la disposition nouvelle de ses meubles [. . .], il parvint peu à peu, à mesure que le souvenir de son salon d'homme marié s'atténuait, à trouver que cette chambre était claire et gaie' (disturbed and a little offended at first by the new arrangement of his furniture [. . .], he gradually succeeded, as the memory of his living room as a married man faded away, in finding this room bright and happy) (Huysmans [1881] 2009: 107). While, for a short time, Mélanie seems to be enough to replace the presence of a wife or lover, André falls again into his nostalgia for a family household: 'il désirait la femme [. . .] pour le frôlement de sa jupe, la cliquette de son rire, le bruissement de sa voix, pour sa société, pour l'air enfin qu'elle dégage. Sans elle, son logement lui semblait maussade' (he desired a woman [. . .] for the rustle of her skirt, the clatter of her laughter, the rustle of her voice, her company, the atmosphere she creates. Without her, his home seemed gloomy) (Huysmans [1881] 2009: 127). André's situation shows with cynicism the paradox of a culture strongly based on a traditional and static domesticity, while becoming something else. André's only way to cope with the situation seems to be a frantic change of houses and women in the hope of recovering the mythical meaning of home. André's domestic experience suggests a compulsion to repeat, as well as being illustrative of how the dynamic aspect of modernity made its way through domestic space, permeating all realities of social life from streets to homes. In this context, as Rita Felski states, 'the so-called private sphere, often portrayed as a domain where natural and timeless emotions hold sway, is shown to be radically implicated in patterns of modernization and processes of social change' (1995: 3). The representations of homes in *En ménage* are, indeed, spatial projections of mobile and shifting emotions that cannot be hosted within a stable architecture. Such homes are totally involved in the process of domestic and sexual modernisation characterised by instability. Besides, as domestic space was traditionally assumed to be part of the female sphere, *En ménage* shows how women were also a part of the process of modernisation, as it is Berthe who unsettles domestic life in the first place. In contrast, André appears to be a victim of modern life, as he finds difficulties in, for example, continuing with his work as a writer due to his ephemeral domestic experiences: '[André] ne pouvait travailler que dans un logement qu'il connaissait bien [...]. Il avait donc tout d'abord usé de longues heures à examiner [...], puis à en embrasser l'ensemble [...]. C'était une affaire de quinze jours au moins' ([André] could only work in a place he knew well [...]. He had, therefore, first spent long hours examining [...], then embracing the whole [...]. It was at least a fortnight's affair) (Huysmans [1881] 2009: 110). André's longings for the duration of space and time contrast with a new mobile Paris. Thus, *En ménage* presents what Philippe Geinoz (2016: 118–19) defines as a schizophrenic representation of the city, where there is a radical separation between the public and private life:

> Huysmans apparaît donc, plus que tout autre, comme l'écrivain de ce qu'on peut appeler la schize haussmannienne – soit cette coupure stricte, spatialement sans intermédiaire, entre l'extérieur public, conçu en fonction d'une obsession, celle de la circulation (de l'air, des marchandises, des personnes ou des troupes), et l'intérieur privé, cloisonné et potentiellement rempli d'objets – une schize que l'œuvre met en crise. (2016: 118–19)

> (Therefore, Huysmans appears, more than anyone else, as the writer of what we can call the Haussmannian schism – that is, this strict separation between the public exterior, conceived with an obsession for circulation (of air, goods, people or troops), and the private interior, partitioned and potentially filled with objects – a schism that in this work appears in crisis.)

En ménage, however, represents this 'coupure stricte' (strict separation) between the urban and domestic spaces in a psychological form; in other words, it is André who tirelessly tries to reproduce this suffocating interior: 'du plafond au plancher, les murs disparaissaient sous un fouillis de faïences, de tableaux, de cuivres, de porcelaines du Japon, au milieu duquel deux aquarelles impressionnistes étincelaient dans leurs barres d'or sur le fond bistré du papier de tenture' (from the ceiling to the floor the walls disappeared under a jumble of earthenware, paintings, brass and porcelain from Japan, in the middle of which two impressionist watercolours sparkled in their gold frames against the dark background of the wallpaper) (Huysmans [1881] 2009: 108). Geinoz fails to note that in *En ménage* domestic space resists the 'clôture' (enclosure) André wishes for. Although André puts all his efforts into maintaining a radical separation between the exterior and the interior, the latter is permeated by the same values of circulation, especially those of sexual circulation. This last one is, in fact, the only trigger that causes André's own movement through the city looking for a new place, and afterwards, for other places. The circulation of interiors in the text is first caused by Berthe's change of sexual partner, who is significantly defined as 'un danseur qui l'invitait à valser dans les bals' (a dancer who invited her to waltz) (Huysmans [1881] 2009: 95). The lover himself, as well as the context in which Berthe and he meet, reinforce the idea of movement.

Glass and André's loss of gender

Regarding women, André does eventually put Cyprien's words in practice – 'on n'a rien à soi' (one owns nothing) (Huysmans [1881] 2009: 52) – and decides to change his strategy, visiting several lovers: 'persuadé enfin que la possession d'une femme à soi seul, à Paris, était chose impraticable, [André] se décida à adopter cette combinaison [. . .]. Au lieu d'aller toujours chez la même, il en visitait, chaque fois, une différente' (finally convinced that the possession of a woman all for himself was impossible in Paris, [André] decided to adopt this other strategy [. . .]. Instead of always going to the same woman, he would visit a different one each time) (Huysmans [1881] 2009: 135–6). André's perambulations in Paris become, thus, sexualised; in Solal's words, 'Huysmans [. . .] place son récit sous l'égide d'une spatialisation de la sexualité en même temps que d'une sexualisation de l'espace' (Huysmans [. . .] places his story under a spatialisation of sexuality at the same time as a sexualisation of space) (2009: 606). The circulation around Paris and each one of the interiors André visits are permeated with sexual meaning. This becomes especially highlighted during one of André's walks after he receives a letter from his former mistress Jeanne, and goes to meet her on Rue Sauval: '[André] chercha enfin, sur son plan de Paris, où était située la rue Sauval' ([André] looks for Rue Sauval on his map of Paris) (Huysmans [1881] 2009: 167). The view of Paris on the map graphically projects André's sexual tour as he looks for his way to Jeanne. His sexuality and desires are literally mapped onto the city, which thus clearly becomes a sexual space, bringing back the idea of sexual circulation as André moves around the streets of Paris to find an old lover.

The particularity of this walk, different to André's walks with Cyprien, lies in the fact that the streets of Paris are signposted by glass and light, in other words, by modernity: 'ennuyé et joyeux tout à la fois, il se mirait dans les pans de glace des magasins et vérifiait la tenue de sa cravate et de son col' (bored and joyful at the same time, he stood in front of the shop windows to check his tie and collar) (Huysmans [1881] 2009: 168). Glass, in this instance, builds sexual masculinity with connotations that differ from those traditionally found in the nineteenth century. The shop windows work as mirrors that allow André to arrange his physical aspect before his encounter with Jeanne. Thus, while shop windows become sexualised, André's sexuality – or sexual appeal – becomes imbedded with a sense of commercialisation. We have seen this relationship between commerce and sexuality in the domestic construction of the hôtel Saccard and the figure of Renée Saccard, but in *En ménage* it is the male character who is represented as entering the world of sexual exchange. This double aspect of sexuality and economy now focalised on a male figure affects gender roles. In fact, André is surprised when he finds out that Jeanne did not want to meet him in order to become lovers and, thus, help her own economic situation, but André knows that 'elle avait toujours travaillé depuis leur rupture' (she had always worked since their separation) (Huysmans [1881] 2009: 175). André finds Jeanne's autonomy unexpected as his insecurity shows: '[il] marmottait, le nez baissé' ([he] mumbled, his head down) (Huysmans [1881] 2009: 176). His role as provider is lost, and with it his role as man. But this gender inversion is already introduced during his walk towards Jeanne:

Derrière une vitrine, une demoiselle de magasin le dévisageait avec un sourire et il reprit son va-et-vient, perdant son rôle d'homme, prenant celui d'une fille battant son quart, observé derrière les marchandises des montres par de jeunes femmes qui se chuchotaient à l'oreille, dans un éclat de rire: 'Encore un poireau!' (Huysmans [1881] 2009: 171)

(Behind a window, a young lady from the store was staring at him with a smile while he resumed his comings and goings, losing his role as a man, taking that of a girl doing the street, observed, standing behind the displayed watches, by young women who whispered in each other's ears, in a burst of laughter: 'Another chick!')

André's sexual promenade around Paris signifies a process of loss of gender forms. While at the beginning of his plan, André seemed to be on the hunt for Jeanne, looking for her street on the map, he is progressively transformed by the city into a sexual and passive object. The city's new spaces and forms, i.e., the shops with their shop windows, unsettle André's masculinity as he marches in front of female shop assistants. In fact, like Jeanne, other women have taken jobs, and they are employed in the new shops. André is objectified by the employees' gazes and words as he exhibits his body just after arranging his looks in front of one of the shop windows. Besides, André is attracted to the goods on display in a way that recalls Emma Bovary fascinated by Monsieur Lheureux's material, or the female passers-by in front of Octave Mouret's department store in Zola's *Au Bonheur des Dames* (1883): 'il tirait encore sa montre, arrivait dans ce carré à colonnes qui sert de vestibule à la galerie d'Orléans et il demeurait extasié devant cette boutique' (he took out his watch again, arrived at the square with columns which served as a vestibule of the Orléans Gallery and he remained ecstatic in front of this shop) (Huysmans [1881] 2009: 169). Paris seems to awaken André's interest in shopping, which is traditionally represented as a female activity. In fact, while most scholarship focuses on the impact of nineteenth-century shopping centres on bourgeois women, *En ménage* inverts the gender of female shoppers in André.[3] Besides, the galerie d'Orléans was one of the first large galleries built in Europe with iron and glass, and presenting arcades, which Benjamin defines as 'house no less than street' (2002: 10). Thus, commercial architecture in André's promenade introduces a sense of blurred boundaries, not only in gender and sexual terms, but also between private and public spaces. The domestic is again permeated with values belonging to the public sphere. In the next chapter, however, we will see how it is the private sphere that permeates the public space with notions of intimacy.

Jeanne is also one of the girls who works in the shops. Her economic autonomy becomes socially exhibited when, after their dinner, André offers to pay for Jeanne and her friend, but Jeanne rejects his offer: 'André tira son porte-monnaie et réclama l'addition, mais les deux femmes s'y opposèrent. Il insista sans plus de succès [. . .], un peu honteux de laisser payer les femmes devant le garçon' (André took his wallet and asked for the bill, but the two women objected. He insisted without any success [. . .], a little embarrassed to let the women pay in front of the waiter) (Huysmans [1881] 2009: 175). From the beginning of André's sexual tour, Paris is represented as a city that emasculates him due to the changes in urban structure and the consolidation of a new job market where women have become part of the new capitalism. Although in the 1880s women were still a small part of the employees in shops, as Michael B. Miller shows in his analysis of the history of department stores in Paris (1981: 78), *En ménage* focuses on representing a female commercial world which inverts gender roles and attitudes around business: women are callers of attention of potential male buyers, who need to be seduced by the displayed merchandise, a fact that also recalls prostitution. *En ménage* seems to represent in a new light a new moral anxiety around salesgirls at the time, as Elizabeth Wilson notes: 'the newly independent women customers caused as much moral anxiety as the salesgirls' (2013: 150). In fact, the salesgirls in Huysmans' text are associated with a sexualisation of Paris through a new economic activity pursued en masse by middle-class citizens. Wilson defines shopping as 'almost sexualised' (2013: 150), and André does indeed relate to the architecture of the shops – when he looks himself at the shop windows – and to the shop girls in a sexualised manner.

En ménage represents commercial spaces as threatening for the male authority and the patriarchal structure through an inversion of gender roles. Although Wilson argues that this was caused by the fact that shopping centres gave women a space of socialisation outside home (2013: 150), *En ménage* represents the assimilation of male roles by women and vice-versa, locating the problem in male subjectivity. Shopping can in fact be listed among the activities Patrick Bergeron points at as being on the list of traditional female doings, which, he argues, are present in the general work of Huysmans and his tendency to represent a new masculinity:

Avec la correction du vêtement, du mobilier, des manières, de l'hygiène et de la diète de vie [...], s'accentue une dévirilisation. Alors que traditionnellement, l'homme est déchargé des soins de l'intérieur, les domaines de compétence virile étant l'affrontement, le risque, la guerre, les durs travaux, les héros au centre de proses narratives qui nous intéressent ont troqué la force et le risque contre l'ordre et l'accumulation domestiques. La recherche d'une bonne, d'un rosbif ou d'un concept d'ameublement est l'équivalent métaphorique d'une chasse. (2009: 115)

(With the correction of clothing, furniture, manners, hygiene and lifestyle [. . .], a devirilisation is emphasised. While traditionally, man had been relieved of the care of the interior, and the fields of manly competence were confrontation, risk, war and hard work, the heroes at the centre of the narrative that concerns us have exchanged strength and risk for domestic order and accumulation. The search for a maid, roast beef or furniture is the metaphorical equivalent of a hunt.)

Indeed, André's main concern, as we have seen, is that of creating a complete interior, taking into account aesthetic and practical issues. André's task is to reproduce home, its layout and decoration, as well as the accomplishment of all domestic activities within the home. *En ménage* presents this unsettlement of the male role, mentioned by Bergeron, as going hand in hand with a lack of traditional definitions of femininity and masculinity.

Architecture and women in movement

In *En ménage*, historicist architecture is referred to as constituting a public space where, Cyprien complains, 'nous sommes imbibes et saturés de toute une lavasse de lieux communes et de formules!' (we are imbibed and saturated with a lavish of commonplaces and formulas!) (Huysmans [1881] 2009: 112). The expression 'lieux communes et formules' (commonplaces and formulas) can be read as referring both to established ways of living and to institutionalised aesthetics, which are now empty of meaning and express common bourgeois forms of organising one's personal life and relationships. As example of historicist architecture, Cyprien mentions 'l'art grec' (Greek art), the 'Parthénon' and 'la Place de la Concorde' (Huysmans [1881] 2009: 113). Those works are represented as the materialisation of a rather normative domesticity that reflects and translates into public architecture. Cyprien's views are contextualised in a larger cultural apprehension towards Second-Empire architecture. In the 1880s, *La Revue générale de l'architecture* showed its contempt towards historicist buildings:

> Si, au moins, à travers les masses blanchâtres d'immeubles suant le froid et l'humidité, perçait un peu d'art; si, le long de ces rues nouvelles, nous pouvions découvrir les marques d'un travail artistique, d'une pensée neuve [. . .]. Mais non; rien que d'éternelles rééditions de fenêtres aux lourds frontons chargés de fruits et de guirlandes à

l'emporte pièce [. . .]. Voilà tout ce que les imitations de façades de boulevard alignées sous Napoleón III. (Rivoalen 1883: 67)

(If, at least, through the white blocks of buildings sweating cold and humidity, a little art could be seen; if, along these new streets, we could discover the traces of artistic work, of pioneer thinking [. . .]. But no; nothing but eternal reproductions of windows with heavy pediments loaded with fruit and cookie-cutter garlands [. . .]. These are all the imitations of boulevard façades we find aligned under Napoleón III.)

The lack of originality and the impossibility of creating new architectural ideas were common critiques of Haussmannian architecture. We have seen in *La Curée* how private buildings were also part of the architectural aesthetics of the Second Empire, and we find how Cyprien includes on his infamous list 'chalets en pierres de taille' (dressed stone chalets) (Huysmans [1881] 2009: 113). In this case, we find stone homes as representative of the traditional ways of living, shaped by the established domestic discourse.[4] This includes a difference in perspective between the texts of Huysmans and Zola: while Cyprien's critique of historicism is based on the use of stone, the narrator of *La Curée* places the problematics on glass. Thus, if glass in *La Curée* appears to unsettle domestic values, Cyprien criticises Haussmannian architecture for perpetuating those same values through the use of stone. Cyprien's alternative to Second-Empire urbanism should present 'du pittoresque, des architectures à effet, des rues bizarres avec des clairs de lune, des montagnes et des forets' (picturesque, architecture effects, bizarre streets with moonlight, mountains and forests) (Huysmans [1881] 2009: 122–3). This statement bears striking resemblances with Viollet-Le-Duc's overall work, where the picturesque is strongly present and encouraged through the use of local material, what in architecture is called the genius loci of the place. Cyprien's references to landscape elements are also present in many of Viollet-Le-Duc's drawings in strong relation to the singularity of the place,[5] which contrasts with the uniformity of Paris.

Despite the common characteristics between Cyprien and Viollet-Le-Duc's discourses, Cyprien seems to move a step forward in terms of sexual liberalism, while Viollet-Le-Duc seems reluctant to any model different from the traditional one. In fact, Viollet-Le-Duc's *Histoire d'une maison* (1873) depicts the history of a family where, although women's opinions are being considered in order to build a proper house for them, traditional and patriarchal family forms prevail. These differences could have a historical cause: there are almost ten years between the publication of *Histoire d'une maison* and *En ménage*, the Second Empire ended in 1870, and divorce was reinstated in 1884. Indeed, the topic of divorce had been discussed during the years prior to its legalisation, and this shows a change of mentality starting in the late 1870s (Pedersen 2004: 15). Moreover, Alain Corbin notes how there was an increase of adultery in France from 1884, which he explains as follows: 'les nouvelles voluptés conjugales, l'essor des pratiques contraceptives, voire la revendication du droit de la femme au plaisir [. . .] dégradent le modèle de l'épouse vertueuse' (the new marital pleasures, the rise of contraceptives, even the demand for a woman's right to pleasure [. . .] damage the model of the virtuous wife) (1999: 511). In this context, the reasons behind the critiques of both Viollet-Le-Duc and Cyprien of Haussmannian architecture are found in different ideas of family and, by extension, womanhood. For Viollet-Le-Duc, Paris in the Second Empire is immoral and unethical. The architect's theories, simultaneously romantic and modern, seem to mythologise the domestic interior placed in a timeless past. Viollet-Le-Duc's modernity does not consist of new views on family politics but of a recovery of 'authentic' bourgeois values through a modern treatment of architecture based on its fusion with engineering and the respect of materials. However, Cyprien sees the legacy of Second-Empire Paris as obsolete and bourgeois, and looks forwards rather than backwards for a solution. Cyprien aims at living in a more dynamic city instead of the static historicist constructions.

For Cyprien it is the idea of architectural and sexual movement that characterises modernity, something the old Paris of Haussmann fails at providing. As examples of modern architecture, Cyprien mentions 'la gare du Nord' and 'le nouvel hippodrome' (Huysmans [1881] 2009: 113). In an article of 1882, *La Revue générale de l'architecture* included the neighbourhood of l'Hippodrome among the new constructions of Paris (Rivoalen 1882: 258). Cyprien's views on architecture partly echoed those of Huysmans, who expresses his hate for historicist architecture: 'brûler la Bourse, la Madeleine, le ministère de la Guerre, l'église Saint-Xavier, l'Opéra et l'Odéon, tout dessus du panier d'un art infâme!' (burn the Stock Exchange, the Madeleine, the Ministy of War, the Church of Saint-Xavier, the Opera and the Odeon, all this is infamous art!) (1889:

413). Geinoz notes the author's opinion on Second-Empire Paris: 'La ville haussmannienne est pensée comme un ensemble fonctionnel à unifier – ou à uniformiser' (The Haussmannian city is conceived as a functional whole to unify – or standardise) (2016: 121). However, in contrast to Cyprien, Huysmans attacks iron architecture, calling the Eiffel Tower 'mesquine' (wretched) (1889: 416), and stating that, 'le fer est encore incapable de créer une œuvre personnelle entière, une véritable œuvre' (iron is still incapable of creating a personal, complete work, a true work) (1889: 418). Huysmans' scepticism about iron structures, including railways (1889: 414), relates to his views on domesticity, which we have seen in the static representations of the domestic ideal in Dutch painting. Railways, like 'la gare du Nord' and 'le nouvel hippodrome', which Cyprien praises (Huysmans [1881] 2009: 113), are places of movement. For Cyprien movement is what relates to a modern concept of female beauty and he locates it in the figure of the *flâneuse*: 'la Vénus que j'adore à genoux comme le type de la beauté moderne, c'est la fille qui batifole dans la rue' (the Venus that I adore on my knees as the type of modern beauty is the girl wandering the streets) (Huysmans [1881] 2009: 113). Far from the static representations of women at home in Dutch paintings, the idea of urban movement also evokes the image of the prostitute. It is in the modern woman – a woman in movement – where circulation and sexuality are found together. Thus, this new femininity is permeated with ideas of sexual movement and it blurs the difference between prostitutes and middle-class women.

This location of woman in the street implies a deformation of the architectural structures that in the traditional domestic culture aimed at shaping woman's body and sexuality, as we have seen in the previous chapters. There is, in fact, an association of different kinds of women in André's memories that represents a movement through classes, as well as a de-housing of the middle-class wife. When André, after leaving Berthe and feeling again the need for a woman, remembers his past lovers before marrying, one of those is Jeanne, 'une petite ouvrière un peu incompréhensible, très corrompue ou très naïve, mais, dans tous les cas, attachée où elle broutait et tendre' (a cute worker, a little incomprehensible, very corrupt or very naïve, but, in any case, contented and tender) (Huysmans [1881] 2009: 129). However, Jeanne and Berthe appear as partaking in the same kind of sexuality: 'la comparaison s'établissait forcément entre Berthe, Jeanne et ces femelles qui, levant la chemise et la jupe d'un coup, pressaient l'extase, se dépêchaient de le renvoyer pour descendre dans la rue ou dans le salon' (the comparison was necessarily established between Berthe, Jeanne and these females who, suddenly lifting their skirt, with urged ecstasy, hurried to send him away to go down to the street or the living room) (Huysmans [1881] 2009: 131). In this image, the street and the living room become permeated with the same sexual connotations; in other words, there is no difference between female bourgeois sexuality and that of a working-class girl, or prostitute. The identification of the street and living room also reflects the unification of private and public spaces with their respective domestic and public sexualities. Brian Nelson notes how 'the problem in the nineteenth-century urban life was whether every woman in the new, disordered world of the city was not a public woman' (2008: xvii). This is in fact related to a new construction of the private and public domains, which we have already seen in *L'Adultera*, where glass in domestic architecture unsettles the interior/exterior boundary. In *En ménage* domestic architecture appears thus as a failure to define the domestic ideal André desires.

The private and the public spheres are confused with each other: domestic space is unshaped; it loses its static meaning to become a moving space framed by dynamic structures. The glass culture seen in the previous two chapters seems to expand in the Paris of the 1880s. In fact, Eleb states how in that decade, 'les façades au travers desquelles le soleil peut pénétrer se multiplient. Les fenêtres sont de plus en plus souvent élargies par des panneaux de verre latéraux' (the façades through which the sun can penetrate are multiplying. Windows are increasingly enlarged by adjacent glass panels) (1995: 254). With this, the domestic and sexual discourses architecture has framed become also mobile, flexible and confused with non-architectural sexualities: the difference between bourgeois sexualities and those at the margins of bourgeois discourses diffuse. For Cyprien, such confusion is in fact what characterises the modern woman, who is represented as a dynamic subject in movement and outside the confines of domestic architecture. Locating the modern woman in the street also breaks with the static domestic imaginary that placed women at home, where her movements are necessarily constrained by the space's limits. In the context of *En ménage*, movement implies promiscuity and home moving.

Although with a slight difference, notions of movement are also present in Viollet-Le-Duc's work. Michelle Perrot notes how 'dans

[. . .] *Histoire d'une maison* (1873), [Viollet-Le-Duc] accorde le plus grand soin aux vestibules, couloirs, escaliers, qui doivent être moyens de circulation et de communication autant que d'évitement' (in [. . .] *Histoire d'une maison* (1873), [Viollet-Le-Duc] gives the greatest possible attention to vestibules, corridors, staircases, which must function as means of circulation and communication as well as of avoidance) (1999: 164). Although noting the importance of circulation, Viollet-Le-Duc shows awareness of the dangers of a space of free movement as it might lead to the dissolution of domestic boundaries, in particular of class, as much as Jeanne and Berthe are represented as a single type of woman.

Corridors and stairways are in fact very present in the apartment buildings of Paris, and are represented in nineteenth-century domestic literature such as Zola's *Pot-Bouille* (1882),[6] published a year after *En ménage*, as spaces of deceit and confusion. The importance of the topic of architectural circulation is antedated by *Pot-Bouille* and *En ménage*. Indeed, it would not be until approximately twenty years later that Guadet would make an extensive description of the design and use of elements of circulation, such as corridors and stairways, in *Éléments et théorie de l'architecture* (1901). According to Guadet, 'le corridor [est] destiné uniquement à la circulation, il faut éviter tout ce qui serait une entrave; ainsi les saillies, occasions de chocs, sont incompatibles avec l'idée de corridor' (the corridor [is] intended only for circulation, it is necessary to avoid anything which would be an obstacle; thus obtrusions, opportunities for shocks, are incompatible with the idea of a corridor) (381). But for André this idea of domestic circulation is turned into a parody. In fact, André is victim to rumours about the causes of his separation, which he learns from the concierge of his new apartment building: '[la concierge] révéla des détails inattendus sur la femme d'André; alors, les langues qui commençaient à s'arrêter, tournèrent de plus belle' ([The concierge] revealed unexpected details about André's wife; then, the rumours that had begun to stop, started again) (Huysmans [1881] 2009: 122). In opposition to the housekeeper of a family house, the concierge in an apartment building does not work for the interests of any of the families living there. Although of an inferior status and position, the concierge enjoys an important degree of freedom, and his or her situation at the building's door turns him or her into an important mediator of the building's life. In *En ménage*, the concierge regulates the circulation of rumours that challenge André's self-confidence, and influence André's views on his public representation. However, the concierge also acts as an accomplice in finding information for André about his wife: 'Je m'en informerai; si tu veux, auprès du concierge, proposa Cyprien' (I will find out; if you want, through the concierge, proposed Cyprien) (Huysmans [1881] 2009: 146). The concierge appears, thus, as a neutral but valuable figure, who moves information through space. However, the most significant trait of the concierge is that he or she relegates the head of the household to an inferior position in terms of power and control. In this context, the ground floor of the apartment building is a liminal space for gender relationships, which suffer a power transfer: as men become less powerful, women gain power. The concierge is, thus, a shifting point in power-gender relationships.

In *En ménage*, the sense of mobility of André's apartment building and the apartment itself is enacted by the presence of the concierge and the servant respectively. In fact, the impression of a complex structure with passages and doors is first represented when André brings Jeanne home, and wants to avoid being seen with her:

> Voici la maison: ici la porte cochère et une allée aboutissant en ligne directe à un grand mur; de chaque coté de cette allée, un corps de bâtiment; eh bien, c'est dans le bâtiment de droite, juste à ce point-ci, là où j'écrase du noir, que débouche mon escalier, tu n'as qu'à grimper jusqu'au dernier étage. (Huysmans [1881] 2009: 182–3)

> (Here is the house: here the carriage entrance and an alley leading directly to a large wall; on each side of this alley, a main building; well, it's in the building on the right, just at this point, where it's all dark, that the staircase comes out, you just have to climb up to the top floor.)

André's directions for Jeanne to find his place show the complicated space of the apartment building, which is controlled by the concierge and, therefore, Jeanne needs to learn her way to André's apartment door. The building's structure is the expression of the concierge's power, as Jeanne's question shows: 'ah bien, et si le concierge s'informe où je vais?' (Well, what if the concierge finds out where I am going?) (Huysmans 2009: 183). Mobility appears again as a consequence of André's lost domestic peace and lack of spatial control. The apartment building is turned into a labyrinth due to the concierge's presence, and it is not experienced as André's own space.

Once inside the apartment, however, André is no more at peace as now it is his servant Mélanie who seems to take control over the space. Thus, the sense of mobility in André's apartment is caused by Jeanne's desire to hide herself from the servant: 'Jeanne n'osait plus maintenant entrer dans le cabinet de toilette; elle avait peur que la bonne n'ouvrit la porte de communication' (Jeanne no longer dared to enter the bathroom; she was afraid that the maid would open the communicating door) (Huysmans [1881] 2009: 190). While doors aimed at communicating servants and landlords, André's 'porte de communication' (communicating door) is turned into the opposite: an element to avoid the servant, who rules the space through this door. At the same time, the door becomes an architectural handicap for the intimacy between André and Jeanne precisely because its main function is to communicate with the servant.

Towards the sexualisation of domestic space

The last of André's home moving takes place after Jeanne leaves him, and he returns to Berthe. This last part of the text works as a theoretical conclusion in presenting the cultural outcome of the many topics explored throughout the novel: domestic instability, sexual circulation, the domestic and sexual values brought out by the concept of a modern architecture, the unsettlement of traditional gender roles, and the deconstruction of traditional representations of the domestic. Such an outcome leads to the configuration of a new marriage and domestic life marked by a strong sense of the erotic.

After his relationship with Jeanne, André imagines again a new interior with a new woman:

À l'occasion d'un fauteuil qu'il avait donné à réparer la veille, des projets d'ameublement le hantèrent et il se figurait les bibelots qu'il achèterait, les toiles rares, et il pensait aussi à une cave splendide et à une femme charmante. (Huysmans [1881] 2009: 255)

(On an occasion on which the day before he had taken an armchair to be repaired, he felt haunted by furnishing projects and imagined the knick-knacks he would buy, the rare fabrics, and he also thought of a splendid cellar and a lovely woman.)

This new domestic project, however, is characterised by André's final awareness of the domestic myth that seems to make possible a new reality: 'quel imbécile je suis avec toutes mes rêveries!' (What an imbecile I am with all my daydreaming!) (Huysmans [1881] 2009: 255). The novelty resides in the fact that this project will be accomplished, and in so doing will modify the image of the domestic ideal by introducing an open erotic relationship with André's wife, Berthe. Thus, when Berthe visits André he behaves as if sexually approaching one of his mistresses:

> Il s'étira les doigts qui craquèrent, pris d'évanouissement, ayant la subite récurrence, sous la chemise de sa femme, d'une mignonne tache fauve, arrondie comme une pastille entre les deux seins.
> Énervée elle aussi [. . .], elle eut un brusque réveil et elle se tendit, les joues en feu et les yeux noyés [. . .]. Elle sourit à son mari dans la glace. (Huysmans [1881] 2009: 263)

> (He stretched out his cracking fingers, fainted, having the sudden recurrence, under his wife's shirt, of a cute tawny spot, rounded like a pellet between the two breasts.
> Angry, too [. . .], she woke up suddenly and she stretched, her cheeks on fire and her eyes wet [. . .]. She smiled at her husband in the mirror.

By introducing the erotic in the domestic imaginary, the unsettlement of boundaries between a bourgeois marriage and non-traditional relationships is confirmed. In fact, André consciously equates Berthe to Jeanne: 'c'est peut-être la seule fois que je me sois conduit comme il le fallait avec ma femme. Oui, avoir plus de laisser-aller, moins de retenue et plus d'abandon [. . .], gentil, bon garçon, comme je l'ai été avec Jeanne' (this may be the only time that I have behaved properly with my wife. Yes, to be careless, to show less restraint and more abandonment [. . .], nice, good boy, as I was with Jeanne) (Huysmans [1881] 2009: 264). Besides, glass, which related to an inversion of gender roles, is also part of the sexualisation of marriage: 'elle sourit à son mari dans la glace' (she smiled at her husband in the mirror) (263). The introduction of the sexual in the representation of the domestic sphere contrasts with the construction of womanhood seen still in publications of the 1880s and

1890s. Mme Louise D'Alq, for example, was the author of a series of essays recollected in *Feuilles éparses* (1880–1895), which were didactic texts addressed to young women. This genre was called savoir-vivre, and gave indications on how to behave socially and in private, and how to run the house properly. In *Feuilles éparses*, Mme D'Alq reproduces the domestic ideal, and defines women with the following words: 'pour être réellement la véritable compagne de son mari et le rendre heureux, il faut posséder surtout la douceur, l'abnégation, la soumission et l'indulgence' (to truly be the companion of one's husband and to make him happy, it is necessary above all to be gentle, and to possess self-sacrifice, submission and indulgence) (1880–1895: 92). Abnegation and submission clearly stand against Berthe's characteristics. Besides, the sexual aspect of marriage is not mentioned in the book's more than two hundred pages. Thus, 'abnégation', 'soumission' and 'indulgence' do not relate to an eroticisation of women.

The removal of boundaries between the concepts of wife and lover makes possible the substitution of one for the other. This mostly entails the normalisation of sexualised marriage and the legitimisation of relationships based on sexual affinities. Both these facts are represented by André's renewed marriage with Berthe and Cyprien's partner, Mélie, with whom he cohabits: 'ton papa Cyprien et ta maman Mélie [. . .] vivent simplement ensemble, comme toi tu aurais pu le faire avec une chatte, sans en avoir préalablement obtenu l'autorisation d'un deuxième chat' (Cyprien, your dad, and Mélie, your mum [. . .] simply live together, as you could have done with a cat, without having previously obtained the authorisation of another cat) (Huysmans [1881] 2009: 228). Although the legal frameworks of André's and Cyprien's respective relationships are different, *En ménage* shows how their function and meaning are the same. In sexualising middle-class women, the equivalence between marriage and cohabitation grants women independence: 'les sorties mesurées de [Mélie] continuèrent sans qu'elle les expliquait et sans que [Cyprien] eut le courage de l'interroger' ([Mélie's] few outings continued without explanation and without [Cyprien] having the courage to question her) (Huysmans [1881] 2009: 233). Thus, the representation of women as sexual beings within the parameters of middle-class ways of living works as a means to construct equality between men and women. In fact, Mélie shows how women's position is empowered when she comments on André and Berthe's situation:

> Je suis bien sure [...] que dans l'histoire de votre ménage, le plus à plaindre c'est votre dame. Quand on a eu ses petites habitudes, son chez-soi, c'est bien pénible, allez, d'être chez les autres. Non, les hommes ne sont pas justes, ils ne veulent pas comprendre ce qui en est. (Huysmans [1881] 2009: 250)

> (I am quite sure [...] that in the history of your household, your lady is the one to be pitied. When you have had your little habits, your home, it is very painful, come on, to live at others' places. No, men are not righteous, they do not want to understand what righteousness is.)

Mélie's words show complicity with Berthe, as well as undermining Berthe's adultery, which is not even mentioned. Mélie shows a female perspective within the private realm, and focuses the attention on Berthe's struggles after her separation instead of on the act of adultery itself. But, as in the case of *L'Adultera*, Huysmans' text leaves room for irony, or, at least, a certain cynicism. In fact, the author's admiration for Dutch painting puts into question a genuine defence of non-traditional ways of living. Mélie's words in the above passage can very well be read as a warning against the autonomy women are gaining and men's new submissive position in the domestic sphere. The irony permeating the text, however, does not invalidate the representation of new domestic cultures and their consequences for men and women. On the contrary, it illustrates the complexity of a transitional moment.

*

En ménage represents a new domestic culture based on the deconstruction of the domestic ideal in opposition to a still present normative way of dwelling defined in moral and architectural texts. André experiences the complexities of accomplishing normative domesticity when he finds out about his wife's adultery. The male subject becomes, thus, the focus of experience of a domestic transition from an ideal, regulated domesticity to a less defined and stable life. André's constant mobility to find a new place and a woman illustrates the difficulties of constructing home as traditionally represented. In contrast, André will change space and women as typical of the new era of circulation and mobility that affect the private realm.

Important to this instability of private life is the mobility of gender roles. While women take on traditional male roles men experience female concerns. André, for example, is mainly concerned with the constitution of a household. This shows how the boundaries between male and female, defined by the activities both genders performed, became de-regularised. This blurring of boundaries does not take place only regarding gender but also in terms of class and types of romantic relationships. In fact, the figures of mistress and wife are identified with each other, hence representing marriage as an erotic reality. This eroticisation of the domestic introduces a sexual equality between middle-class men and women that stands in opposition to common discourses of the time.

Domestic mobility finds an aesthetic correlation with new architectural constructions defined as modern by the magazines of the period. Thus, places such as the hippodrome and train stations are characterised by a sense of mobility. Similarly, the *flâneuse*, who entails movement, is seen as a modern woman and representative of a new type of beauty. The dynamism of architecture, domestic space and sexuality is characteristic of *En ménage* and the novel introduces what will become more common ways of living in the twentieth century. In the next chapter we will see how eroticism and the blurring of boundaries become an even more prominent part in the life of a middle-class marriage.

Notes

1 The most recent article about the nostalgic presence of the Dutch tradition on Huysmans is: Geinoz, Philippe. 2016. 'L'americanisation de la ville et l'intimité perdue: Huysmans et le nouveau Paris', *Romantisme* (2) 172, 118–27.
2 Bryden and Floyd 1999; Chase and Levenson 2000; Rosner 2005.
3 Particularly important on the rise of consumer culture is the overall work of Rachel Bowlby, specifically, *Just Looking: Consumer Culture in Dreiser, Gissing and Zola* (1985; rpt. 2010).
4 Frank Caucci mentions how stone was also seen as belonging to the old tradition in 1880s Chicago, and how skyscrapers became associated with modernity. See Caucci's essay 'Huysmans, Wilde, d'Annunzio et l'école de Chicago: esthetiques de fin de siècle' (1989).
5 See Viollet-Le-Duc's *L'habitation moderne* (1875).
6 Sylvie Thorel-Cailleteau goes further and defines *Pot-Bouille* as a sequel of *En ménage* as some character types, such as '[le] célibataire, [...] la femme adultère et [...] l'employé de bureau' appear in both novels (2009: 144).

5

Vienna: Towards a New Domestic Imaginary

This chapter approaches Vienna as the place where the evolution of nineteenth-century domesticity culminates. Architecture and the sexual discourses being produced in early twentieth-century Vienna were significant as they articulated a new domestic culture, which is found at the beginning of a new middle-class domesticity. The cultural production of turn of the century Vienna illustrates the final transformation of a nineteenth-century domestic discourse into a massive European middle-class culture.[1] It also shows the end of the 'bürgerliche Ordnung' (bourgeois order) (Vorbrugg 2002: 147) as articulated in the nineteenth century. Different issues concerning the domestic were explored among Viennese architects, doctors and writers. The expression of female sexuality, the sexualisation of the nuclear family, the articulation of home as a sexual space, the introduction of open spaces and an architecture that played with notions of familiarity and unfamiliarity were some of the topics present at the turn of the century. In this context, the previous chapters have shown the progressive modifications of the domestic experience during the second part of the nineteenth century, while the cultural milieu of Vienna at the beginning of the twentieth century meant the consolidation of a series of changes in the domestic sphere that slightly shifted away from the logic of domestic discourses that originated in the eighteenth century.

Those progressive modifications of the domestic were a determinant for the eventual redefinition of the actual concept of domesticity. Such a redefinition was finally pushed by the following factors: the formulation of the Freudian unconscious, the representations of an erotic private sphere and the opening of sexual and spatial boundaries. In Vienna the sexual discourse articulated by psychoanalysis signified a real disturbance of a concept of domesticity based mainly on stable limits. Freud's definition of both the unconscious and perversion introduced the continuity between normal and perverse sexuality and abolished the clear opposition between them. Although part of Freud's thought was based on an already existent medical tradition, which included Auguste A. Tardieu (1818–1879), Richard von Krafft-Ebing (1840–1902) and Jean-Martin Charcot (1825–1893) among others, the novelty of his discourse resided in the way in which perversion was being narrated, and the fact that his discourse was widely and commonly used. Far from using specialised and obscure terms, psychoanalysis presented a narrative form in which ideas and terminology reached far beyond the medical field.[2] This facilitated the access to, and appropriation of, medico-sexual concepts by the average public, and hence a wider awareness of the sexual issues addressed by the medical field.

The importance of psychoanalysis also resided in the way in which it problematised family relationships, displacing desire within the limits of domestic space. Thus, psychoanalysis unsettled a discourse in which each family member had a defined place in terms of his or her sexuality, as Krafft-Ebing's statement shows: 'Während der Mann zunächst das Weib und in zweiter Linie die Mutter seiner Kinder liebt, sich im Bewußtsein der Frau im Vordergrund der Vater ihres Kindes und dann erst der Mann als Gatte' (While the man first loves the woman as wife and then as the mother of his children, it is the other way around for the woman, who first loves the man as the father of her child and only after that, as a husband) (1894: 14). The psychoanalytical disturbance of theoretical boundaries, although aiming at reinforcing the traditional role of family life, as Eli Zaretsky shows in his analysis of Freud's Victorian thought (2005: 46), had as a consequence the opening of sexual limits and the transformation of home into an 'uncanny' space in relation to the performance of sexual deviance. Besides, female sexuality was deeply explored, and that seemed to facilitate its expansion out of the confines of domestic space as mostly theorised until then. The new form psychoanalysis gave to family sexuality incorporated changes that led to domestic modifications in the middle classes but did not, altogether, alter the essential structures of bourgeois life articulated around notions of work, family, home and leisure.

Regarding the architectural context, similar disputes to those found in the countries discussed in the previous chapters took place in Austria. As in the capital cities of England, France and Germany, in Vienna debates about old and new styles became very prominent in the 1890s. Otto Wagner (1848–1918) published his seminal work *Moderne Architektur* (1896) stating that, 'die Hauptursache, warum die Bedeutung des Architekten nicht voll gewürdigt wird, liegt in der von ihm bisher verwendeten Formenwelt, in seiner an die Menge gerichteten Sprache, welche derselben in den meisten fällen völlig unverständlich blieb' (the main reasons for which the importance of the architect is not fully appreciated lie in the forms he has hitherto used, in his language which, addressed to the crowd, remained completely incomprehensible in most cases) ([1896] 1902: 28). We have seen how Viollet-Le-Duc also echoed this statement. Wagner was one of the first architects in Austria to openly attack historicism. This is, however, later than in the other European capitals, where before the proper emergence of a clearly different style such as Art Nouveau, other important architects, such as Viollet-Le-Duc in France, presented the first consistent critique of historicism.

During the second half of the nineteenth century Vienna experienced similar urban developments to those of Paris and Berlin. The most significant construction of the second half of the nineteenth century was the Ringstrasse, which Carl E. Schorske defines as 'a vast complex of public buildings and private dwellings, [that] occupies a wide belt of land separating the old inner city from its suburbs' (1980: 24). The Ringstrasse symbolised the modernisation of the city in the 1860s, the same period in which Haussmann started the modernisation of Paris.[3] However, the Ringstrasse project also showed the differences between the history of the middle classes in Vienna and Paris. Being built when the liberals, who represented the middle class, enjoyed more political influence in the 1860s, the Ringstrasse surrounded the inner city and remained related to the imperial and aristocratic tradition, showing the limited power of the bourgeoisie (Schorske 1980: 24). While the renovations of Paris were essentially bourgeois, and took place at the city's heart, Vienna's middle class needed to settle outside it. Schorske defines the difference between the inner city and its belt in aesthetic terms: 'the inner city was dominated architecturally by the symbols of the first and second estates [. . .]. In the new Ringstrasse development, the third estate celebrated in architecture the triumph of constitutional *Recht* over imperial *Macht*' (1980: 31). As in Paris, the citizens of the new Vienna represented by the Ringstrasse lived in apartment buildings, which 'were conceived as multiple-family dwellings, whose "aristocratic" character was established first and foremost by their facades' (Schorske 1980: 49). Indeed, this aspect of highly ornamental façades in the new apartment buildings is repeatedly found in Zola's *Pot-Bouille* (1882) and its descriptions of new Parisian residences. In Vienna, the new apartments were influenced by the aristocratic baroque palace and presented a historicism which most early twentieth-century architects would reject.

The key transitional figure from historicism to the so-called Modern Style in Vienna was Wagner, who, as Elana Shapira mentions, 'began his architectural career on the Ringstrasse, and though he endorsed the European perspective he would turn against the eclectic historicist style [. . .]. He rejected the educational program of the historicist period in favour of art nouveau aesthetic schemes' (2016: 11). Wagner presents a similar evolution to that of Viollet-Le-Duc: although the French architect did not completely break with historicism, he both openly challenged it and wrote new architectural theories that have been equally significant for the definite settlement of Art Nouveau. However, as Shapira notes, Wagner did not present an eclectic style, while France did reject Haussmann's architecture through eclecticism during the 1890s as we have seen in the previous chapter. In this context, France seemed to experience a longer transition before something as radical as Art Nouveau arrived.

The architectural scene, however, was very rich and complex in Vienna. Eventually, architects such as Adolf Loos (1870–1933) would present a fierce critique of Art Nouveau and the modern architecture represented by Wagner. Loos stated that historicism could not be radically avoided but should be used as a source of inspiration for a new modern style (1931: 137). Loos would also echo Viollet-Le-Duc in defining the relationship between material and form in 1898: 'Ein jedes material hat seine eigene formensprache, und keines kann die formen eines anderen materials für sich in anspruch nehmen' (Each material has its own language and form, and none of them can claim the forms of another material) (Loos 1932: 111). Other figures, such as Oskar Strnad (1879–1935) who was a key figure in the Wiener Wohnkultur, and Josef Frank (1885–1967), would also be prominent in creating a different style more similar to that of Loos than Art Nouveau and historicism. For the purpose of this chapter, and in order to simplify the complexity of the architectural scene in Vienna, I will look at one of the common aspects of all these architects: the alteration of the sexual normal through architectures that enacted non-normative sexual experiences.

Regarding sexuality, most scholarship has approached early twentieth-century architecture in terms of gender and space. Christopher Reed's seminal work *Not at Home* (1996) looks at how twentieth-century architecture unsettled the traditional male and female parts of the house, that is, the place of men and women at home: 'if the domestic is the main arena for the enforcement of conventional divisions of masculinity and femininity (along with their complement, heterosexuality), however, the modern home has also been a starting ground for rebellion against these norms' (1996: 16). Reed refers here to the way in which new homes in the twentieth century structured gender by structuring space. Hilde Heynen and Gülsüm Baydar's edited book *Negotiating Domesticity: Spatial Productions of Gender in Modern Architecture* (2005) continues the exploration between space and gender along the same lines. However, scholarship has not paid attention to the ways in which architecture created spaces for the experience of non-normative sexual practices, which were considered perverse in the medical field.

All the innovations in the fields of architecture and sexual discourse find a literary representation in Schnitzler's *Traumnovelle* (1926). This novella, based in Vienna, represents the story of Fridolin, a bourgeois citizen who after listening to his wife's erotic confessions, leaves home for a night. During his night walk Fridolin lives different experiences that raise questions of fidelity and sexuality. *Traumnovelle* conveys modified experiences of sexuality and the domestic as part of the emerging twentieth-century middle-class culture. Although *Traumnovelle*, unlike nineteenth-century novels, is not rich in detailed representations of interiors, it does conceptualise a new domestic experience that is also shaped in the architecture of the time. In this sense, through Fridolin, *Traumnovelle* conveys the subjective, male impression of sexual and domestic issues being articulated in architecture and psychoanalysis. As in *En ménage*, the text conveys a domestic transition from a male point of view, exploring the relationship between man and home.

New forms, new content

French and German anxieties around notions of interior and exterior space, the use of glass and the dissolution of boundaries in the late nineteenth century became confirmed by new architectures in twentieth-century Vienna, where external boundaries became far less prominent, and internal ones disappeared. The concept of the glass house seen in *L'Adultera* finds an expression in new homes where the boundary between interior and exterior blurs. In fact, Austrian architects of the new twentieth century were not concerned with spatial and architectural prescriptions, nor with static structures, but with free and spacious rooms. The new homes presented substantial amounts of glass, for example, through the use of French doors, which helped to dissolve the boundary between the inside and the outside. In his design for the Stiegl House (1924) Josef Frank pursued a project without boundary between the interior and exterior: 'a wall of French doors on the south façade of the house [...] served to break down the distinction between interior and exterior, allowing free access to the terrace and veranda' (Long 2002: 88). Inside the house Frank removed the walls between the living areas, creating one single space. This lack of internal boundaries dissolves the increased specialisation and division of rooms of the previous century, which was the defining trait of common bourgeois houses and apartments. With this modification of the bourgeois house a freer way of dwelling was introduced. The dweller was not meant to be constantly defined by the space he occupied, instead, he or she needed to interpret, and give meaning and function to space. Inhabiting became a more creative practice.

The new Viennese architecture dissolved the possibility of a homogeneous domestic discourse, that is, of a discourse that aimed at a homogeneous way of dwelling, supported by a static and normative conception of rooms. In the new Viennese architecture, the correct way of dwelling melted in an architectural space where boundaries were not defined, and different spaces merged into one. Such space resists regulation: it cannot be normative as the dweller enjoys more freedom to inhabit a space which can function as different spaces at the same time. This means that space needs to be interpreted before being inhabited, and, therefore, by its very nature cannot reflect or create one single usage. Besides, the main division created by nineteenth-century domestic discourses, that of the inside and outside, disappears. From here on, the domestic imaginary sustained by such division struggles to hold on. In this new context, concepts such as perversion or vice, which we have seen present in nineteenth-century architectural treatises, lose validity. Architects do not employ judgemental words of sexual character anymore to prescribe ways of living and warn against architectural misuses. Sexuality disappears altogether from architectural discourses, which started employing new terminology such as modern, machine or practical. This fact shows that the anxieties around a domestic ideal are not found among the new architects to the same degree: although the new Viennese architects would still try to convey, for example, privacy, putting in practice the domestic ideal through strict regulations was not an issue anymore. A more immediate concern would be finding an architecture which could express the modern age in new terms.

Viennese architects, however, did not aim at breaking with the traditional concept of domesticity altogether. Ideas such as privacy were important for Loos, who designed houses that resembled opaque blocks, such as the Müller House (1930). By erasing all decoration and using concrete as the construction's main material, the Müller House's façade does differ from nineteenth-century constructions, although privacy is still conveyed. Nevertheless, this idea of privacy is not free from a new interpretation when it is considered together with the interior of the house. The interior structure of the Müller House is what creates a new domesticity, in this case, imbued with a sense of the erotic. The Müller House, like many of Loos's designs, is territory for a game of gazes. Inside the massive cube, which this house is, the dweller engages in a visual game formed by different levels and apertures that veil and unveil the different parts of domestic space.

The wall separating the salon from the stairs behind presents several levels that lead the gaze through the house in a sensual way by progressively covering or uncovering – depending on the direction – what is on the other side of the wall. This dynamism contrasts with the façade that appears as an immobile massive block with small and gated windows. Thus, the sense of privacy and protection the façade constructs acquires its entire dimension when juxtaposed to the interior: privacy serves the sense of mystery, eroticism and freedom that takes place inside. Privacy in the Müller House does not protect the domestic ideal but rather

Figure 5.1 Müller House © The Albertina Museum, Vienna

transgresses it by creating a playful erotic space. The Müller House illustrates how traditional features of domesticity were not rejected but used to convey a new sense of interior.

Recent scholarship on early twentieth-century architecture has argued that architects were concerned with creating a new place called home rather than dissolving it. In this regard, Reed defined twentieth-century architecture as permeated with notions of the domestic rather than approaching it as anti-domestic. Regarding the Bloomsbury Group, for example, Reed says that its members experienced '[an] alienation from the conventional home and the determination to imagine new forms of domesticity' (1996: 147). Thus, the concept of bourgeois domesticity continued its development during the twentieth century. Architects such as Wagner, Loos, Strnad or Frank were concerned with recovering a domesticity in a similar way to that seen in Viollet-Le-Duc. That is, Austrian architects were preoccupied with conveying authentic and original bourgeois values such as privacy and modesty through a modern architecture.

In this context, Christopher Long situates the influence of nineteenth-century English architecture, especially channelled through Hermann Muthesius's *Das englische Haus* (1905), on Austrian architecture: 'the matter-of-factness of English houses, their lack of pretension and, above all, their avoidance of a controlling theory seemed to [Frank] to pose an alternative to the rigid formality and ostentatiousness of Central European historicism' (2002: 33). Modern architecture did not originate from an anti-bourgeois perspective but the opposite, and like psychoanalysis, it might be defined as rather reactionary although the consequences of such new forms led to new and unforeseen definitions of domesticity. In fact, architectural theories and texts show a romantic view in placing the ideal architecture in the old days just as the bourgeoisie placed the ideal home in a recent past: 'Statt lügnerischen schlagworten wie, "heimatkunst" zu folgen, entschließe man sich doch endlich zu der einzigen wahrheit zurückzukehren, die ich immer verkünde: zur tradition. Man gewöhne sich, zu bauen wie unsere väter gebaut haben, und fürchte nicht, unmodern zu sein' (Instead of using inaccurate catchphrases like 'regional art,' one finally decides to return to the only truth that I have always proclaimed: tradition. Get used to building like our fathers built and do not be afraid of be out of fashion) (Loos 1931: 143). The strong oppositions between Loos and Wagner, for example, did not belong to a wider discussion on being bourgeois or not, but on properly expressing bourgeois and domestic values, and freeing them from the tyranny of historicism. In fact, Wagner used the word 'comfort' to express the need for a new architecture:

Einfach, wie unsere Kleidung, sei der Raum, den wir bewohnen. Hiermit ist aber nicht gesagt, daß der Raum nicht reich und vornehm ausgestattet sein könne [...]. Reichtum und Vornehmheit sind aber nicht durch Formen auszudrücken, welchen mit unseren Anforderungen von Komfort [...] disharmonieren. (1902: 170)

(The space we inhabit should be like our clothes. This does not mean, however, that the room cannot be richly and elegantly furnished [...]. However, wealth and refinement cannot be expressed through forms that disagree with comfort.)

Rybczynski has shown how comfort was one of the defining traits of a new consolidated bourgeoisie in the eighteenth century (1988: 22). Viennese architects did not alter the basic structure of the bourgeois discourse but in exploring new architectural forms they would alter some of the traditional meanings of domesticity. Thus, the emergence of so many different styles after 1900 is the expression of a crisis of domesticity, which in itself included the definition of the middle class and comes from the second half of the nineteenth century: in the last decades of the nineteenth century all stylistic debates regarding historicism can be ultimately defined as a crisis of identity in a culture strongly based on domesticity. At the beginning of the twentieth century each architectural variation would then be a response to that one crisis and to the bourgeois need for self-definition.

Wandering and the male crisis of domesticity

As in *En ménage*, *Traumnovelle* presents the modifications to domestic culture from a male point of view. Fridolin, a Viennese doctor, starts wandering the streets of Vienna after listening to the erotic confessions of his wife, Albertine, and having himself narrated his own fantasies to her. Albertine's tale turns into an uneasy experience for Fridolin, who becomes upset at his wife's fantasies with other men and walks Vienna for one night in order to avoid coming back home. Wandering, an activity that André also performs in *En ménage*, seems in fact to represent the male crisis of domesticity.[4] However, if André walks the streets of Paris in order to find a home, Fridolin wanders in Vienna as a means to avoid home. Nevertheless, in both texts the cause of wandering remains the same: an unsettling female sexuality. André finds his wife with a lover while Fridolin listens to his wife's desires, which threatens the stability of the family:

> [Der Beamte] hatte mich flüchtig gemustert, aber erst ein paar Stufen höher blieb er stehen, wandte sich nach mir um, und unsere Blicke mußten sich begegnen. Er lächelte nicht, ja, eher schien mir, daß sein Antlitz sich verdüsterte, und mir erging es wohl ähnlich, denn ich war bewegt wie noch nie [. . .]. Wenn er mich riefe – so meinte ich zu wissen –, ich hätte nicht widerstehen können. Zu allem glaubte ich mich bereit; dich, das Kind, meine Zukunft. (Schnitzler 1926: 7–8)

> ([The officer] glanced at me, but only stopped a few steps higher, turned to me, and our eyes met. He was not smiling, rather it seemed to me that his face looked concerned, and it was probably the same for me, because I was moved like never before [. . .]. If he had called me – I thought – I could not have resisted. I thought I was ready to give up everything; you, the child, my future.)

Albertine's desires towards a stranger during a holiday with her husband and daughter, and her potential willingness to abandon her family, are represented as a dangerous possibility for the dissolution of the nuclear family that so much characterised the rise of the bourgeoisie.[5] It is not Fridolin's confession of his attraction to other women but Albertine's attraction to other men which appears as menacing. Albertine's erotic desires are represented as the other to Fridolin, who senses his lack of control over his wife's seeming irrationality. Moreover, Albertine herself seems to lack control over her desires. Her incapacity to resist – 'ich hätte nicht widerstehen können' (I could not have resisted) (7) – and the distance with which she refers to her own self in that particular moment as different to her present self introduces a sense of dispossession in regard to the sexual. In this case, the sexual refers both to Albertine's particular sexuality and that of the marriage, i.e., the marriage's sexual life. This places marriage in an even more vulnerable position as there is a third element that becomes part of conjugal life, and it is expressed as a kind of sexual unconscious. In clear difference to, for example, Melanie van der Straaten, who appears fully conscious of her choices and desires, Albertine is rather a victim of them. Although both husbands, Ezechiel and Fridolin, experience the same lack of control towards their wives' sexualities, *Traumnovelle* adds another turn of the screw: Albertine's lack of control of her own sexuality.

What is represented as Albertine's irrational sexuality contrasts, on one hand, with a social and medical aim at constructing sexual norms, and on the other hand, with the expression of sexuality – especially female sexuality – as a cultural construct. In fact, Krafft-Ebing grants women the mission of building civilisation, saying '[daß] die Liebe des Menschen auf höherer Civilisationsstufe nur eine monogamische sein kann und sich auf einen dauernden stützen muß' ([that] man's love on a higher level of civilisation can only be monogamous and must be based on a permanent partner) (1894: 4–5), for which man needs 'eine Lebensgefährtin für die Hauswirtshcaft, eine Hausfrau in dem Weibe zu besitzen' (a life companion to take care of the house, having a housewife in the woman) (3). The concept of wandering appears as opposed to a strict sense of settlement, which in this case is shaken by Albertine. As Ernesto Acevedo-Muñoz states: '*Dream Story* [...] tells the story of a man who, insulted by his wife's confession of an imagined infidelity, goes through a series of increasingly bizarre erotic encounters that tempt him to violate his own moral code' (2002: 120). Female sexuality and culpability appear thus intertwined, and Albertine is represented as bearing the weight of her husband's moral integrity.

Like Paris in the previous chapter, Vienna in *Traumnovelle* appears as a sexualised space as Fridolin maps his erotic desire onto the space of the city. However, Vienna is not only sexualised but also dangerous and unfamiliar: 'Die Lage in der ambivalent besetzen Josefstadt macht sie zu einem Ort der Geborgenheit wie der Krise. Sie ist Ausgangs- und Bezugspunkt und Gegenpol zu den Stationen, die der Held durchläuft' (The situation in the ambivalent and busy Josefstadt makes it a place of security as well as of crisis. It is both the starting and reference point and the opposite of the areas through which the hero passes) (Vorbrugg 2002: 146). It is not only home but also the neighbourhood that is perceived as a changing and insecure reality. In *Traumnovelle* such perception is explored through the lenses of sexuality as Fridolin's wandering is triggered by erotic narration, and it is then signposted by erotic encounters with unknown women. From Rathausplatz, Fridolin walks towards the Josefstadt district where he meets a prostitute, Mizzi, and enters her apartment. Once in her room, Fridolin's thought illustrates the erotic unconscious, which seems to direct his wandering: 'Wer auf der Welt möchte vermuten [...] daß ich mich jetzt gerade in diesem Raum befinde?' (Who in the world might guess [...] that I am in this room right now?) (Schnitzler 1926: 34). Fridolin's own surprise at finding himself in a prostitute's room echoes Albertine's feelings of surprise at being at the officer's disposal. However, Albertine remains the cause of Fridolin's wandering, and therefore, of his potential loss of control over his sexuality. Male wandering appears, thus, as undomesticated sexuality which is caused by a prior undomesticated female sexuality. The latter causes a domestic crisis that expels man from his home, and reminds us of the main role women had in protecting the integrity of the domestic sphere: 'seit dem Abendgespräch mit Albertine rückte er immer weiter fort aus dem gewohnten Bezirk seines Daseins in irgendeine andere, ferne, fremde Welt' (since the evening conversation with Albertine he had moved further and further away from the familiar area of his existence into some other, distant, alien world) (Schnitzler 1926: 36). This all expresses the dangers of an autonomous female sexuality, and its capacity to dissolve domestic culture by expelling man.

Albertine's sexuality leads Fridolin into an open space with less obvious architectural limits, which in *Traumnovelle* finds a correlation with the potentiality – never fully realised – for Fridolin to cross his own sexual limits. Although the city is a kind of architectural space, as it is defined by pavements and buildings that convey meaning, it is a far less constraining space than an apartment or house. Besides, the urban space constituted the outside in domestic discourse. This means that normative sexuality and sex were placed within the limits of domestic architecture. Thus, in sexual terms, Fridolin turns into an outsider.

We saw in Chapter One how domestic space limits and constrains the sexual expression of Emma Bovary, and how Flaubert's text illustrates the opposition between domestic space and the open field. In this case, Fridolin's temptation to fulfil his erotic encounters with women at the margins of domestic sexuality places the sexual tension in men. This change of roles illustrates the sexual empowerment of women, especially as Albertine remains within the limits of domestic architecture despite her dubious fidelity. This gives her control over the home as well as the capacity to regulate the home as (a) sexual space, contrasting with those male medical discourses which approached women's sexuality as the other. In this context, women are the departing point for the constitution of a new sexual and domestic culture. Ester Saletta uses the expression 'femminile *borderline*' (2014: 179) to define Albertine. In fact, in *Traumnovelle* Albertine is represented in terms of her sexuality and desire, which are found at the boundary between the licit and the illicit and, thus, she herself embodies the transition from the domestic to the undomestic where Fridolin is led. It is Albertine who opens up the home into a new space represented by the city. This is key to the configuration of a male crisis of domesticity, as we have also seen in *En ménage*. In fact, even the same act of wandering, which had been traditionally represented as a privileged male activity in the nineteenth century, appears here as imposed on a man that cannot go back home.

Prostitutes and wives: the homogenisation of women and spaces

During his wandering, Fridolin encounters other domestic spaces such as Mizzi's apartment and the secret house where he witnesses a naked masked ball. Those spaces are the result of Fridolin's expulsion from home, and are strongly eroticised and associated with sin.[6] Mizzi's apartment and bedroom are conceptually at the other end of those of Fridolin, who leaves his room to enter Mizzi's. The apartments of Fridolin and Mizzi mirror each other, as the women inhabiting each of those spaces also do. As it is Albertine's telling of her erotic fantasies that acts as the reason for Fridolin's wandering, it is also Albertine who pushes him towards Mizzi as if both women were in alliance. Due to Schnitzler's awareness of psychoanalysis and his close relationship with Freud[7] it has been common among scholarship to read the relationship between Albertine and the rest of the women in *Traumnovelle* from a psychological perspective.[8] This methodology, which contrasts with my historic-cultural approach, implies a psychological reading of Fridolin himself, and does not take into account cultural and social alterations of the time regarding the relationship between spouses, or the introduction of a new domestic-sexual culture. From the cultural point of view of this chapter, in *Traumnovelle*, as in *En ménage*, the relationship between middle-class women and prostitutes is problematised. Although the comparison between them is not as explicit in *Traumnovelle* as it is in Huysmans' text, Schnitzler's novella invites a reading that equates the middle-class wife to a prostitute by means of their sexualised natures, and spaces. That is, both women present different forms of illicit desire or sexuality that escape the traditional domestic culture or are placed at its margins. In this regard, Saletta notes how 'Albertine, come tutte le altre donne incontrate da Fridolin nella sua notte brava, è fattore di destabilizzazione della struttura sociale, a partire dalla sua cellula più piccola, la famiglia' (Albertine, like all the other women Fridolin meets on his night walk, is a factor in the destabilisation of the social structure, starting with its smallest cell, the family) (2014: 180). Following Saletta's argument, in *Traumnovelle* the middle-class wife becomes a destabilising element of the nuclear family by means of her own sexuality. Although this fact is also represented in the adulterous novel, the novelty here resides in the non-expulsion, or punishment, of the wife from the home, something that we have seen in the previous section, representing a new approach to relationships between the sexes.

Albertine and Mizzi are women that Fridolin desires but with whom he only converses – the same will happen with his dancing partner at the masked ball. Albertine and Mizzi are represented as accomplishing the same function of perpetuating Fridolin's sexual frustration. Besides that, and in a more subtle way, the text represents both apartments with the same minimal descriptions: the room where Albertine talks presents a window and door as the unique architectural framework that helps to identify and limit the space: '[Fridolin] stand am Fenster, das Antlitz im Dunkel' ([Fridolin] stood by the window, his face in the dark) (Schnitzler 1926: 9), and '[Fridolin] stand immer noch am Fenster, unbeweglich' ([Fridolin] was still standing by the window, motionless) (11). In the first case, the window punctuates the end of Albertine's erotic story and, in the second case, the beginning of Fridolin's own fantasy with a girl he saw once. Finally, the bedroom scene ends with 'es klopfte' (there was a knock) (15). While in Mizzi's case, the brief mention of a door, a bed and a chair work as concrete signposts: '"Ich [Fridolin] bin wirklich müd, und ich finde es sehr angenehm, hier im Schaukelstuhl zu sitzen und dir einfach zuzuhören" [. . .] sie saß auf dem Bett und schüttelte den Kopf' ('I [Fridolin] am really tired, and I find it very pleasant to sit here in this rocking chair and just listen to you' [. . .] she sat on the bed and shook her head) (34). The door in this case opens the bedroom scene instead of closing it: 'Plötzlich stand [Fridolin] neben ihr, das Tor fiel hinter ihm zu, sie sperrte ab, zündete ein Wachskerzchen an und leuchtete ihm vor' (Suddenly

[Fridolin] was standing next to her, with the gate closed behind him, she locked the door, [and] lit a wax candle shining in front of him) (53). Doors close one conversation with a woman to open another conversation with a different woman. In both cases, doors work as architectural framework, and highlight the privacy of both conversations, as well as uniting an imaginary space within one single apartment. This is highlighted by the fact that both rooms are made similar by a lack of representation: if represented in more detail, differences in wealth and class might have been expressed. But those rooms are not differentiated by class; instead they are associated through the power of female sexuality over Fridolin. The lack of spatial difference correlates with the lack of difference between the sexualities of two women who should appear as opposite expressions of femininity with different social roles. There is a democratisation of space that occurs at the same time as that of sexuality.

The representation of architectural signposts echoes the design of Austrian architect Oskar Strnad (1879–1935) who used 'markers' as points of reference in his architectural constructions (Long 2016: 20). In Strnad's designs, markers are very specific objects, or trees in some cases, which signpost a way and are used as references to inform the dweller where he is, or what path to take. The use of markers was due to the deviations Strnad introduced in his works. Such deviations consisted in employing unexpected architectural forms or patterns, such as not aligning conjoining spaces, and making the user shift when the path is expected to continue in a straight line. In these architectural experiences markers remind us of the place we are in, even if such a space appears distorted. In other words, markers are identifying elements. In the same way, the rooms in *Traumnovelle* described above present architectural markers – doors, windows, a chair – which are the only spatial references for the reader.[9] However, in *Traumnovelle* architectural markers do not distinguish spaces but rather homogenise them. In both cases, though, the use of markers makes the architectural experience an uncanny one, and relates to deviation: in Strnad's case, it is assumed that home becomes a disturbing and unfamiliar space, which could not be inhabited without particular references. In *Traumnovelle* the use of markers makes domestic spaces unfamiliar. In both cases a new concept of the domestic is being constructed that undermines the security, continuity and stability theorised in the preceding century.

For Fridolin, however, the domestic distortion is experienced through female sexuality. This experience will continue from Mizzi's apartment to a house where Fridolin will be part of a masked ball. Moving forwards in his walk through Vienna, Fridolin encounters Nachtigall, an old friend, in a coffee house. Nachtigall tells Fridolin that he is playing piano for a cohort: 'Ich spiele heute in einem Privathaus, aber wem es gehört, weiß ich nicht' (Today I am playing in a private house, but I do not know who it belongs to) (Schnitzler 1926: 44). Anonymity is the characteristic of this new domestic space Fridolin will visit. In fact, not only the house is anonymous but also the people who temporally inhabit it in order to perform a ritual in the form of a masked dance: 'Frauen standen unbeweglich da, alle mit dunkeln Schleiern um Haupt, Stirn und Nacken, schwarze Spitzenlarven über dem Antlitz, aber sonst völlig nackt' (Women stood there motionless, all with dark veils around their heads, foreheads and necks, black lace larvae over their faces, but otherwise completely naked) (Schnitzler 1926: 61). In the masked ball while the faces are unrecognisable the bodies remain visible; this creates an animalistic sexuality where subjectivity disappears, and for Fridolin it opens the door to a highly promiscuous experience where partners are exchanged.

The sense of promiscuity is conveyed not only through the representations of the body but also through space, as the ritual takes place every time in a different house: '"Du spielst also heute zum erstemal dort?" fragte Fridolin mit steigendem Interesse. "Nein, das drittemal. Aber es wird wahrscheinlich wieder ein anderes Haus sein."' ('So this is your first time playing there?' asked Fridolin with increasing interest. 'No, the third time. But it will probably be another house again') (Schnitzler 1926: 44). The constant change of house, as well as the anonymity in which all of them remain, is the architectural representation of the anonymous promiscuity the participants engage in. In the masked ball itself, the anonymous change of partners undermines the individualistic aspect of the subject, i.e., the face and name are unknown, which opposes traditional bourgeois matchmaking.

Fridolin's experience of the house strikes us in its similarity with the impression conveyed by the Müller House where the façade empowers anonymity and mystery while the inside is playful and erotic. In *Traumnovelle* privacy seems modified in the same way as in the Müller House, that is, incorporating the erotic and sexual. In fact, the sexual and domestic anonymity represented in *Traumnovelle* finds an architectural correlation with many of the domestic houses designed by Loos. *Ornament und Verbrechen* (1908), in which Loos strongly criticised Art Nouveau for its excess, stands as one of the leading figures of a clean architecture without ornaments. This is expressed especially in the façades of his buildings which appear as a hermetic mass. Shapira mentions how the ideas of both privacy and anonymity are conveyed through Loos's façades (2016: 13). For Loos, the façade, i.e., the house's face, should not present any mark that characterises the house's owner. The façade gives no information either about the interior of the house or its inhabitants.

The sense of anonymity in Loos is also associated with social equality (Shapira 2016: 13). From a sexual point of view, the masked ball means the homogenisation of all the participants in the ball which erases differences of class and position: 'Konnten alle diese Weiber etwas andere sein? Dirnen – kein Zweifel. Auch wenn sie alle noch irgendein zweites, sozusagen bürgerliches Leben neben diesem führten, das eben ein Dirnenleben war' (Could all these women be something else? Whores – no doubt. Even if they all lead some second, so to speak, bourgeois life besides this one, which is a prostitute's life) (Schnitzler 1926: 73). As in the case of Albertine and Mizzi, all women at the ball become one and the same by means of their sexual potential and their anonymous representation. This representation of women from an erotic point of view is important within an early twentieth-century middle-class context as the regulation of sexuality had been key in the previous decades to classify women – wife, prostitute, bachelorette etc. In this context, the masked ball represents the construction of a new sexual culture, one of its consequences being – according to Fridolin's experience – the homogenisation of sex and eroticism that goes beyond issues of class and civil status. Moreover, it introduces what will become a mass production culture of sex later in the century. The homogeneous aspect of sexuality, as represented in *Traumnovelle*, makes impossible the classification of female sexuality according to women's status, and this implies the suspension of rules. Fridolin's tone, in referring to the dancers as whores, shows a disdain towards the female condition both as prostitutes and wives. Followed by his anger at Albertine, the masked ball gives him another chance to expand his own fears surrounding Albertine's sexual autonomy. Albertine becomes one among those female dancers, who are all of them sexualised women.

This representation of middle-class wives and prostitutes is located within a broader cultural context where psychoanalytical discourse was being formulated, and family relationships were being shaped in a new fashion. In fact, Freud discusses the relationship between mothers and prostitutes in his work on the psychology of love, 'Beiträge zur Psychologie des Liebeslebens' (1910). In order to explain the possible association between both terms, Freud begins by noticing the 'schärfstem Gegensatze zwischen der "Mutter" und der "Dirne"' (sharpest contrast between the 'mother' and the 'whore') ([1924] 1973: 72), an opposition that was particularly acute during the nineteenth century. Freud's explanation of the reason that allows continuity between what were considered two separate types of women – in regard, again, to the use of their sexuality – lies in the unconscious:

> Dieses Verhältnis von schärfstem Gegensatze zwischen der 'Mutter' und der 'Dirne' wird uns aber anregen, die Entwicklungsgeschichte und das unbewußte Verhältnis dieser beiden Komplexe zu erforschen, wenn wir längst erfahren haben, daß im Unbewußten häufig in Eines zusammenfällt, was im Bewußtsein in zwei Gegensätze gespalten vorliegt. (72)

(This relationship of sharp contrast between the 'mother' and the 'prostitute' will stimulate us to research the history of development and the unconscious relationship of these two complexes when we have long since learned that the unconscious often collapses into one thing that in the consciousness is two split opposites.)

The importance of the above passage resides in the fact that sexual boundaries dissolve at the theoretical level in sharp contrast to what happened in nineteenth-century medico-sexual discourses, such as those of Auguste A. Tardieu, Krafft-Ebing, Carl F. O. Westphal or Charles Féré. Although degeneration theories of the late nineteenth century placed the possibility of perversion in the 'normal' subject, perversion was understood to occur in a separate moment than that of normality: both states did not co-exist. The formulation of the unconscious introduced the constant presence of the perverse in the normal. Thus, psychoanalysis was an important cultural phenomenon for the blurring of boundaries between what had been defined as different sexualities. In this context, *Traumnovelle* represents the anxieties surrounding the bourgeois family which was being defined in a new way.

The deconstruction of the sexual normal

The deconstruction of the domestic ideal, as illustrated in *Traumnovelle*, finds a correlation with the deconstruction of the sexual normal. Albertine's desire, for example, opposes Krafft-Ebing's words: 'Anders das Weib. Ist es geistig normal entwickelt und wohlerzogen, so ist sein sinnliches Verlangen ein geringes. Wäre dem nicht so, so müßte die ganze Welt ein Bordell und Ehe und Familie undenkbar sein' (The woman is different. If she is spiritually developed and well-bred, her sensual desire is low. If this were not the case, the whole world would be a brothel and marriage and family would be unthinkable) (1894: 14). The domestic ideal could not be sustained without a regulated female sexuality. Both domesticity and sexuality were further integrated by architecture, which needed to allow their accomplishment. In 'On a Case of Female Impotency' (1896), which American Dr R. W. Shufeldt sent to Krafft-Ebing, Shufeldt studies a case of a female patient for whom it is impossible to perform coitus. This case illustrates the views on the role, and use, of architecture in destabilising female sexuality: '[her letters] show her to be of a low order intellectually; that she has been *melancholic* from girlhood; has led largely a monotonous life, mostly in one place, and had a room to herself' (12). For this reason, the doctor continues, 'the presence of such a person in a true home simply means its ruin in very short order' (18). The reasons for the impossibility of consummating marriage are placed in a misuse of domestic space during girlhood: a room of one's own. Enjoying a room by herself is associated with masturbation as Dr Shufeldt notes in the same letter: 'a physician, was soon convinced that this acidity of the genital secretions in her case was due to onanism' (4). Although Dr Shufeldt refers to the practice of onanism during the patient's adulthood, by mentioning the patient's own room during her childhood, the doctor suggests that she started this sexual practice prior to her marriage. The distribution and use of domestic space are seen as key to the performance of (non-)normative sexual practices. In this patient's case, her marriage is endangered by a misuse of space in the past.

Against this background, the extensive formulation of the unconscious by psychoanalysis seemed to break down all regulatory and classificatory aims of doctors and architects during the nineteenth century. Although psychoanalysis had similar purposes to those of nineteenth-century sexology, i.e., the healing and avoidance of sexual perversions in order to restore the household, its discourse stood in contrast to the well-defined pathologies of previous decades that were mostly based on binary oppositions. The erasure of such opposition contrasted with the *Weltanschauung* prevailing in the nineteenth century. We have seen, for example, how Monsieur Homais' boxes in *Madame Bovary* represented the systematic and scientific thought of the nineteenth century also found in architecture. In this regard, the theoretical formulation of the unity of the opposites marks the beginning of a new sexual and dwelling culture based on new approaches to sexuality and architecture, which we have seen being introduced in the previous chapters.

Psychoanalysis shook its contemporary domestic discourse and sexual prescriptions not by normalising the traditional perverse but by deconstructing the normal. One of the reasons which allowed this to happen was the formulation of a larger concept of the perverse that complicated the concept of the sexual normal based on heterosexual intercourse within the bounds of marriage. The perverse enters domestic space, and puts into question the concept of normality itself and hence the definition of the normal subject:

> Die Perversionen sind entweder *a)* anatomische Überschreitungen der für die geschlechtliche Vereinigung bestimmten Körpergebiete oder *b)* Verweilungen bei den intermediären Relationen zum Sexualobjekt, die normalerweise auf dem Wege zum endgültigen Sexualziel rasch durchschritten werden sollen. (Freud [1905] 1981: 49)

> (The perversions are either a) anatomical transgressions of the body areas intended for the sexual union or b) lingering in the acts preceding the sexual union; those should be ended quickly on the way to the final sexual goal.)

Section (b) of the above passage places perversion in a point of liminality that eventually becomes permanent. Thus, Freud defines such liminal moments as 'Momente [. . .] welche die Perversionen an das normale Sexualleben anknüpfen lassen' (Moments [. . .]

which link perversions to normal sex life) ([1905] 1981: 49). In Freud's sexual theory, liminal moments stand for erotic and sexual activities that are meant to lead to copulation but are not ends in themselves. In this case, Freud's novelty resides in the way he narrates already existing content. Krafft-Ebing, for example, did not present a clear and concise definition of perversion in *Psychopathia Sexualis* but the whole text was a description of perversions, which by exclusion defined the normal. In Krafft-Ebing the relationship between the normal and the perverse is one of absence and opposition: what is not the normal is the perverse and vice-versa. However, Freud bridged both the normal and the perverse in quite a delicate way as in his definition everybody becomes aware of the possibility of lingering in the liminal activity. Perversion is theorised in a way that makes it accessible and recognisable to all.

The new mobility of the term 'perversion' turns sexuality into a more fluid experience, which consequently makes the boundaries of marital sex more vulnerable and less defined. Due to the importance of the opposition between normal and marginalised sexualities in the nineteenth century, the impact of the new definition of perversion on marriage was notorious: it allowed the possibility of redefining marriage in new ways, and, therefore, allowed new ways of living. Freud's approach to sexuality in terms of liminality facilitates the definite dissolution of a boundary between the normal and the perverse, in other words, between domestic sexuality and un-domestic sexualities (e.g., outsiders). We have seen the relationship between architectural liminal spaces and perversion in the previous chapters: architectural liminal spaces have been analysed as spaces leading to potential sexual transgression, especially windows and doors, i.e., boundaries between the inside and the outside, and therefore points in strict need of regulation. Such architectural regulation correlated with a sexual one. Freud, however, by articulating the existence of perversion within normal sexuality, i.e., the foreign within the familiar, invades the security of domestic space in sexual terms, and architectural liminal spaces lose their association with perverse sexuality.

Family space was also unsettled by the extended definition of infantile sexuality psychoanalysis provided. Freud's development of the sexuality of children from an early age, and the formulation of the Oedipus complex, added a totally new aspect to the concept of family. The nuclear family, which was a central part of bourgeois domesticity, as well as key to the development of bourgeois homes in their continuous subdivision and specialisation of rooms,[10] was being redefined in sexual and erotic terms affecting the relationships between parents and children.[11] Quoting American psychologist Phyllis Blanchard in 1910, Zaretsky notes the sexualisation of marriage: 'one of the most disturbing innovations of modernity, [Blanchard] added, was "the emergence of the sex element in marriage"' (2005: 55). While home had been understood in terms of male and female spaces during the nineteenth century, now sex and the sexual were becoming an integral part of domestic space. Besides, the sexualisation of the domestic and all its dwellers was not free from danger as family relationships were theorised in terms of rivalry. This meant a direct attack on the idealised representation of the domestic in the previous centuries, and clearly handicapped attempts at constructing the domestic ideal.

Constructing new bourgeois sexualities

If psychoanalysis unsettled the normal by theorising its inherent perversity, Loos's architecture was constructing new sexual experiences within the domestic, and normalising sexual perversions. The expression of new forms of the sexual normal in psychoanalytical discourse finds a correlation with the new architectural forms in the domestic sphere. New domestic architecture created space for new sexual experiences, as shown by, for example, Loos's architectural plans for Josephine Baker. In 1927, Loos worked on the plans for a house for the singer and although the plan never became a reality, it presents very interesting features: it was overall a voyeuristic project. Christopher Long and Beatriz Colomina call attention to the construction of the indoor swimming pool, which is surrounded on all four sides by an ambulatory: '[the ambulatory] is raised along one side; it is at the same height as the salon on two sides; along the fourth is a second stair' (Long 2016: 130). The peculiarity of this path around the swimming pool is that it presents four windows, 'permitting an observer to peer inside into the water' (Long 2016: 130). The windows surrounding the swimming pool suggest that Baker could have been seen while moving in the water, and she might have been able to return the gaze from the swimming pool. Thus, this house allows a play of gazes on both sides of the windows. Both Long and Colomina, however, believe that the windows allowed looking in only one direction – from outside the pool into it. For this reason, Long argues that the project was both 'voyeuristic and exhibitionistic. It is about seeing and being seen' (2016: 130). But, in fact, the swimmer might have been able to look back into the salon.

Colomina uses the word 'tension' (1992: 95) to describe Loos's manipulation of boundary elements such as walls. In the Baker house, the ambulatory pierced with windows expresses such a tension between the inhabitant and her own enclosure. In this regard, Colomina states: 'the subject of Loos' houses is a stranger, an intruder in his own space' (1992: 95). Colomina assumes that the windows unsettle a desired sense of discretion. Unlike Long, she fails to speculate about the possibility of enjoyment through exhibitionism. But, besides that, Colomina ignores the possibility of the fact that in the Baker house a new sense of domesticity was being constructed. Arguing that the inhabitant might feel a stranger in his own house due to the visual elements is assuming a domestic discourse that does not consider the possibility of an erotic space. However, Loos is constructing the exhibitionism of the female body in a way that empowers it as the female subject can look back at the person who is watching her. This grants an important degree of consciousness to the fact of being seen that stops the female body from being a passive object.

It is important to note that Loos designed the Baker house with the potential owner in mind. In fact, in this case architecture constructs a sexual concept with a direct impact on female subjectivity. As in *Traumnovelle*, in the Baker house there is a change of perspective in the representation of a female gaze looking back. Albertine's gaze in the holiday resort moves in the captain's direction: 'Er blickte nicht zu mir her, ich aber spielte mit dem Gedanken, aufzustehen, an seinen Tisch zu treten und ihm zu sagen: "Da bin ich, mein Erwarteter, mein Geliebter"' (He did not look at me but I flirted with the idea of getting up, going to his table and saying to him: 'Here I am, my beloved') (Schnitzler 1926: 8). The narration of the memory in fact starts with Albertine's active gaze: 'ich hatte ihn schon des Morgens gesehen' (I had already seen him that morning) (7). In both quotations Albertine looks at the object of her desire, actively searching for him.

The play around the window and the gaze in the Baker house, as well as Albertine's active gaze, stand in opposition to what we have seen in Chapter One, where the active female gaze through the window constructs the adulteress. The domestic architecture represented in *Madame Bovary* and Loos's plans for Baker's house construct different female subjectivities. This is achieved first of all in a literal and material way, by structuring space in a way that allows, or does not allow, the body and the gaze to move freely; and, secondly, by changing the meaning of windows by giving them a new use. Such meaning, however, is a consequence of the more immediate experience of the window caused by its position and use: new architectural meaning comes directly from the material experience of architecture. We have seen how architectural treatises of the second half of the nineteenth century strongly defined windows in terms of their function, and their use was regulated. In the Baker house's designs, however, windows became part of a visual game rather than giving a solution to problems of ventilation and illumination. Seeing the window as an element in a game rather than as an architectural element with clear regulations allows the window to be free from a strict normative use. Although games present a set of rules, the degree of choice and use is greater; moreover, the sense of play allows a space free from moral connotations. For the user of the window this means engaging with it in a new way, which introduces creativity. In this context, the relationship between architecture and sexuality appears in a fresh way: the windows in the Baker house transgress, in fact, the architectural regulations of the previous decades. This leads to the construction of voyeuristic and exhibitionistic scenes. Both voyeurism and exhibitionism were seen as improper uses of the body, and as perversions. Therefore, from a late nineteenth-century perspective, the transgression of architectural regulations leads to sexual transgressions, or at least, to a new formulation of the sexual within the domestic domain. However, it is especially important to note that in the Baker house it is the architect who defines the windows; in such a space voyeurism and exhibitionism would not be a misuse of the windows, as has been the case in the previous chapters, but the correct use of them. This suggests a naturalisation of what were first considered architectural and sexual transgressions. The inhabitant of the Baker house would use the windows properly if he or she used them to look at the semi-naked swimmer, and their experience as voyeur would be the correct outcome. In contrast, to be transgressive in the Baker house would mean to avoid looking through the windows. This indicates a complete change in architecture and its relationship to sexuality, and, ultimately, we see the construction of a new domestic space. This echoes the change of meaning in the term perversion, which we have seen in the previous section, defined by Freud. In both architectural and psychoanalytical cases, perversion depends on the subject's perspective; it is a relative fact.

The vulnerability of the bourgeois marriage and the representation of intimacy

Both new sexual discourses and architecture represented the vulnerability of the bourgeois family, the end of the nineteenth-century sense of domesticity, and the beginning of a wider and common twentieth-century middle class. On one hand, domestic vulnerability is particularly explored in terms of sexual and erotic boundaries, as we have seen in the representation of a homogeneous female sexuality for all women and the Freudian concept of perversion. The lack of female sexual definition, itself relating to a more fluid idea of perversion, threatens to dissolve one of the characteristics of the bourgeoisie, which participated in the construction of normal sexuality. On the other hand, the literary representation of intimacy exposes the bond between spouses, while in architecture there is an increased interest in constructing the intimate parts of the house: the bedroom and bathroom. Although architects considered those two rooms to be private spaces, the special attention paid to them shows a new approach to intimacy that differed from the previous decades.

In fact, during the second half of the nineteenth century bourgeois apartments were structured in a way in which representational spaces (e.g., mainly the salon and living room) were facing the main street, while the most private spaces were inside the apartment. This distribution protected the private life of the family, but it also allowed the exhibition of wealth and position, as we have seen in France with *La Curée*. In Vienna the situation was the same when Otto Wagner started working on some apartment buildings; as Peter Haiko relates, they had an 'Enfilade der öffentlich-repräsentativen Räumlichkeiten an der Ringfront mit dem Festsaal als Zentrum und den ihn links und rechts begleitenden Räumen' (Enfilade of the public and representational rooms on the front with the ballroom as the centre and the rooms accompanying it on the left and right) (1984: 12). This was particularly characteristic of the Ringstrasse, which as we have seen, was representative of bourgeois architecture in the second half of the nineteenth century. But in 1886, Wagner changed this architectural conception in his design of an apartment for the Heckscher family in which the representational spaces were not facing the main street (Haiko 1984: 14).[12]

However, what seemed to be a move towards a greater sense of privacy at the turn of the century was an architecture that highlighted the sexual body and sexualised domestic space. As in the case of Loos's Müller House, which we have seen in the first section of this chapter, the concept of privacy is modified through eroticism. Haiko refers to the private areas with the following words: 'Das Schlaf- und Badezimmer als Ort der neuen Prächtigkeit' (The bedroom and bathroom [are] the places of the new splendour) (1984: 28). Indeed, Wagner meticulously worked on those spaces, designing all of their elements including the furniture and decoration. Especially interesting was the glass bath he designed for his own house in 1898, which echoes the swimming pool in the Baker house. The intrinsic values of Wagner's glass bath are transparency and nakedness, which are located at the home's heart as the bath is in one of the house's most intimate parts. We have seen how large windows convey a sense of nakedness and the erotic by allowing exhibitionism and accessibility – threatening, thus, traditional domesticity in *La Curée*. In Zola's text, the fact that windows articulate the eroticisation of the interior presents such eroticisation ultimately as a potentiality: protecting home from it is still possible as windows are boundary elements that can be used for regulation. But in Wagner's case, transparency and nakedness are openly brought into the domestic space by the glass bath; those values are assimilated into domestic culture. This means that the sense of erotic nakedness becomes a fact rather than a possibility: hence, a domestic value in itself. The sense of eroticism is incorporated within the very concepts of intimacy and domesticity.

Regarding the glass bath, Haiko argues the following: 'die Desexualisierung der "neu entdeckten" Nacktheit. Der meist mit Rigidität verleugneten Sexualität im hygienischen Bereich antwortet Wagner mit der Umgestaltung des Bades in ein Boudoir. Sein Bad ist Ort des narzißtischen und voyeuristischen Genusses von Körperlichkeit' (the de-sexualisation of the 'newly discovered' nudity. Wagner responds to the rigidity of sexuality present in the hygienic areas with a transformation of the bathroom into a boudoir. His bathroom is a place of narcissistic and voyeuristic enjoyment of the body) (1984: 31). In his association of architecture with a new hygienist mentality in the late nineteenth century,

Haiko paradoxically argues for the lack of sexual sense in the body and for a voyeuristic pleasure. But it is neither: in the first case, hygienist and medical approaches to the body are theoretically de-sexualised. However, domestic space, where the bath is located, is not a neutral space or a medical one, but is charged with emotions; home is a strongly subjective place. Secondly, exhibitionism would scarcely make sense in such an intimate room. Therefore, it is the eroticisation of home itself, enacted by a piece of furniture, that takes place here, and with it, a new way of thinking about home and relationships emerges.

In this regard, the eroticisation of the interior is problematised in *Traumnovelle*, which opens with a recollection of erotic fantasies Fridolin and Albertine share with each other. In *Traumnovelle* the erotic is what makes marriage vulnerable, and it becomes a destabilising element of the constituted domestic space: 'wie Todfeinde liegen wir hier nebeneinander' (we lie next to each other like mortal enemies) (Schnitzler 1926: 93). Fridolin's thought takes place after Albertine tells him her dream while he was away at night. The dream, in which Fridolin is sacrificed, adds to his own uneasiness towards his wife after her erotic confessions. Moreover, Albertine's dream also contains erotic elements: 'ob ich nur jenem einen oder auch andern gehörte, ich könnte es nicht sagen' (whether I belonged to one or the other, I could not tell) (Schnitzler 1926: 88). Fridolin's perception of his wife as mortal enemy is the consequence of Albertine's dangerous sexuality, which stands in contradiction to Fridolin's own representation of a housewife: 'da saß sie ihm [Fridolin], gegenüber, die ihn heute nacht ruhig ans Kreuz hatte schlagen lassen, mit engelhaftem Block, hausfraulich-mütterlich' (there she sat opposite him [Fridolin], with an angelic block, housewife-motherly, she who had quietly crucified him last night) (Schnitzler 1926: 105). For Fridolin, Albertine appears contradictory, as her sexuality cannot coexist with her angelic, domesticated and maternal characteristics. In fact, to Fridolin it seems plausible to associate Albertine's desires with murder. His expectations of Albertine's character are those defined by traditional domestic discourses, and he sees her sexuality as resisting domestication.

From Fridolin's perspective, the representation of Albertine's doubleness illustrates the disassociation of female subjectivity. This female doubleness relates to the doubleness of the interior (e.g., the difference between theory and practice in the domestic space), which we have seen in the previous chapter. In this case, Albertine's double nature represents the doubleness of domesticity, and presents it as an impossible ideal. In fact, Fridolin experiences, 'daß all diese Ordnung, all dies Gleichmaß, all diese Sicherheit seines Daseins nur Schein und Lüge zu bedeuten hatten' (that all this order, all this equilibrium, all this certainty of his existence was only appearance and lies) (Schnitzler 1926: 107). As with André in *En ménage*, the deconstruction of the interior is triggered by undomesticated female sexuality, that is, a sexuality which escapes the order of domestic space. Moreover, in the cultural context of *Traumnovelle*, such order is itself fading away: architecture does not seem to sustain it anymore. Acevedo-Muñoz mentions Fridolin's incapacity to understand female desire, and defines Fridolin's wandering as the search for a solution to the riddle of Albertine's desires:

> *Dream Story* [is] concerned with a man's attempt to understand desire. The twist lies in that this protagonist's search is not for the essence of his own desires, but those of his wife. Thus, the main character [. . .] is doomed to fail [. . .] because he is seeking answers to a question he is not equipped even to ask. (2002: 119)

Acevedo-Muñoz locates Schnitzler's text within a wider context of a medical tradition looking for answers to the question of female desire. Freud, for example, was invested in understanding female sexuality, dedicating an essay to it, 'Über die weibliche Sexualität', in 1931. This context reinforces the male perspective in the representation of a domesticity in crisis which is mostly depicted as being dependent on a particular idea of femininity.

In *Traumnovelle*, intimacy, which is mostly represented through private conversations among the spouses, is unsettling and terrifying. Those moments expose the solid basis of the bourgeois marriage, and become a tool for the deconstruction of traditional domesticity. *Traumnovelle* shows how the paradox of intimacy resided in the fact that while relationships were becoming more liberal, more emphasis was being put on the sexual and emotional lives of spouses. In fact, this, which could be understood as a re-privatisation of domestic space by means of highlighting the most intimate aspects of the couple's life, results in the opposite: an exhibition of intimacy. Richard Sennett's analysis in *The Fall of Public Man* (1977) is based on the theory that the public sphere disappears under the tyranny of the private realm where intimacy and feelings take over civility. The representation of an overwhelming intimacy in *Traumnovelle* points likewise at an overwhelming domesticity, so much so that by dissolving the boundaries between interior and exterior the private realm takes over the public one. The fears of nineteenth-century architects and writers of exposing the interior to an intrusive and menacing exterior resulted in a movement in the opposite direction. While such writings advanced the dissolution of spatial boundaries, they underestimated the power of the interior in imposing its rules over the outside.

This clarifies the fact that the weight of Schnitzler's text is put on the opening bedroom scene with Fridolin and Albertine. This moment is charged with meaning, emotions and consequences for Fridolin and his understanding of marriage. The bedroom has been traditionally represented in architecture and literature as the most private space of the apartment, and in *Traumnovelle*, the representation of the bourgeois apartment is absolutely focused on the bedroom: it seems to suggest that what happens in the bedroom is enough to explain and understand the marriage. However, this reclusion within the most interior part of the apartment leads to the opening of sexual boundaries and endangers the solidness of marriage. As we have seen with the changes in architectural structure, which diminished the representational parts of the house, home loses its social meaning and becomes exclusively the space of the couple. By charging the bedroom with emotional and semantic importance, sexuality acquires an important role in the couple's life. Architecturally, this fact illustrates the dominance of the private over the public realm. Reducing the social function of home means transforming the domestic space into a more sexual and emotional place charged with pressures and expectations for and from both partners. Besides, the loss of social function isolates the marriage from a wider context in which the constitution of the traditional marriage was based. If family and business relationships were part of the support of a new nuclear family, emotions and sexuality take over as the main pillars for matchmaking. Sennett argues how by the end of the twentieth century sexuality did not present a social aspect anymore: 'the modern term "affair" [. . .] represses the idea that physical love is a social act; it is now a matter of an emotional affinity which *in esse* stands outside the web of other social relationships in a person's life' (1977: 8).

Traumnovelle introduces a new marriage culture by focusing on the emotional and sexual explorations of Albertine and Fridolin: their relationship is defined in the bedroom. Marriage is not represented as being a small part of a wider structure but as being on its own and placed in the middle of a city full of temptations. In this sense, Fridolin struggles to maintain a traditional middle-class way of living within the emergence of a new social and cultural context. From Albertine's perspective, this shift in sexual and domestic culture is alienating, and *Traumnovelle* gives us a critical view of this development.

*

By the end of the nineteenth century and during the first decades of the twentieth century, crucial changes in domestic culture were taking place in Vienna. While Vienna's architectural evolution had been slightly behind other European capitals (such as Paris) during the second half of the nineteenth century, at the turn of the century it presented many conditions which transformed the city into a focus of change. Vienna hosted doctors, writers and architects who introduced important modifications to the traditional definition of domesticity which had prevailed during the nineteenth century. Although trying to prevent traditional domestic values, such as privacy, intimacy and comfort, architects created innovative designs that opened the possibility of interpreting domestic space in new ways. This brought new meanings to home and deeply modified the conceptualisation of the domestic.

Inherent in the new articulation of the domestic was the modification of sexual discourse. New architectures, especially Loos's designs, created spaces that allowed the exhibitionism of the body and facilitated voyeuristic experiences. The possibility of such experiences impacted the perception of domestic sexuality as understood in the late nineteenth century and still in part of the twentieth. Thus, home was being transformed into an erotic space in contrast to its nineteenth-century definitions in which erotic and sexual aspects were not mentioned. Besides architecture, the field of medicine also had an influence on this new erotic aspect of home. With the birth of psychoanalysis, the nuclear family started being theorised in terms of sexual desire, which applied to all members of the household and to their mutual relationships. Besides this, Freud also modified the concept of perversion as it turned into a more slippery and porous reality, which, far from being associated with abnormal subjects, became an intrinsic part of the bourgeois family. Thus, the sense of remoteness associated with perverts was lost, and perversion became a familiar concept to be found within the walls of middle-class homes.

But, at the same time as perversion became familiar, home was experienced as unfamiliar space by those who struggled to maintain a traditional way of living. In this context, *Traumnovelle* explores the alienation of a middle-class husband who feels threatened by his wife's erotic impulses and sexual desires. Fridolin represents the male crisis of domesticity at a time when the domestic culture was changing. Such a crisis is focalised on female sexuality and the new role middle-class housewives were taking on. Thus, Albertine appears as a complex subject with a sexual impulse unknown even to herself, in contrast to other heroines seen in this book. This uncontrollable part of Albertine makes Fridolin feel alienated in his own space and, by extension, the city. This also leads Fridolin to identify Albertine with the prostitutes he encounters later in the night. Such an identification comes from a progressive dissolution of boundaries between domestic and marginal sexualities.

The weight Schnitzler's text puts on the intimate life of marriage points at the central part sex and intimacy will play in the configuration of love relationships. Thus, literature represents intimacy more deeply. In architecture, this turn to intimacy translates into an emphasis placed on the intimate parts of the house rather than representational spaces.

Notes

1. See Gay 2002.
2. See Fine 1979 and Zaretsky 2005.
3. See Schorske 1980: 24–115.
4. Celestino Delyto's analysis of the crisis of masculinity as represented in *Eyes Wide Shut* illustrates the contemporaneity of *Traumnovelle* and one of the ways in which Schnitzler's text introduced many domestic issues that became common ground in the twentieth and twenty-first centuries: 'los planos sostenidos de Tom Cruise [...] pasan a representar la crisis contemporánea de una masculinidad que no acaba de encontrar su lugar tras los cambios producidos en las últimas décadas en las relaciones entre hombres y mujeres' (2005: 70).

5 Vorbrugg notes how *Traumnovelle* starts with a harmonic family scene that represents the 'bürgerliche Ordnung' (2002: 147).
6 Within a context of a strong domestic and Judeo-Christian culture, the representation of woman as the cause of man's expulsion from home echoes the biblical passage of Eve's sin and the consequent expulsion of Adam and Eve from paradise.
7 Regarding Schnitzler and Freud's relationship see Loewenberg 2006: 255–79.
8 Acevedo-Muñoz, for example, argues that Albertine is constantly projected by Fridolin onto other women (2002: 135); Celestino Deleyto presents the same approach (2005: 72).
9 Miriam Vorbrugg notes the use of markers in all the stops Fridolin makes in his wandering: 'Die Stationen sind außer durch ihre topographische Lage auch durch bestimmte Eigenschaften gekennzeichnet' (2002: 145).
10 See Eleb and Debarre (1999) and Chase and Levenson (2000).
11 The period of consolidation and highest development of the bourgeoisie actually starts and ends with the formulation of opposed childhood theories: those of Rousseau and Freud. The first one stressed the innocence and purity of children while the second one introduced sexuality and sexual knowledge in children.
12 Parisian architecture experienced the same modifications in the 1880s, where bourgeois residences started losing their sense of exhibitionism, and seemed to move into a more private architecture. See Eleb and Debarre (1995).

Bibliography

[Anon.]. 1856a. 'Provincial News', *The Builder*, 12 Jan., vol. XIV, no. 675, pp. 13–24
[Anon.]. 1856b. 'The Abbey Kitchen at Fontevraut', *The Builder*, 9 Feb., vol. XIV, no. 679, p. 73
[Anon.]. 1871. 'Berliner Neubauten: VI. Wohnhaus mit Fabrikgebäude in der Zentralstrasse, von Ende und Böckmann', *Deutsche Bauzeitung*, 27 April, 17, pp. 132–4
[Anon.]. 1873. 'Berliner Neubauten: Die Flora zu Charlottenburg bei Berlin von Baumeister Hubert Stier', *Deutsche Bauzeitung*, 19 April, 32, pp. 121–2
Acevedo-Muñoz, Ernesto R. 2002. 'Don't Look Now: Kubrick, Schnitzler, and "The Unbearable Agony of Desire"', *Literature, Interpretation, Theory*, 13 (2), pp. 117–37
Adams, Annmarie. 1995. 'The Eichler Home: Intention and Experience in Postwar Suburbia', *Perspectives in Vernacular Architecture*, 5, pp. 164–78
Adert, Laurent. 1996. *Les mots des autres: Flaubert, Sarraute, Pinget* (Paris: Presses Universitaires du Septentrion)
Agacinski, Sylviane. 1992. *VOLUME: Philosophies et politiques de l'architecture* (Paris: Galilée)
Ariès, Philippe and Duby, Georges (ed.). 1985–1987. *Histoire de la vie privée*, 4 vols (Paris: Seuil)
Armstrong, Nancy. 1987. *Desire and Domestic Fiction: A Political History of the Novel* (New York: Oxford University Press)
d'Aurec, Prince. 1894. 'Les usages mondaines de notre temps', *La Grande Dame: Revue de l'élégance et des arts*, pp. 361–5
Auslander, Leora. 1996. *Taste and Power: Furnishing Modern France* (London: University of California Press)

Bachelard, Gaston. 1949. *La Psychanalyse du feu* (Paris: Gallimard)
— 1967. *La poétique de l'espace*, 5th edn (1st edn, 1958) (Paris: Presses Universitaires de France)
Badinter, Elisabeth. 1980. *L'Amour en plus* (Paris: Flammarion)
Bauman, Zygmunt. 2000. *Liquid Modernity* (Cambridge: Polity)
Baydar, Gülsüm. 2005. 'Figures of Wo/man in Contemporary Architectural Discourse', in *Negotiating Domesticity: Spatial Productions of Gender in Modern Architecture*, eds Hilde Heynen and Gülsüm Baydar (Abingdon: Routledge), pp. 30–46
Beatty, Claudius J. P. 2004. *The Part Played by Architecture in the Life and Work of Thomas Hardy* (Plush Publishing)
Belenky, Masha. 2013. 'Disordered Topographies in Zola's *La Curée*', *Romance Notes*, 53, pp. 27–37
Bender, Niklas. 2010. *La Lutte des paradigmes: La Littérature entre histoire, biologie et médicine (Flaubert, Zola, Fontane)* (Amsterdam: Rodopi)
Benjamin, Walter. 2002. *The Arcades Project* (Cambridge, MA: Harvard University Press)
Bergeron, Patrick. 2009. 'Huysmans, Barrès et la mélancolie domestique', in *J.-K. Huysmans chez lui*, ed. Marc Smeets (Amsterdam: Rodopi), pp. 101–19
Berman, Marshall. 2010. *All That Is Solid Melts into Air* (London: Verso)
Bonnet, Gilles. 2006. 'La Parodie transesthétique comme fiction critique: Huysmans et *L'Art moderne*', in *Poétiques de la parodie et du pastiche de 1850 à nos jours*, eds Catherine Dousteyssier-Khoze and Floriane Place-Verghnes (Lausanne: Peter Lang), pp. 163–74
Bowlby, Rachel. 2010. *Just Looking: Consumer Culture in Dreiser, Gissing and Zola* (Abingdon: Routledge)
Brauer, Fae. 2009. 'Wild Beasts and Tame Primates: "Le Douanier" Rousseau's Dream of Darwin's Evolution', in *The Art of Evolution: Darwin, Darwinisms, and Visual Culture*, eds Barbara Larson and Fae Brauer (Hanover: Dartmouth College Press), pp. 194–225
Brown, Julia, P. 2008. *The Bourgeois Interior* (Charlottesville: University of Virginia Press)
Bryden, Inga and Floyd, Janet (ed.). 1999. *Domestic Space: Reading the Nineteenth-century Interior* (Manchester: Manchester University Press)
Cabanès, Jean-Louis. 2013. 'Sublime et réalisme dans les romans de Flaubert', in *Flaubert hors de Babel*, eds Michel Crouzet and Didier Philippot (Paris: Eurédit), pp. 33–55

Camp, Maxime du. 1875. *Paris: Ses organes, ses fonctions et sa vie. Tome sixième* (Paris: Hachette)

Campmas, Aude. 2013. 'Exposition et reconnaissance de la femme-fleur dans *La Curée*: Variations sur les tableaux vivants, mise en scène de stérilité', in *The Art of Theatre: Word, Image and Performance in France and Belgium, c. 1830–1910*, ed. Claire Moran (London: Peter Lang), pp. 165–82

Caron, Mathieu. 2015. '"Une loge dans le théâtre du monde": De la conception de l'intérieur entre immanence et transposition (1779–1848)', *Romantisme*, 168, pp. 15–27

Caucci, Frank. 1989. 'Huysmans, Wilde, d'Annunzio et l'école de Chicago: Esthétiques de fin de siècle', in *Actes du congrès national de la Société française de littérature générale et comparée*, ed. G. Ponnau (Toulouse: Presses universitaires du Mirail), pp. 223–30

Chase, Karen and Levenson, Michael. 2000. *The Spectacle of Intimacy: A Public Life for the Victorian Family* (Princeton: Princeton University Press)

Colomina, Beatriz (ed.). 1992. *Sexuality and Space* (New York: Princeton Architectural Press)

— 1992. 'The Split Wall: Domestic Voyeurism', in *Sexuality and Space*, ed. Beatriz Colomina (New York: Princeton Architectural Press), pp. 73–128

Corbin, Alain. 1999. 'La Relation intime ou les plaisirs de l'échange', in *Histoire de la vie privée, 4: De la Révolution à la Grande Guerre*, eds Philippe Ariès and Georges Duby (Paris: Seuil), pp. 461–518

— 2008. *L'Harmonie des plaisirs: Les manières de jouir du siècle des Lumières à l'avènement de la sexologie* (Paris: Perrin)

Crook, Mordaunt J. 1987. *The Dilemma of Style: Architectural Ideas from the Picturesque to the Post-Modern* (London: John Murray)

Cryle, Peter. 2002. *The Telling in the Act: Sexuality as Narrative in Eighteenth- and Nineteenth-Century France* (Newark: University of Delaware Press)

Cryle, Peter and Stephens, Elizabeth. 2017. *Normality: A Critical Genealogy* (Chicago: University of Chicago Press)

D'Alq, Louise. 1880–1895. *Feuilles Éparses* (Paris: Au Bureau des Causeries Familières)

Daly, César. 1855. 'Maison d'habitation de Londres', *Revue générale de l'architecture et des travaux publics*, no. 2, pp. 57–63

— 1855. 'Maison d'habitation de Londres', *Revue générale de l'architecture et des travaux publics*, no. 4, pp. 144–9

— 1864. *L'Architecture privée au XIXe siècle sous Napoleon III*, 3 vols (Paris: A. Morel)

Darby, David. 2016. '"Nicht zu nah und nicht zu weit": Windows and the Domestication of Modernity in Fontane's Berlin', in *The Window: Motif and Topos in Austrian, German and Swiss Art and Literature*, eds Heide Kunzelmann and Anne Simon (Munich: Iudicium), pp. 85–109

De Mare, Heidi. 2006. 'Domesticity in Dispute: A Reconsideration of Sources', in *At Home: An Anthropology of Domestic Space*, ed. Irene Cieraad (Syracuse: Syracuse University Press), pp. 13–30

Del Lungo, Andrea. 2014. *La Fenêtre: Sémiologie et histoire de la représentation littéraire* (Paris: Seuil)

Deleuze, Gilles. 2001. 'Zola et la fêlure', in *La Bête humaine*, ed. Henri Mitterand (Paris: Gallimard), pp. 7–24

Deleyto, Celestino. 2005. 'De mascaras, puntos de vista y fantasias sexuales: *Relato soñado* y *Eyes wide shut*', *El Cuento en Red: Estudios sobre la Ficción Breve*, 12, pp. 67–75

Derrida, Jacques. 1972. *La Dissémination* (Paris: Seuil)

Dezalay, Auguste. 2003. 'Préface', in Émile Zola, *Nana* (Paris: Gallimard), pp. 7–18

Donald, Moira. 1999. 'Tranquil Havens? Critiquing the Idea of Home as the Middle-Class Sanctuary', in *Domestic Space: Reading the Nineteenth-century Interior*, eds Inga Bryden and Janet Floyd (Manchester: Manchester University Press), pp. 103–20

Downey, Georgina (ed.). 2013. *Domestic Interiors: Representing Homes from the Victorians to the Moderns* (London: Bloomsbury)

Downey, Georgina and Taylor, Mark. 2015. 'Impolite Reading and Erotic Interiors in Eighteenth-Century France', in *Designing the French Interior: The Modern Home and Mass Media*, eds Anca I. Lasc, Georgina Downey and Mark Taylor (London: Bloomsbury), pp. 13–28

Duffy, Larry. 2005. *Le Grand Transit Moderne: Mobility, Modernity and French Naturalist Fiction* (Amsterdam: Rodopi)

— 2015. *Flaubert, Zola, and the Incorporation of Disciplinary Knowledge* (London: Palgrave)

Eleb, Monique and Debarre, Anne. 1999 [1989]. *Architecture de la vie privée: Maisons et mentalités XVII–XIX siècles* (Brussels: Hazan)

— 1995. *L'Invention de l'habitation moderne: Paris 1880–1914* (Brussels: Hazan)

Emptaz, Florence. 2001. 'La Pharmacopée de Monsieur Homais, ou la pharmacie dans tous ses états', in *Centre Flaubert CEREdI*, <http://www.nakala.fr//nakala/data/11280/e2aa316b>

Etymology Dictionary <http://www.etymonline.com/>
Facos Michelle. 1999. 'The Ideal Swedish Home: Carl Larsson's Lilla Hyttnäs', in *Not at Home: The Suppression of Domesticity in Modern Art and Architecture*, ed. Christopher Reed (New York: Thames and Hudson), pp. 81–91
Feldman, Jessica. 2002. *Victorian Modernism: Pragmatism and the Varieties of Aesthetic Experience* (Cambridge: Cambridge University Press)
Felski, Rita. 1995. *The Gender of Modernity* (Cambridge, MA: Harvard University Press)
Féré, Charles. 1899. *L'Instinct sexuel: Évolution et dissolution* (Paris: Félix Alcan)
Fine, Reuben. 1979. *A History of Psychoanalysis* (New York: Columbia University Press)
Flaubert, Gustave. 2001. *Madame Bovary*, ed. Thierry Laget (Paris: Gallimard)
Fontane, Theodor. 1959. 'L'Adultera', in *Sämtliche Werke*, 4, ed. Edgar Gross (Munich: Nymphenburger), pp. 7–125
Foss, Colin. 2017–2018. 'Love and Real Estate: The Matchmaker and the Real Estate Developer as Social Types in Zola and Gaboriau', *Nineteenth-Century French Studies*, 46 (1&2), pp. 58–72
Foster, Thomas. 2002. *Transformations of Domesticity in Modern Women's Writing: Homelessness at Home* (Basingstoke: Palgrave Macmillan)
Foucault, Michel. 1975. *Surveiller et punir: Naissance de la prison* (Paris: Gallimard)
— 1976. *Histoire de la sexualité: La Volonté de savoir* (Paris: Gallimard)
Franklin, Jill. 1981. *The Gentleman's Country House and Its Plan, 1835–1914* (London: Routledge and Kegan Paul)
Freud, Sigmund. 1973. 'Beiträge zur Psychologie des Liebeslebens', in *Gesammelte Werke, vol. 8*, ed. (missing) (Frankfurt: Verlag), pp. 66–91
— 1976. 'Über die weibliche Sexualität', in *Gesammelte Werke, vol. 14*, ed. (missing) (Frankfurt: Verlag), pp. 515–37
— 1981. 'Drei Abhandlungen zur Sexualtheorie: die sexuellen Abirrungen', in *Gesammelte Werke, vol. 5*, ed. (missing) (Frankfurt: Verlag), pp. 27–145
Garber, Marjorie. 2000. *Sex and Real Estate: Why We Love Houses* (New York: Pantheon Books)
Gay, Peter. 2002. *Schnitzler's Century: The Making of Middle-Class Culture, 1815–1914*. (New York: Norton)

Geinoz, Philippe. 2016. 'L'Américanisation de la ville et l'intimité perdue: Huysmans et le nouveau Paris', *Romantisme*, 2 (172), pp. 118–27

Gillian, Rose. 2007. *Feminism and Geography: The Limits of Geographical Knowledge* (Oxford: Polity Press)

Girouard, Mark. 1979. *The Victorian Country House* (London: Yale University Press)

Glinoer, Anthony. 2015. 'La Bohème chez elle: Étude sur l'imaginaire de l'intérieur bohème', *Romantisme*, 168, pp. 61–9

Godo, Emmanuel. 2007. *Huysmans et l'évangile du réel* (Paris: Cerf)

Goncourt, Edmond, and Goncourt, Jules. 1956. *Journal: Mémoires de la vie littéraire, vol. I, 1851–1863*, ed. Robert Ricatte (Paris: Flammarion)

Görner, Rüdiger. 2001. 'Fontane and the European Context: Introduction', in *Theodor Fontane and the European Context: Literature, Culture and Society in Prussia and Europe*, eds Patricia Howe and Helen Chambers (Amsterdam: Rodopi), pp. 11–14

Guadet, Julien. 1901. *Éléments et théorie de l'architecture* (Paris: Librarie de la Construction Moderne)

Gurlitt, Cornelius. 1888. *Im Bürgerhaus* (Dresden: Gilbers'sche Königl)

H. L. 23 February 1867. 'Der Mensch und sein Haus', *Deutsche Bauzeitung*, 8, pp. 62–4

Haiko, Peter. 1984. 'Otto Wagners Interieurs: Vom Glanz der französischen Könige zur Ostentation der "modernen Zweckmäßigkeit"', in *Otto Wagner: Möbel und Innenräume*, eds Paul Asenbaum et al. (Vienna: Residenz Verlag), pp. 11–63

Hamon, Philippe. 1992. *Expositions: Literature and Architecture in Nineteenth-Century France* (Oxford: University of California Press)

Hardy, Thomas. 2004. 'How I Built Myself a House', in *An Indiscretion in the Life of an Heiress and Other Stories*, ed. Pamela Dalziel (Oxford: Oxford University Press), pp. 3–10

— 2008. *The Return of the Native* (Oxford: Oxford University Press)

Harrow, Susan. 2000. 'Exposing the Imperial Cultural Fabric: Critical Description in Zola's *La Curée*', *French Studies*, 54 (4), pp. 439–52

— 2010. *Zola, the Body Modern: Pressures and Prospects of Representation* (London: Legenda)

Harvey, David. 1990. *The Condition of Postmodernity: An Enquiry into the Origins of Cultural Change* (Cambridge, MA: Blackwell)

— 2006. *Paris, Capital of Modernity* (New York: Routledge)

Haussmann, Georges-Eugène. 1985. *Mémoires: Grands Travaux de Paris, I, 1853–70* (Paris: Guy Durier)

Havard, Henry. 1884. *L'Art dans la maison: Grammaire de l'ameublement* (Paris: Ed. Rouveyre et G. Blond)

Hennessy, Susie S. 2015. *Consumption, Domesticity, and the Female Body in Émile Zola's Fiction* (Lewiston: The Edwin Mellen Press)

Heynen, Hilde. 2005. 'Modernity and Domesticity: Tensions and Contradictions', in *Negotiating Domesticity: Spatial Productions of Gender in Modern Architecture*, eds Hilde Heynen and Gülsüm Baydar (Abingdon: Routledge), pp. 1–29

Heynen, Hilde and Baydar, Gülsüm (ed.). 2005. *Negotiating Domesticity: Spatial productions of gender in modern architecture* (Cornwall: Routledge)

Hillebrand, Bruno. 1971. *Mensch und Raum im Roman: Studien zu Keller, Stifter, Fontane* (Munich: Verlag)

Hollier, Denis. 1974. *La Prise de la Concorde: Essais sur Georges Bataille* (Paris: Gallimard)

Honig, Bonnie. 1994. 'Difference, Dilemmas, and the Politics of Home', *Social Research*, 61 (3), 563–97

Howe, Patricia. 2001. '"A visibly-appointed stopping-place": Narrative Endings at the End of the Century', in *Theodor Fontane and the European Context: Literature, Culture and Society in Prussia and Europe*, eds Patricia Howe and Helen Chambers (Amsterdam: Rodopi), pp. 137–52

Hughes, John. 2004. 'Visual Inspiration in Hardy's Fiction', in *Thomas Hardy Studies*, ed. Phillip Mallett (Basingstoke: Palgrave Macmillan), pp. 229–54

Huysmans, Joris-Karl. 1875. '*Le Cellier* de Pierre de Hoock', in *Écrits sur l'art (1867–1905)*, ed. Patrice Locmant (Paris: Bartillat), pp. 46–8

— 1877. 'Les Peintres hollandais', in *Écrits sur l'art (1867–1905)*, ed. Patrice Locmant (Paris: Bartillat), pp. 73–6

— 1889. '*Le Muse des Arts décoratifs et l'architecture cuite*', in *Écrits sur l'art (1867–1905)*, ed. Patrice Locmant (Paris: Bartillat), pp. 409–13

— 2006. 'Le Fer', in *Écrits sur l'art (1867–1905)*, ed. Patrice Locmant (Paris: Bartillat), pp. 413–18

— 2009. *En ménage: En rade* (Paris: Éditions du Boucher)

Irigaray, Luce. 1983. *L'Oubli de l'air chez Martin Heidegger* (Paris: Minuit)

Kerr, Robert. 1865. *The Gentleman's House; or How to Plan English Residences from the Parsonage to the Palace*, 2nd edn (London: John Murray)

Kleinberg, S. J. 1999. 'Gendered Space: Housing, Privacy and Domesticity in the Nineteenth-century United States', in *Domestic Space: Reading* the Nineteenth-century Interior, eds Inga Bryden and Janet Floyd (Manchester: Manchester University Press), pp. 142–61

Knoepflmacher, U. C. 1990. 'Hardy Ruins: Female Spaces and Male Designs', *PMLA* 105 (5), pp. 1055–70

Kohlmaier, Georg and Sartory, Barna von. 1991. *Das Glashaus: Ein Bautypus des 19. Jahrhunderts. Houses of Glass: A Nineteenth-Century Building Type* (Cambridge, MA: MIT Press)

Krafft-Ebing, Richard von. 1894. *Psychopathia Sexualis* (Stuttgart: Verlag)

Kritzman, Lawrence. 1989. 'L'Architecture du corps utopique', in *Littérature et Architecture*, ed. Philippe Hamon (Rennes: Centre d'histoire et d'analyse des textes, Interférences), pp. 37–45

Kulper, Amy C. 2009. 'Private House, Public House: Victor Horta's Ubiquitous Domesticity', in *Intimate Metropolis*, ed. Vittoria Di Palma, Diana Periton and Marina Lathouri (Abingdon: Routledge), pp. 110–31

Lafon, Henri. 1989. 'Espace privé, espace public dans le roman du XVIIIe', in *Littérature et Architecture*, ed. Philippe Hamon (Rennes: Centre d'histoire et d'analyse des textes Interférences), pp. 65–73

Lasc, Anca, I. 2015. 'Angels and Rebels: The Obsessions and Transgressions of the Modern Interior', in *Designing the French Interior: The Modern Home and Mass Media*, eds Anca I. Lasc, Georgina Downey and Mark Taylor (London: Bloomsbury), pp. 47–58

Lasc, Anca I., Downey, Georgina, and Taylor, Mark (ed.). 2015. *Designing the French Interior: The Modern Home and Mass Media* (London: Bloomsbury)

Lloyd, Fran and O'Brien, Catherine (ed.). 2000. *Secret Spaces, Forbidden Places: Rethinking Culture* (New York: Berghahn Books)

Loewenberg, Peter. 2006. 'Freud, Schnitzler, and *Eyes Wide Shut*', in *Depth of Field: Stanley Kubrick, Film, and the Uses of History*, eds Geoffrey Cocks, James Diedrick and Glenn Perusek (Madison: The University of Wisconsin Press), pp. 255–79

Long, Christopher. 2002. *Josef Frank: Life and Work* (Hong Kong: The University of Chicago Press)

— 2016. *The New Space* (New Haven: Yale University Press)

Loos, Adolf. 1932. 'Das Prinzip der Bekleidung', in *Die Schriften von Adolf Loos, 1897–1900*, vol. 1, ed. (missing) (Innsbruck: Brenner), pp. 110–17

— 1931. 'Heimatkunst', in *Die Schriften von Adolf Loos, 1900–1930*, vol. 2, ed. (missing) (Innsbruck: Brenner), pp. 133–44

Lucae, Richard. 1869. 'Über die Macht des Raumes in der Baukunst', *Zeitschrift für Bauwesen*, 19, pp. 294–306

Lucas, Charles. 1878. 'Sur l'habitation à toutes les époques', *Comptes Rendus Sténographiques*
Luria, Sarah. 1999. 'The Architecture of Manners: Henry James, Edith Wharton and The Mount', in *Domestic Space: Reading the Nineteenth-century Interior*, eds Inga Bryden and Janet Floyd (Manchester: Manchester University Press), pp. 186–209
Mantz, Paul. 1883. 'Les meubles du XVIII siècle', *Revue des arts decoratifs*, 4, pp. 312–25
Marcus, Sharon. 1999. *Apartment Stories* (Berkeley: University of California Press)
— 2007. *Between Women: Friendship, Desire, and Marriage in Victorian England* (Princeton: Princeton University Press)
Massey, Doreen. 2007. *Space, Place and Gender* (Oxford: Polity Press)
Matz, Wolfgang. 2014. *Die Kunst des Ehebruchs: Emma, Anna, Effi und ihre Männer* (Göttingen: Wallstein)
Mays, Kelly J. 2014. 'How the Victorians Un-Invented Themselves: Architecture, the Battle of Styles, and the History of the Term Victorian', *Journal of Victorian Culture*, 19 (1), pp. 1–23
Michelet, Jules. 1870. *L'Amour*, 7th edn (Paris: Hachette)
Miller, Michael B. 1981. *The Bon Marché: Bourgeois Culture and the Department Store, 1869–1920* (Princeton: Princeton University Press)
Nelson, Brian. 2008. 'Introduction', in *The Ladies' Paradise* (Oxford: Oxford University Press)
Nottinger, Isabel. 2003. *Fontanes Fin de Siècle: Motive der Dekadenz in L'Adultera, Cécile, und Der Stechlin* (Würzbug: Verlag Königshausen & Neumann)
Olsen, Donald J. 1986. *The City as a Work of Art: London, Paris, Vienna* (New Haven: Yale University Press)
Oosterhuis, Harry. 2012. 'Sexual Modernity in the Works of Richard von Krafft-Ebing and Albert Moll', *Medical History*, 56 (2), pp. 133–55
Patmore, Coventry. 1862. *The Angel in the House* (London: Macmillan and Co.)
Pedersen, Jean E. 2004. *Legislating the French Family: Feminism, Theater, and Republican Politics, 1870–1920* (New Brunswick: Rutgers University Press)
Periton, Diana. 2009. 'Urban Life', in *Intimate Metropolis*, eds Vittoria Di Palma, Diana Periton and Marina Lathouri (Abingdon: Routledge), pp. 9–40
Perrot, Michelle. 1999. 'Avant et ailleurs', in *Histoire de la vie privée*, 4:

De la Révolution à la Grande Guerre, eds Philippe Ariès and Georges Duby (Paris: Seuil), pp. 15–18

—— 1999. 'Figures et rôles', in *Histoire de la vie privée, 4: De la Révolution à la Grande Guerre*, eds Philippe Ariès and Georges Duby (Paris: Seuil), pp. 109–65

—— 1999. 'Drames et conflits familiaux', in *Histoire de la vie privée, 4: De la Révolution à la Grande Guerre*, eds Philippe Ariès and Georges Duby (Paris: Seuil), pp. 243–63

Philippot, Didier. 2013. 'Flaubert et le mythe du "Livre sur rien"', in *Flaubert hors de Babel*, eds Michel Crouzet and Didier Philippot (Paris: Eurédit), pp. 83–143

Phillips, Roderick. 1988. *Putting Asunder: A History of Divorce in Western Society* (New York: Cambridge University Press)

Pinon, Pierre. 2002. *Atlas du Paris haussmannien: La ville en heritage du Second Empire à nous jours* (Paris: Parigramme)

Reed, Christopher (ed.). 1996. *Not at Home: The Suppression of Domesticity in Modern Art and Architecture* (New York: Thames and Hudson)

—— 1999. '"A Room of One's Own": The Bloomsbury Group's Creation of a Modernist Domesticity', in *Not at Home: The Suppression of Domesticity in Modern Art and Architecture*, ed. Christopher Reed (New York: Thames and Hudson), pp. 147–60

Reverzy, Éléonore. 2015. 'Présentation', *Romantisme*, 168 (2), pp. 5–14

Reynaud, Léonce. 1867. *Traité d'architecture: Art de batir. Études sur les matériaux de construction et les éléments des edifices* (Paris: Dunod), 3rd edn

Rice, Charles. 2007. *The Emergence of the Interior: Architecture, Modernity, Domesticity* (Abingdon: Routledge)

Rimmer, Mary. 2004. 'Hardy, Victorian Culture and Provinciality', in *Thomas Hardy Studies*, ed. Phillip Mallett (Basingstoke: Palgrave Macmillan), pp. 135–55

Rivoalen, Émile. 1882. 'À travers Paris', *La Revue générale de l'architecture* (3), pp. 111–22

—— 1882. 'Promenades à travers Paris: Maisons et locataires', *La Revue générale de l'architecture* (6), pp. 258–63

—— 1883. 'Promenades à travers Paris', *La Revue générale de l'architecture* (2), pp. 65–71

Rosario, Vernon A. 1997. *The Erotic Imagination: French Histories of Perversity* (New York: Oxford University Press)

Rosenbaum, Jonathan. 2006. 'In Dreams Begin Responsibilities', in

Depth of Field: Stanley Kubrick, Film, and the Uses of History, eds Geoffrey Cocks, James Diedrick and Glenn Perusek (Madison: The University of Wisconsin Press), pp. 245–54
Rosner, Victoria. 2005. *Modernism and the Architecture of Private Life* (New York: Columbia University Press)
Rousseau, Jean-Jacques. 1993. *Julie, ou la nouvelle Héloïse, vol. II* (Paris: Gallimard)
Rouvillois, Frédéric. 2007. 'Préface', in Blanche-Augustine-Angèle Soyer, *Usages du monde: Règles du savoir-vivre dans la société moderne*, ed. Frédéric Rouvillois (Paris: Broché), pp. 15–25
Roy-Reverzy, Éléonore. 2013. 'La Statue mutilée: Flaubert dans le naturalisme', in *Flaubert hors de Babel*, eds Michel Crouzet and Didier Philippot (Paris: Eurédit), pp. 57–82
Rudolph, Nicholas C. 2015. *At Home in Postwar France: Modern Mass Housing and the Right to Comfort* (New York: Berghahn Books)
Ruskin, John. 1989. *The Seven Lamps of Architecture* (London: Constable)
Rybczynski, Witold. 1988. *Home: A Short History of an Idea* (London: Heinemann)
Saletta, Ester. 2014. 'Arthur Schnitzler: Immaginare il femminile. Esempi letterari e cinematografici', *Studia Austriaca*, 22, pp. 161–90
Scheidig, Katrin. 2012. *Raumordnungen bei Theodor Fontane* (Marburg: Verlag)
Schenker, Heath M. 1995. 'Parks and Politics During the Second Empire in Paris', *Landscape Journal*, 14 (2), pp. 201–19
Schnitzler, Arthur. 1926. *Traumnovelle* (Berlin: Fischer)
Schorske, Carl E. 1980. *Fin-de-siècle Vienna: Politics and Culture* (New York: Alfred A. Knopf)
Seiler, Bernd W. 2011. *Fontanes Berlin: Die Hauptstadt in seinem Romanen* (Berlin: Verlag für Berlin-Brandenburg)
Sennett, Richard. 1977. *The Fall of Public Man* (London: Penguin Books)
Shapira, Elana. 2016. *Style and Seduction* (Waltham: Brandeis University Press)
Shufeldt, R. W., MS Case histories on deviant sexual behaviour, pertaining correspondence, 1886–1898, Professor Richard Freiherr von Krafft-Ebing collection, PP/KEB/A/14, Wellcome Collection, London
Sidlauskas, Susan. 1996. 'Psyche and Sympathy: Staging Interiority in the Early Modern Home', in *Not at Home: The Suppression of Domesticity in Modern Art and Architecture*, ed. Christopher Reed (New York: Thames and Hudson), pp. 65–80

Simon, Jules and Simon, Gustave. 1892. *La Femme du vingtième siècle*, 8th edn (Paris: Calmann Lévy)

Smeets, Marc. 2009. 'Joris-Karl Huysmans chez lui – en guise d'introduction', in *J.-K. Huysmans chez lui*, ed. Marc Smeets (Amsterdam: Rodopi), pp. 7–13

Solal, Jérôme. 2009. 'Le Divin lait de Lydwine: Érotique du chez-soi et théorie du dehors', in *J.-K. Huysmans chez lui*, ed. Marc Smeets (Amsterdam: Rodopi), pp. 122–36

Spurr, David. 2012. *Architecture and Modern Literature* (Ann Arbor: University of Michigan Press)

Spurr, Sam. 2009. 'Drawing the Body in Architecture', *Architectural Theory Review*, 14 (3), pp. 322–32

Steltler, Ed., 1856. 'Nouvelles et faits divers', *Revue générale de l'architecture et des travaux publics*, no. 4, pp. 216–24

Takaï, Nao. 2013. *Le Corps féminin nu ou paré dans les récits réalistes de la seconde moitié du XIXe siècle: Flaubert, les Goncourt et Zola* (Paris: Honoré Champion)

Tanner, Jessica. 2015. 'Speculative Capital: Zola's Repossession of Paris', *L'Esprit Créateur*, 55 (3), pp. 114–26

Tanner, Tony. 1979. *The Novel of Adultery: Contract and Transgression* (Baltimore: John Hopkins University Press)

Tardieu, Ambroise. 1857. *Étude medico-légal sur les attentats aux moeurs* (Paris: J. B. Billière et Fils)

Texier, Edmond. 1877. *Les Femmes et la fin du monde* (Paris: Calmann Lévy)

Thomas, Jane. 2013. *Thomas Hardy and Desire: Conceptions of the Self* (Basingstoke: Palgrave Macmillan)

Thorel-Cailleteau, Sylvie. 2009. 'Intimisme', in *J.-K. Huysmans chez lui*, ed. Marc Smeets (Amsterdam: Rodopi), pp. 137–47

Tschumi, Bernard. 2012. *Architecture Concepts: Red Is not a Color* (New York: Rizzoli)

Turner, Paul. 2001. *The Life of Thomas Hardy: A Critical Biography* (Oxford: Blackwell)

Une Parisienne. 1894. 'La Comtesse de Puiseux', *La Grande Dame: Revue de l'élégance et des arts*, pp. 1–3

Viollet-Le-Duc, Eugène. 1863–1872. *Entretiens sur l'architecture* (Paris: A. Morel)

— 1875. *L'Habitation moderne, première partie* (Paris: Morel et Cie, Libraires-Éditeurs)

— 1877. *L'Habitation moderne, deuxième partie* (Paris: Morel et Cie, Libraires-Éditeurs)

— 1978. *Histoire d'une maison* (Liège: Pierre Margada)

Vorbrugg, Miriam. 2002. 'Imagination des Begehrens: Arthur Schnitzlers *Traumnovelle* und Stanley Kubricks *Eyes Wide Shut*', *Literatur für Leser*, 25 (3), pp. 143–67

Wagner, Otto. 1902. *Moderne Architektur*, 3rd edn (1st edn 1896) (Vienna: Anton Schroll & Co.)

Walker, John. 2011. *The Truth of Realism: A Reassessment of the German Novel 1830–1900* (Oxford: Legenda)

White, Nicholas. 1999. *The Family in Crisis in Late Nineteenth-Century French Fiction* (New York: Cambridge University Press)

Wigley, Mark. 1992. 'Untitled: The Housing of Gender', in *Sexuality and Space*, ed. Beatriz Colomina (New York: Princeton Architectural Press), pp. 327–89

Willsdon, Claire A. P. 2003. '"Promenades et plantations": Impressionism, Conservation and Haussmann's Reinvention of Paris', in *Soil and Stone: Impressionism, Urbanism, Environment*, eds Frances Fowle and Richard Thomson (Guildford: Ashgate), pp. 107–24

Wilson, Elizabeth. 2013. *Adorned in Dreams: Fashion and Modernity* (London: Tauris)

Wolfreys, Julian. 2009. *Thomas Hardy* (Basingstoke: Palgrave Macmillan)

Woods, May and Warren, Swartz. 1988. *Glass Houses: A History of Greenhouses, Orangeries and Conservatories* (Hong Kong: Aurum Press)

Young, Iris M. 1997. 'House and Home: Feminist Variations on a Theme', in *Intersecting Voices: Dilemmas of Gender, Political Philosophy, and Policy* (Princeton: Princeton University Press), pp. 134–64

Zaretsky, Eli. 2005. *Secrets of the Soul: A Social and Cultural History of Psychoanalysis* (New York: Vintage)

Ziegler, Robert E. 1993. 'Huysmans' *En ménage* and the Unwritable Naturalist Text', *Forum for Modern Language Studies*, 29 (1), pp. 18–30

Zijdeman, Richard et al. 2014. 'Working Women in France, Nineteenth and Twentieth Centuries. Where, When, and Which Women Were in Work at Marriage?', *The History of the Family*, 19 (4), pp. 537–63

Zola, Émile. 1981. *La Curée*, ed. Henri Mitterand (Paris: Gallimard)

— 2003. *Nana*, ed. Auguste Dezalay (Paris: Le livre de poche)

Index

adultery, 5, 13–14, 17–18, 28–9, 33, 38, 43, 45, 47, 52, 80, 82–5, 87–90, 95, 98–100, 102, 107, 109, 120–1, 123–4, 136, 144

architectural design, 2, 5, 24, 85, 89

architecture, 1–6, 8–10, 14–15, 17–20, 22–6, 28–30, 32–3, 35–6, 38–40, 45–7, 49, 51–2, 56, 60–5, 68, 71–4, 76, 78–80, 82–4, 90, 92, 95, 101–2, 107, 109, 113–14, 122, 128, 133–8, 141, 145–6, 149–4, 158, 163, 165–6, 168–2, 174–7

body, 2, 5–6, 10–11, 14, 17, 29, 35, 37, 43, 47, 51–2, 57–62, 64, 66, 73–6, 79–80, 84, 89, 109, 125, 132, 137, 162, 166, 169–70, 172–3, 176

boundary, 10–11, 29, 31, 33, 41, 43, 59, 67, 84, 91–3, 108–9, 138, 151, 159, 167, 169, 172

bourgeois, 3, 10,15, 25, 56, 58–59, 64–6, 69, 73, 77, 79, 91, 100, 108–9, 112–13, 117–19, 132, 134, 136, 138, 142, 146–8, 150–1, 154–5, 162–3, 165, 167–8, 171, 174–5, 177

discourses, 1, 3, 4–5, 12–14, 27, 29, 40, 46–7, 57, 60–1, 65, 68–9, 74, 76, 78–9, 82, 86–7, 89–90, 94, 104–5, 113–14, 118–19, 135, 138, 145–6, 152, 158, 164, 171, 173

domestic architecture, 1, 4, 6, 8–10, 17, 19, 24–5, 28–29, 35–6, 39, 47, 60, 64, 71–2, 82, 95, 113–14, 138, 158, 168–9

domestic culture, 6–8, 10, 24, 58, 63–4, 79–80, 87, 90–1, 102, 109, 111, 137, 144, 146, 155, 158–60, 172, 176–7

domestic ideal, 2, 7–8, 10–11, 13–14, 33, 39, 47, 52, 63, 65, 87, 89–91, 111–16, 118–19, 122–3, 137–8, 142–4, 152, 165, 168

domestic imaginary, 10, 32, 89, 91, 94, 105, 116, 119, 138, 142, 146, 152

domesticity, 1, 3, 6–8, 10–11, 13–14, 25–6, 36, 38–40, 45, 47, 50, 56, 58, 63, 65, 76–80, 82, 89–94, 97–8, 100, 102–3, 105, 108–9, 111, 114–22, 125, 128, 134, 137, 144, 146–7, 150, 152–5, 159, 165, 167, 169, 171–2, 174–7

door, 12, 27–9, 36–8, 41–45, 139–41, 160–2

doubleness, 7, 118, 173–4

erotic, 12–13, 15, 56, 58, 72, 110, 122, 141–2, 145–6, 150, 152–3, 155–60, 162–3, 167–9, 171–3, 176–7

exhibitionism, 5, 51, 53–4, 58–9, 61, 64, 72, 78, 83, 169–70, 172–3, 176

Index

female body, 5–6, 10, 14, 17, 37, 51–2, 58–60, 62, 125, 169
female sexuality, 5, 9, 11–14, 17–18, 39–40, 47, 83, 97, 107, 110, 146–7, 155, 157–8, 161–3, 165, 171, 174, 177
Flaubert, G., 5, 17, 26–9, 31, 34–5, 37–8, 42–7, 51, 116, 120, 158
Fontane, 81, 83–4, 87–90, 95–6, 99, 101–7
Foucault, M., 2–3, 9
form, 1, 5, 14–15, 20, 22–5, 27, 46, 51, 54, 60, 62, 65, 74, 80, 87, 92, 97, 105–6, 108, 124, 129, 147, 149, 162
Frank, J., 15, 149, 151, 154
Freud, S., 3, 13, 164, 166–7, 171, 174, 176
function, 22–4, 29–30, 42, 51, 60, 62, 74, 76, 80, 84, 91, 96–7, 108, 139, 141, 143, 151, 160, 170, 175

gender, 6, 11, 67, 73–5, 78–9, 97, 109, 114, 119, 123–4, 130–3, 140–2, 144–5, 150
glass, 5, 11, 14, 49, 51–4, 56–57, 62, 64–5, 67–70, 78–9, 81–4, 86, 89–91, 93–5, 97, 100–3, 107–10, 130–2, 135, 138, 142, 151, 172

Hardy, T. 3, 16–18, 32–4, 36–7, 39, 41–2, 47
home, 1–2, 4, 7–12, 14, 16–18, 23–4, 28–30, 33–4, 39, 41–6, 50–3, 58, 60, 62–6, 70, 76, 78–9, 85–6, 88–9, 93–4, 97, 104–6, 111–12, 114, 117–20, 123–5, 127–8, 133–4, 137–8, 140–1, 144, 146–7, 150, 154–5, 157–61, 165, 168, 172–3, 175–7
Huysmans, 3, 63, 77, 111–14, 116–25, 127–44, 159

image, 7, 9–11, 16, 32, 37, 56, 58, 88, 94, 96, 104, 117–19, 123, 137–8, 142

interior, 5, 7, 9, 23, 31–3, 35–7, 42–3, 50–7, 60, 62, 66, 70, 77, 79, 86, 90–4, 96–7, 109, 116–19, 122–3, 126–7, 129–30, 134, 136, 138, 141, 151–3, 163, 172–5

Kerr, R., 2, 8, 18–20, 22–7, 30–3, 35, 37–40, 47, 52, 76
Krafft-Ebing, R., 3, 8, 13, 21, 23–4, 27, 30, 40, 75, 147, 157, 164–5, 167

Loos, A., 6, 15, 46, 149–50, 152, 154, 163, 168–9,

medicine, 2, 22–3, 27, 68, 176
men, 10–12, 40, 70, 114–15, 121, 140, 143–5, 150, 155–6, 158
middle classes, 1, 7, 12, 69, 105, 147–8
misuse, 2, 4, 6, 14, 25, 28, 30, 33, 41–2, 46–7, 90–1, 165, 170
mother, 8, 11, 62, 75, 88, 94–5, 99, 105–6, 147, 164

norm, 4–6, 9, 14–15, 37, 50, 112, 121, 126
normal, 1–3, 13, 23, 30–1, 67–69, 80, 147, 150, 164, 165–8
normality, 2, 4, 30–1, 164, 166
normative sexuality, 2–3, 6, 8, 33, 46, 68, 102, 109, 158
normativity, 1–2, 6, 14, 17, 37, 45, 61, 68, 110
non-normative sexuality, 3, 33, 46, 102, 109

pathology, 1–2, 166
pathological, 1–3, 21, 26, 66, 79
perverse, 3, 21, 66, 69, 147, 150, 164, 166–7
perversity, 2–3, 21, 23, 25, 33, 47, 49, 60, 68, 76, 168
prescriptive, 2–4, 6, 12, 14, 17–18, 20, 25, 27, 29, 33, 47, 53
prescriptiveness, 2, 4, 6, 16–19, 21, 25–6, 29, 39, 47, 51–3, 93, 96–7

privacy, 5, 8, 10, 12, 22, 26, 30–1, 35–36, 41, 45, 47, 51, 53–4, 59, 61–2, 65, 70, 79, 86, 90, 92–3, 97–8, 109, 119, 122–3, 152, 154, 161–3, 172, 176
private life, 2, 12, 53, 108, 114, 129, 144, 171
promiscuity, 5, 74, 138, 162

Rice, C., 118, 7

Schnitzler, A., 3, 15, 150, 156, 158–60, 162–3, 169, 173–4
Second Empire, 1, 25, 35, 45, 49–52, 60–1, 64–5, 69–71, 73, 77, 80, 114, 134–7
sexology, 1, 3, 13, 79, 166
sexual culture, 5–6, 8, 10, 25–6, 51, 60, 82, 159, 163
sexual practice, 3, 165
sexuality, 1–3, 5–6, 8–15, 17–18, 20, 26–7, 29–30, 33, 35, 37, 39–40, 43, 46–7, 49, 51–2, 60–1, 66–70, 73, 75–80, 82–4, 96–7, 102, 104–5, 107–2, 115, 125, 130–1, 137–8, 145–7, 150, 152, 155–7, 170–7
space, 1–6, 8, 11, 14, 17–19, 23–5, 28–9, 31, 33, 35–7, 39–47, 51–4, 57–62, 67, 69, 71, 73–4, 78–9, 83, 88–91, 93–6, 102–6, 108–12, 114, 118–19, 122, 124–5, 127–30, 132–4, 138–41, 144–7, 150–3, 155, 157–62, 165–70, 172–7
spatial practices, 7, 47

transgression, 2, 5–6, 8, 10, 13, 17, 25, 28–9, 31, 33–4, 41, 45, 167, 170
Tschumi, B., 4–5, 8, 52

usage, 4, 25, 32, 151

Viollet Le Duc, E., 19, 24–6, 45–6, 51, 60, 62, 65, 74, 92, 135–6, 138–9, 148–9, 154
voyeurism, 5–6, 31, 51, 53, 170

Wagner, O., 15, 56, 148–9, 154, 171–2
women, 1, 8, 10–14, 33, 39–40, 52, 58, 66, 70, 74, 78–9, 87–90, 95, 104, 111, 114–15, 121, 123, 125, 128, 130–4, 137–8, 140, 143–5, 150, 156–64, 171
window, 4–6, 25, 29–33, 35, 40, 53–4, 60, 62, 65–6, 72, 82, 84–6, 88–92, 94–6, 109–10, 117, 127, 131–3, 135, 138, 152, 161, 167–70, 172

Zola, 1, 5, 14, 35, 49–54, 56–7, 59, 61, 63, 65–7, 69, 72–4, 76, 78, 81, 103, 122, 132, 135, 139, 149, 172

EU representative:
Easy Access System Europe
Mustamäe tee 50, 10621 Tallinn, Estonia
Gpsr.requests@easproject.com